# Praise for *Design Patterns Java™ Workbo*

"An excellent book...I'm incredibly impressed with how readable it is. I understood every single chapter, and I think any reader with any Java familiarity would. This book is going to be required reading in a lot of places, including my office."

—Joshua Engel

"Provides a new, more Java-literate way to understand the 23 GoF patterns."

—Bob Hanmer

"This book translates *Design Patterns* into what Java programmers need to know. It is full of short, engaging programming and design problems with solutions—making it easy for programmers to work through solutions and really make patterns 'stick.'"

—Rebecca Wirfs-Brock

"This is one exciting book. It's approachable, readable, interesting, instructive, and just plain valuable. It'll eclipse all other books purporting to teach people the GoF patterns in Java—and perhaps any other language."

—John Vlissides

# Design Patterns
## Java™ Workbook

# The Software Patterns Series

Series Editor: John M. Vlissides

**The Software Patterns Series** (SPS) comprises pattern literature of lasting significance to software developers. Software patterns document general solutions to recurring problems in all software-related spheres, from the technology itself, to the organizations that develop and distribute it, to the people who use it. Books in the series distill experience from one or more of these areas into a form that software professionals can apply immediately. *Relevance* and *impact* are the tenets of the SPS. Relevance means each book presents patterns that solve real problems. Patterns worthy of the name are intrinsically relevant; they are borne of practitioners' experiences, not theory or speculation. Patterns have impact when they change how people work for the better. A book becomes a part of the series not just because it embraces these tenets, but because it has demonstrated it fulfills them for its audience.

**Titles in the series:**

Please see our web site at http://www.awl.com/cseng/swpatterns
for more information on these titles.

# Design Patterns
## Java™ Workbook

**Steven John Metsker**

✦Addison-Wesley

Boston • San Francisco • New York • Toronto • Montreal
London • Munich • Paris • Madrid
Capetown • Sydncy • Tokyo • Singapore • Mexico City

The publisher offers discounts on this book when ordered in quantity for special sales. For more information, please contact:

Pearson Education Corporate Sales Division
201 W. 103$^{rd}$ Street
Indianapolis, IN 46290
(800) 428-5331
corpsales@pearsoned.com

Visit Addison-Wesley on the Web:
www.aw.com/cseng/

Pearson Education, Inc.
Rights and Contracts Department
75 Arlington Street, Suite 300
Boston, MA 02116
Fax: (617) 848-7047

ISBN 0-201-74397-3
Text printed on recycled paper
1 2 3 4 5 6 7 8 9 10—CRS—0605040302
First printing, March 2002

*Library of Congress Cataloging-in-Publication Data*
Metsker, Steven John.
  Design patterns Java workbook / Steven John Metsker.
    p. cm.—(The Software patterns series)
  Includes bibliographical references and index.
  ISBN 0-201-74397-3
  1. Java (Computer program language) I. Title. II. Series

QA76.73.J38 M483 2002
005.13'3—dc21
                                    2002018313

To Alison
    Who fills our house with glimmering light
    With her loving, cozy fire
And Emma-Kate and Sarah-Jane
    Our precious elves, beloved sprites
    Who hop as light as bird from brier.

*Through the house give glimmering light*
*By the dead and drowsy fire;*
*Every elf and fairy sprite*
*Hop as light as bird from brier;*
         —William Shakespeare
           *A Midsummer-Night's Dream*

# CONTENTS

■ **PART VI  APPENDIXES**

# FOREWORD

*Tell me and I forget. Teach me and I remember. Involve me and I learn.*
   —Benjamin Franklin

WITH *Design Patterns Java™ Workbook*, Steve Metsker has done something truly amazing: He's packed a book with extensive coding examples and dozens of exercises that challenge you to truly grok design patterns. It uses software for a fictional company that manufactures and sells fireworks and puts on firework displays as an example. Not only are the coding examples more entertaining than the tired old ATM machine examples, but you'll find yourself learning obscure firework facts as you learn design patterns. The book is fun as well as inviting! And because it describes how each design pattern fits in with and extends Java language constructs, you may find yourself learning more about Java, too!

   A pattern is a way of doing something, a way of pursuing an intent. A design pattern is a way of pursuing an intent using object technology: classes and their methods, inheritance, and interfaces. Each pattern has a name. If you and your teammates know about design patterns, you can work more effectively—because you share a common vocabulary, it's like speaking in shorthand! You can discuss your intentions without groping for the right words. And developers who routinely apply design patterns to their code end up with code that is more flexible and easier to read and modify.

Design patterns were originally described in the book *Design Patterns*, written by Erich Gamma and his colleagues (Addison-Wesley, 1995). That book presents a catalog of 23 proven design patterns for structuring, creating, and manipulating objects. In *Design Patterns Java™ Workbook*, Steve clearly explains each original design pattern from a Java programmer's perspective.

If you take up the challenges in this book, you'll have plenty of opportunity to learn patterns by writing and extending existing code, answering questions that force you to think carefully, and solving some interesting design problems. No matter how much you read about something, the best way to really learn is to put it to practice.

Rebecca Wirfs-Brock
Sherwood, Oregon
January 2002

# PREFACE

At OOPSLA[1] 2000 in Minneapolis, Minnesota, I asked Mike Hendrickson of Addison-Wesley what types of books he thought readers wanted. I was interested to hear that he felt that there is still a market for books to help readers understand design patterns. I suggested the idea of a Java workbook that would give readers a chance to expand and to exercise their understanding of patterns. This sounded good to Mike, and he introduced me to Paul Becker, who supports Addison-Wesley's Software Patterns series. Paul's immediate response was that such a book "should have been written five years ago." I would like to thank Mike and Paul for their initial encouragement, which inspired me to take on this task.

Since that initial meeting, Paul has supported me throughout the entire development process, guiding this book toward publication. Early on, Paul asked John Vlissides, the Software Patterns series editor, for his views on the project. John's reply was that Paul should support the project "in all wise," inspirational words that have stayed with me throughout.

John Vlissides is also, of course, one of the four authors of *Design Patterns*. John and his coauthors—Erich Gamma, Ralph Johnson, and Richard Helm—produced the work that is in every way the foundation of this book. I referred to *Design Patterns* nearly every day that I worked on this book and can hardly overstate my reliance on it.

---

1. OOPSLA is a conference on object-oriented programming, systems, and applications, sponsored by the Association for Computing Machinery.

I have also relied on many other existing books, which are listed in the bibliography at the end of this book. In particular, I have depended on *The Unified Modeling Language User Guide* (Booch, Rumbaugh, and Jacobson 1999) for its clear explanations of UML. For accuracy in Java-related topics I have consulted *Java™ in a Nutshell* (Flanagan 1999b) almost daily. I have also repeatedly drawn on the insights in *Patterns in Java™* (Grand 1998) and *Java™ Design Patterns* (Cooper 2000).

During the months that I was working on this book, I also worked at a financial services institution that has facilities in many locations. As the book emerged, I developed an instructor's course to go with it. I taught the course in Richmond, Virginia, and my associates Tim Snyder and Bill Trudell taught the course concurrently at other locations. I would like to thank these instructors and the students from all three courses for their inspiration and their many insights. In particular, I would like to thank Srinivasarao Katepalli, Brad Hughes, Thiaga Manian, Randy Fields, Macon Pegram, Joe Paulchell, Ron DiFrango, Ritch Linklater, Patti Richards, and Ben Lewis for their help and suggestions. I would also like to thank my friends Bill Wake and Gagan Kanjlia for their reviews of this book in its early stages and Kiran Raghunathan for his help in the later stages. Finally, I'd like to thank my friend Jeff Damukaitis for his suggestions, particularly his insistence that I make the code for this book available to readers. (It is, at oozinoz.com).

As the book came along, Paul Becker arranged for many excellent reviewers to help guide its progress. I'd like to thank John Vlissides again for his reviews. In every review, John somehow convinced me that he liked the book while simultaneously pointing out scores of significant improvements. I'd like to thank Luke Hohmann, Bob Hanmer, Robert Martin, and Joshua Kerievsky for their help at various stages. Each of them made this book better. I'd like to thank Joshua Engel, who has an amazing ability to blend sharp insight with a gentle touch. Finally, I'd like to thank Rebecca Wirfs-Brock, who had many great suggestions, including completely reorganizing the book. I had initially not taken care to put important but understandable patterns up front. The book is much stronger now because of Rebecca's advice and the help of all the book's reviewers.

Steve Metsker (Steve.Metsker@acm.org)

## 1

# INTRODUCTION TO PATTERNS

THIS BOOK is for developers who know Java and who have had some exposure to the book *Design Patterns* (Gamma et al. 1995). The premise of this book is that you want to

- Deepen your understanding of the patterns that *Design Patterns* describes
- Build confidence in your ability to recognize these patterns
- Strengthen your ability to apply these patterns in your own Java programs

## Why Patterns?

A **pattern** is a way of doing something, or a way of pursuing an intent. This idea applies to cooking, making fireworks, developing software, and to any other craft. In any craft that is mature or that is starting to mature, you can find common, effective methods for achieving aims and solving problems in various contexts. The community of people who practice a craft usually invent jargon that helps them talk about their craft. This jargon often refers to patterns, or standardized ways of achieving certain aims. Writers document these patterns, helping to standardize the jargon. Writers also ensure that the accumulated wisdom of a craft is available to future generations of practitioners.

Christopher Alexander was one of the first writers to encapsulate a craft's best practices by documenting its patterns. His work relates to architecture—of buildings, not software. *A Pattern Language: Towns, Buildings,*

**1**

*Construction* (Alexander, Ishikawa, and Silverstein 1977) provides patterns for architecting successful buildings and towns. Alexander's writing is powerful and has influenced the software community, partially because of the way he looks at intent.

You might state the intent of architectural patterns as "to design buildings." But Alexander makes it clear that the intent of architectural patterns is to serve and to inspire the people who will occupy buildings and towns. Alexander's work showed that patterns are an excellent way to capture and to convey the wisdom of a craft. He also established that properly perceiving and documenting the intent of a craft is a critical, philosophical, and elusive challenge.

The software community has resonated with Alexander's approach and has created many books that document patterns of software development. These books record best practices for software process, software analysis, and high-level and class-level design. Table 1.1 lists books that record best practices in various aspects of software development. This list of books is not comprehensive, and new books appear every year. If you are choosing a book about patterns to read you should spend some time reading reviews of available books and try to select the book that will help you the most.

## Why Design Patterns?

A **design pattern** is a pattern—a way to pursue an intent—that uses classes and their methods in an object-oriented language. Developers often start thinking about design after learning a programming language and writing code for a while. You might notice that someone else's code seems simpler and works better than yours does, and you might wonder how that person achieves this simplicity. Design patterns are a level up from code and typically show how to achieve a goal, using one to ten classes. Other people have figured out how to program effectively in object-oriented languages. If you want to become a powerful Java programmer, you should study design patterns, especially those in *Design Patterns*.

**TABLE 1.1:** Books Conveying Software Development Wisdom in the Form of Patterns

| PATTERN CATEGORY | TITLE | AUTHORS/EDITORS |
|---|---|---|
| SOFTWARE PROCESS | *Process Patterns: Building Large-Scale Systems Using Object Technology* | Scott W. Ambler |
| | *More Process Patterns: Delivering Large-Scale Systems Using Object Technology* | Scott W. Ambler |
| OBJECT MODELING | *Analysis Patterns: Reusable Object Models* | Martin Fowler |
| | *Object Models: Strategies, Patterns and Applications* | Peter Coad<br>Mark Mayfield<br>David North |
| ARCHITECTURE | *CORBA Design Patterns* | Thomas J. Mowbray<br>Raphael C. Malveau |
| | *Core J2EE™ Patterns: Best Practices and Design Strategies* | Deepak Alur<br>John Crupi<br>Dan Malks |
| | *Pattern-Oriented Software Architecture, Volume 1: A System of Patterns* | Frank Buschmann<br>Regine Meunier<br>Hans Rohnert<br>Peter Sommerlad<br>Michael Stal |
| | *Pattern-Oriented Software Architecture, Volume 2: Patterns for Concurrent and Networked Objects* | Douglas Schmidt<br>Michael Stal<br>Hans Rohnert<br>Frank Buschmann |
| DESIGN | *AntiPatterns: Refactoring Software, Architectures, and Projects in Crisis* | William J. Brown<br>Raphael C. Malveau<br>Hays W. McCormick III<br>Thomas J. Mowbray |
| | *Applying UML and Patterns, Second Edition* | Craig Larman |
| | *Concurrent Programming in Java™, Second Edition: Design Principles and Patterns* | Doug Lea |
| | *Design Patterns* | Erich Gamma<br>Richard Helm<br>Ralph Johnson<br>John Vlissides |
| | *Design Patterns for Object-Oriented Software Development* | Wolfgang Pree |
| | *Pattern Hatching: Design Patterns Applied* | John Vlissides |
| | *SanFranciso™ Design Patterns* | James Carey<br>Brent Carlson<br>Tim Graser |

**TABLE 1.1:** Books Conveying Software Development Wisdom in the Form of Patterns, continued

| PATTERN CATEGORY | TITLE | AUTHORS/EDITORS |
|---|---|---|
| SMALLTALK ORIENTED | *The Design Patterns Smalltalk Companion* | Sherman R. Alpert<br>Kyle Brown<br>Bobby Woolf |
| | *Smalltalk Best Practice Patterns* | Kent Beck |
| JAVA ORIENTED | *Java™ Design Patterns: A Tutorial* | James W. Cooper |
| | *Patterns in Java™, Volume 1* | Mark Grand |
| COMPENDIA | *The Pattern Almanac 2000* | Linda Rising |
| | *Pattern Languages of Program Design* | James O. Coplien<br>Douglas C. Schmidt |
| | *Pattern Languages of Program Design 2* | John M. Vlissides<br>James O. Coplien<br>Norman Kerth |
| | *Pattern Languages of Program Design 3* | Robert C. Martin<br>Dirk Riehle<br>Frank Buschmann |
| | *Pattern Languages of Program Design 4* | Neil Harrison<br>Brian Foote<br>Hans Rohnert |

*Design Patterns* describes 23 design patterns—that is, 23 ways of pursuing an intent, using classes and objects in an object-oriented language. These are probably not absolutely the most useful 23 design patterns to know. On the other hand, these patterns are probably among the 100 most useful patterns. Unfortunately, no set of criteria establishes the value of a pattern, and so the identity of the other 77 patterns in the top 100 is a mystery. Fortunately, the authors of *Design Patterns* chose well, and the patterns they document are certainly worth learning.

> ## GoF
>
> You may have noted the potential confusion between design patterns the topic and *Design Patterns* the book. To distinguish between the topic and the book title, many speakers and some writers refer to the book as the "Gang of Four" book or the "GoF" book, referring to the number of its authors. In print, this distinction is not so confusing. Accordingly, this book avoids using the term "GoF."

## Why Java?

This book gives its examples in Java because Java is popular and important and will probably be the basis of future generations of computer languages. The popularity of a language is recursive. Developers invest their learning cycles in technology that they believe will last for at least a few years. The more popular a technology becomes, the more people want to learn it, and the more popular it becomes. This can lead to **hype**, or overexcitement about a technology's potential value. But Java is more than hype.

At a superficial level, Java is important because it is popular, but Java is also popular because it is a stride forward in computer languages. Java is a **consolidation language**, having absorbed the strengths and discarded the weaknesses of its predecessors. This consolidation has fueled Java's popularity and helps ensure that future languages will evolve from Java rather than depart radically from it. Your investment in Java will almost surely yield value in any language that supplants Java.

The patterns in *Design Patterns* apply to Java because, like Smalltalk and C++, Java follows a class/instance paradigm. Java is much more similar to Smalltalk and C++ than it is to, say, Prolog or Self. Although competing paradigms are important, the class/instance paradigm appears to be the most practical next step in applied computing. This book uses Java because of Java's popularity and because Java appears to lie along the evolutionary path of languages that we will use for decades ahead.

## Why UML?

Where challenges have solutions in code, this book uses Java. But many of the challenges ask you to draw a diagram of how classes, packages, and other elements relate. You can use any notation you like, but this book uses **Unified Modeling Language** (**UML**) notation. Even if you are familiar with UML, it is a good idea to have a reference handy. Two good choices are *The UML User Guide* (Booch, Rumbaugh, and Jacobson 1999), and *UML Distilled* (Fowler with Scott 2000). The bare minimum of UML knowledge you need for this book is provided in Appendix C, UML at a Glance, page 441.

## Why a Workbook?

No matter how much you read about doing something, you won't feel as though you know it until you do it. This is true partially because until you exercise the knowledge you gain from a book, you won't encounter subtleties, and you won't grapple with alternative approaches. You won't feel confident about design patterns until you apply them to some real challenges.

The problem with learning through experience is that you can do a lot of damage as you learn. You can't apply patterns in production code before you are confident in your own skills. But you need to start applying patterns to gain confidence. What a conundrum! The solution is to practice on example problems where mistakes are valuable but painless.

Each chapter in this **workbook** begins with a short introduction and then sets up a series of challenges for you to solve. After you come up with a solution, you can compare your solution to one given in Appendix B, Solutions, starting on page 359. The solution in the book may take a different slant from your solution or may provide you with some other insight.

You probably can't go overboard in how hard you work to come up with answers to the challenges in this book. If you consult other books, work with a colleague, and write sample code to check out your solution, terrific! You will never regret investing your time and energy in learning how to apply design patterns.

A danger lurks in the solutions that this book provides. If you flip to the solution immediately after reading a challenge, you will not gain much from this book. The solutions in this book can do you more harm than good if you don't first create your own solutions.

## The Organization of This Book

There are many ways to organize and to categorize patterns. You might organize them according to similarities in structure, or you might follow the order in *Design Patterns*. But the most important aspect of any pattern is its intent, that is, the potential value of applying the pattern. This book organizes the 23 patterns of *Design Patterns* according to their intent.

Having decided to organize patterns by intent raises the question of how to categorize intent. This book adopts the notion that the intent of a design pattern is usually easily expressed as the need to go beyond the ordinary facilities that are built into Java. For example, Java has plentiful support for defining the interfaces that a class implements. But if you want to adapt a class's interface to meet the needs of a client, you need to apply the ADAPTER pattern. The intent of the ADAPTER pattern goes beyond the interface facilities built into Java.

This book places design pattern intent in five categories, as follows:

- Interfaces
- Responsibility
- Construction
- Operations
- Extensions

These five categories account for five parts of this book. Each part begins with a chapter that discusses and presents challenges related to features built into Java. For example, Part I, Interface Patterns, begins with a chapter on ordinary Java interfaces. That chapter will challenge your understanding of the Java interface construct, especially in comparison to abstract classes. The remaining chapters of Part I address patterns whose primary intent involves the definition of an interface—the set of methods

**TABLE 1.2:** Categorization of Patterns by Intent

| INTENT | PATTERNS |
|---|---|
| INTERFACES | ADAPTER, FACADE, COMPOSITE, BRIDGE |
| RESPONSIBILITY | SINGLETON, OBSERVER, MEDIATOR, PROXY, CHAIN OF RESPONSIBILITY, FLYWEIGHT |
| CONSTRUCTION | BUILDER, FACTORY METHOD, ABSTRACT FACTORY, PROTOTYPE, MEMENTO |
| OPERATIONS | TEMPLATE METHOD, STATE, STRATEGY, COMMAND, INTERPRETER |
| EXTENSIONS | DECORATOR, ITERATOR, VISITOR |

that a client can call from a service provider. Each of these patterns addresses a need that cannot be addressed solely with Java interfaces.

Categorizing patterns by intent does not mean that each pattern support only one type of intent. A pattern that supports more than one type of intent appears as a full chapter in the first part to which it applies and gets a brief mention in subsequent sections. Table 1.2 shows the categorization behind the organization of this book.

I hope that you will question the categorization in Table 1.2. Do you agree that SINGLETON is about responsibility, not construction? Do you think that COMPOSITE is an interface pattern? Categorizing patterns is somewhat subjective. But I hope that you will agree that thinking about the intent behind patterns and thinking about how you will apply patterns are very useful exercises.

## Welcome to Oozinoz!

The challenges in this book all cite examples from **Oozinoz**, a fictional company that manufactures and sells fireworks and puts on fireworks displays. (Oozinoz takes its name from the sounds heard at Oozinoz exhibitions.) The current code base at Oozinoz is pretty well designed, but many challenges remain for you to make the code stronger by applying design patterns.

## Source Code Disclaimer

The source code used in this book is available at www.oozinoz.com. The code is free. You may use it as you wish, with the sole restriction that you may not claim that you wrote it. On the other hand, neither I nor the publisher of this book warrant the code to be useful for any particular purpose. If you use the oozinoz code, I hope that you will thoroughly test that it works properly with your application. And if you find a defect in my code, please let me know! I can be contacted at Steve.Metsker@acm.org.

## Summary

Patterns are distillations of accumulated wisdom, providing a standard jargon and naming the concepts that experienced practitioners apply. The patterns in *Design Patterns* are among the most useful class-level patterns and are certainly worth learning. This book complements *Design Patterns*, providing challenges to exercise your understanding of the patterns. This book uses Java in its examples and challenges because of Java's popularity and its future prospects. By working through the challenges in this book, you will learn to recognize and to apply a large portion of the accumulated wisdom of the software community.

# PART I

## INTERFACE PATTERNS

# 2

# INTRODUCING INTERFACES

SPEAKING ABSTRACTLY, a class's **interface** is the collection of methods and fields that a class permits objects of other classes to access. This interface usually represents a commitment that the methods will perform the operation implied by their names and as specified by code comments and other documentation. A class's **implementation** is the code that lies within its methods.

Java elevates the notion of interface to be a separate construct, expressly separating interface—what an object must do—from implementation—how an object fulfills this commitment. Java interfaces allow several classes to provide the same functionality, and they open the possibility that a class can implement more than one interface.

The Java interface construct is a powerful tool worth studying in its own right, but your design intent will sometimes go beyond the simple definition of an interface. For example, you might use an interface to adapt a class's interface to meet a client's needs, applying the ADAPTER pattern. You might also create an interface to a collection of classes, applying the FACADE pattern. In this case, you create a new interface by creating a new class rather than a new interface. In these circumstances and others you can apply design patterns to go beyond the ordinary use of interfaces.

## Ordinary Interfaces

*Design Patterns* (Gamma et al. 1990) frequently mentions the use of abstract classes but does not describe the use of interfaces. The reason is that the languages C++ and Smalltalk, which *Design Patterns* uses for its examples, do not have an interface construct. This omission has a minor impact on the utility of the book for Java developers, because Java interfaces are quite similar to abstract classes.

---

**CHALLENGE 2.1**

Write down three differences between abstract classes and interfaces in Java.

*A solution appears on page 359.*

---

The basic definition of Java interfaces is not complex. However, you should be aware of a few subtle points when using them.

Consider the definition of an Oozinoz interface that rocket simulation classes must implement. Engineers design many different rockets, including solid- and liquid-fueled rockets, with completely different ballistics. Regardless of how a rocket is composed, a simulation for the rocket must provide figures for the rocket's expected thrust and **apogee**, or the greatest height the rocket will achieve. Here is the exact code, minus the code comments, that Oozinoz uses to define the rocket simulation interface:

```
package com.oozinoz.simulation;
import com.oozinoz.units.*;
interface RocketSim
{
    abstract Length apogee();
    public Force thrust();
}
```

Classes that provide rocket simulations implement the RocketSim interface. A rocket's apogee and thrust are quantities that combine a magnitude with the physical dimensions of length and force, respectively. (Chapter 3, ADAPTER, has more information about the units package, on page 24.)

CHALLENGE 2.2

Which of the following statements are true?

A. Both methods of the RocketSim interface are abstract, although only apogee() declares this explicitly.
B. Both methods of the interface are public, although only thrust() declares this explicitly.
C. All interfaces are public, so RocketSim is public, although it does not declare this explicitly.
D. It is possible to create another interface, say, RocketSimSolid, that extends RocketSim.
E. Every interface must have at least one method.
F. An interface can declare instance fields that an implementing class must also declare.
G. Although you can't instantiate an interface, an interface definition can declare constructor methods that require an implementing class to provide constructors with given signatures.

*Solutions appear on page 360.*

## Interfaces and Obligations

A developer who creates a class that implements RocketSim is responsible for writing apogee() and thrust() methods that return measures of a rocket's performance. In other words, the developer must fulfill the contract implied by the method names and the code comments.

Sometimes, the methods that an interface designates do not carry an obligation to perform a service for the caller. In some cases, the implementing class can even ignore the call, implementing a method with no body whatsoever.

CHALLENGE 2.3

Give an example of an interface with methods that do not imply responsibility on the part of the implementing class to take action on behalf of the caller or to return a value.

*A solution appears on page 360.*

**FIGURE 2.1:** The
`WindowAdapter` class
makes it easy to register
for window events while
ignoring any events you
are not interested in.

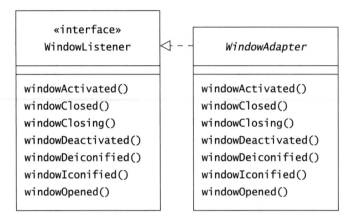

If you create an interface that specifies a collection of notification methods,
you should consider also supplying a **stub**—a class that implements the
interface with methods that do nothing. Developers can subclass the stub,
overriding only those methods in the interface that are important to their
application. The `WindowAdapter` class in `java.awt.event` is an example of
such a class, as Figure 2.1 shows. (For a whirlwind introduction to UML, see
Appendix C, UML at a Glance, on page 441.) The `WindowAdapter` class
implements all the methods in the `WindowListener` interface, but the
implementations are all empty; the methods contain no statements.

---

### CHALLENGE 2.4

What is the value of a stub class like `WindowAdapter`, composed of methods that do nothing?
(Writing out your answer will give you practice at refining and articulating your position.)

*A solution appears on page 361.*

---

## Placing Constants in Interfaces

Interfaces and classes can also cooperate when it comes to defining constants. A **constant** is a field that is static and final.

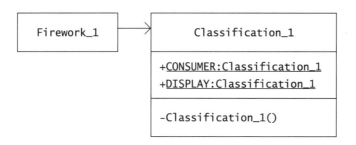

**FIGURE 2.2:** A Firework object has a classification that reflects whether Oozinoz can sell the firework to unlicensed operators.

Consider the definition of the classification of fireworks. In the United States, federal law defines two primary classifications, with each type of **firework** classified as either a consumer or a display type of firework. A *display* firework, any type of firework that is not a consumer firework, may be used only by licensed operators. In federal law, the *consumer* classification defines fireworks that states *may* allow ordinary citizens to purchase and to use. The consumer class is surprisingly large at the federal level, including rockets and aerial shells. State laws specify which consumer fireworks, if any, are legal to purchase and to operate.

Developers at Oozinoz use Classification constants to track whether a firework is federally mandated to be sold only to licensed operators (see Figure 2.2).

The names of the Firework_1 and the Classification_1 classes each end with an underscore and a version number because we will soon **refactor** their code into new versions. When you refactor code, you should not normally include versioning information in class names. Rather, you should use a configuration management system to keep track of versions of your code. However, two versions of the Classification class appear simultaneously in this book, and the naming scheme helps to differentiate these versions.

The Classification_1 class sets up two constants that define a firework's classification:

```
package com.oozinoz.fireworks;
public class Classification_1
{
    public static final Classification_1 CONSUMER =
        new Classification_1();
    public static final Classification_1 DISPLAY =
```

```
            new Classification_1();

        private Classification_1()
        {
        }
    }
```

A typical method that checks the classification constants looks like this:

```
    public void secureOrder(Firework_1 f /*, etc. */)
    {
        //...
        if (f.classification == Classification_1.DISPLAY)
        {
            // issue warning
        }
        else
        {
            // proceed
        }
    }
```

You can make the Oozinoz code a little cleaner if you move the classification constants to an interface and use the Classification class solely for type checking. (The name of the Classification class does not end with a version number, indicating that we won't refactor this class any further.) If you move the constants to an interface, you have to relax the visibility of the Classification constructor:

```
    package com.oozinoz.fireworks;
    public class Classification
    {
        protected Classification()
        {
        }
    }

    public interface ClassificationConstants
    {
        static final Classification CONSUMER
            = new Classification();
        static final Classification DISPLAY
            = new Classification();
    }
```

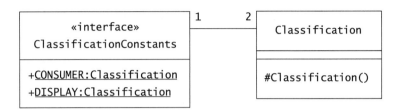

**FIGURE 2.3:** The ClassificationConstants interface defines the two classifications of fireworks that U.S. federal law recognizes.

Figure 2.3 shows the new relationship between ClassificationConstants and Classification. In this arrangement, the Classification class has no purpose other than to provide type checking for parameters of the Classification type. But the ClassificationConstants interface lets you make the secureOrder() code more readable.

---

**CHALLENGE 2.5**

How can you change the secureOrder() method and its class to take advantage of the ClassificationConstants interface?

*A solution appears on page 362.*

---

A Java interface is essentially a purely abstract class, with the provision that a class can implement multiple interfaces. If you think of it in this light, it is logical that a class "inherits" the constants defined in any interface the class implements.

## Summary

The basic purpose of a Java interface is to declare a set of methods that a class implements. This usually implies that the class provides the services that the method names suggest. An exception to this responsibility occurs when the interface lets an object register for event notification. In this situation, the client of the interface bears responsibility for calling the interface methods when the events implied by the method names occur. When you create a registration interface, it is useful to pair the interface with an abstract class that provides empty implementations of the interface methods, simplifying registration. Interfaces and classes can also collaborate in the use of constants, with interfaces providing better readability.

## ■ BEYOND ORDINARY INTERFACES

You can simplify and strengthen your designs with appropriate application of Java interfaces. Sometimes, though, the design of an interface has to go beyond the ordinary definition and use of an interface.

| If you intend to | Apply the pattern |
|---|---|
| • Adapt a class's interface to match the interface a client expects | ADAPTER (Chapter 3) |
| • Provide a simple interface into a collection of classes | FACADE (Chapter 4) |
| • Define an interface that applies to individual objects and groups of objects | COMPOSITE (Chapter 5) |
| • Decouple an abstraction from its implementation so that the two can vary independently | BRIDGE (Chapter 6) |

The intent of each design pattern is to solve a problem in a context. Interface-oriented patterns address contexts in which you need to define or to redefine access to the methods of a class or a group of classes. For example, when you have a class that performs a service you need but with method names that do not match a client's expectations, you can apply the ADAPTER pattern.

# 3

# ADAPTER

As a software developer, you write classes whose methods are called by clients. You may be able to control the interface that the client expects, but often you will not be able to do so. The most common example of an expectation that you must frequently fulfill is the implementation of the `main()` method that the Java interpreter expects. Services such as Swing also often include features that require you to support a predefined interface.

When you need to implement an expected interface, you may find that an existing class performs the services a client needs but with different method names. You can use the existing class to meet the client's needs by applying the ADAPTER pattern. The intent of ADAPTER is to provide the interface a client expects, using the services of a class with a different interface.

## Adapting in the Presence of Foresight

When you need to adapt your code to meet a client's needs, you may find that the client planned for such circumstances. This is evident when the client's developers provide a Java interface that defines the services the client code needs, as in the example shown in Figure 3.1. A client class in a package makes calls to a `service()` method that is declared in a Java interface. Suppose that you have found an existing class with a method that can fulfill the client's needs, but the name of the method is `usefulMethod()`. You can adapt the existing class to meet the client's needs by writing a class that extends `ExistingClass`, implements `ThoughtfulInterface`, and overrides `service()` so that it delegates its requests to `usefulMethod()`.

**21**

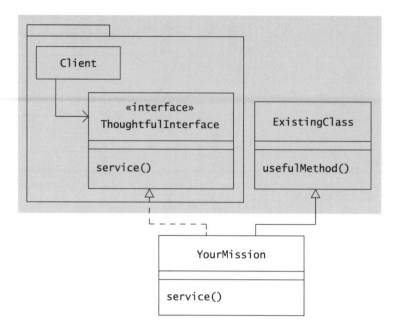

Suppose that you are working with a rocket simulation program at Oozinoz, and you want to include an aerial shell as a "rocket." An **aerial shell** is a firework that is fired from a **mortar**, or tube, and explodes midflight, ejecting and igniting a collection of stars. A **star** is a compressed pellet of a brightly burning, explosive chemical compound. The main difference between shells and rockets is that shells have a lifting charge and no subsequent thrust, whereas rockets have a thrust that is fairly continuous through midflight.

The developer of the rocket simulation has thoughtfully provided an interface that defines the behavior the simulation requires from a rocket:

```
public interface RocketSim
{
    abstract Length apogee();
    public Force thrust();
}
```

This interface is now public, unlike the version in Chapter 2, Introducing Interfaces. The sidebar Units of Measure on page 24 describes how Oozinoz models physical quantities, such as length and force.

A key attribute of a shell is its **muzzle velocity**—the speed at which the shell leaves the mortar it fires from. Given the muzzle velocity, you can calculate the apogee of the shell. (To learn about the chemistry and physics of fireworks, I recommend reading *The Chemistry of Fireworks* (Russell 2000).) The muzzle velocity also lets you calculate the lifting charge force, so you can model thrust as an initial spike that quickly drops to zero.

---

### CHALLENGE 3.1

Complete the class diagram in Figure 3.2 to show the design of a ShellAsRocket class that lets a Shell object participate in a simulation as a RocketSim object.

*A solution appears on page 363.*

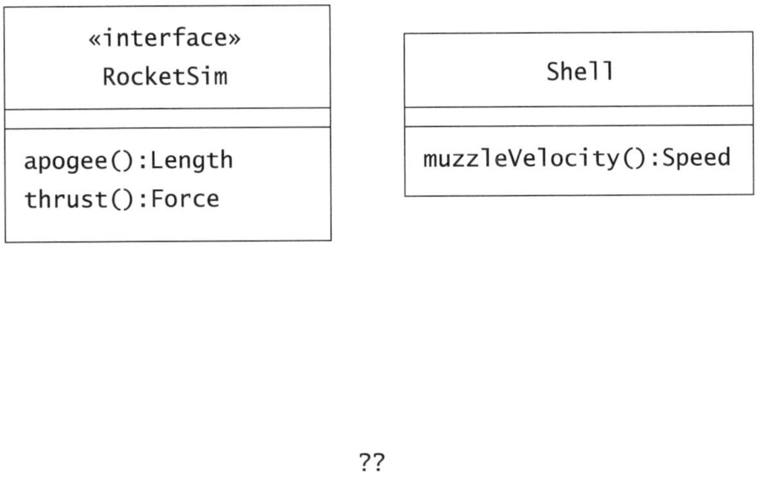

---

| «interface» RocketSim |
| --- |
| apogee():Length<br>thrust():Force |

| Shell |
| --- |
| muzzleVelocity():Speed |

**FIGURE 3.2:** You can adapt a shell's methods to meet the needs of a rocket simulation.

## Units of Measure

The classes and interfaces in the `com.oozinoz.units` package help developers at Oozinoz to prevent unit conversion errors. Rather than using **`double`** to represent everything from inches of length to pounds of force, the Oozinoz developers have created a sophisticated object model for measurements.

A **measure** is a combination of a magnitude and a dimension. A **dimension** is an aggregation of a measure's length, mass, and time exponents. For example, a volume, such as one $ft^3$, is three dimensional in length. An acceleration of 9.8 meters/second$^2$ has a length dimension of 1 and a time dimension of $-2$. The **`units`** package models commonly used dimensions, as Figure 3.3 shows. Note that the subclasses of `Measure` are dimensions, such as **Length** and **Force**, not units, such as inches and pounds.

**FIGURE 3.3:** Oozinoz models units as instances of the `Measure` class, whose subclasses represent particular physical dimensions.

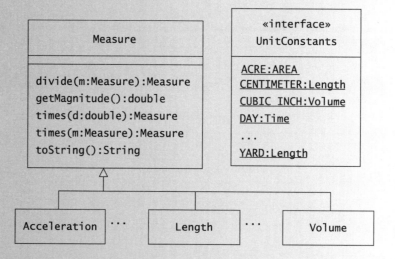

A **unit** is a standard measure—a standard magnitude of a given dimension. For example, a cubic inch is a unit of volume, and a pound is a unit of force. The `UnitConstants` interface supplies units, and the `Measure` hierarchy supplies dimensions for type checking. For example, the `UnitConstants` interface supplies a `CUBIC_INCH` constant whose type is `Volume`.

You can construct new instances of **Measure** by building from the units available in the **UnitConstants** interface. For example, suppose that the cross section of a rocket is 0.75 square inches.

```
Area a = (Area) INCH.times(INCH).times(.75);
```

The **times()** method instantiates whichever subclass of **Measure** reflects the dimension of the new unit. The return type of this method is **Measure**, but you can cast the result to the more specific class that represents the measure's dimension.

To convert a measure to a quantity of a specific unit, divide the measure by the unit. For example:

```
package com.oozinoz.units;
public class ShowConversion implements UnitConstants
{
    public static void main(String[] args)
    {
        Volume v = (Volume) QUART.times(3);
        showVolume(v);
    }

    public static void showVolume(Volume v)
    {
        System.out.println("I see ");
        System.out.println(
            "\t" + v.divide(GALLON) + " gallon(s),");
        System.out.println(
            "\t" + v.divide(CUBIC_INCH) + " cubic inch(es),");
        System.out.println(
            "\t" + v.divide(MILLILITER) + " milliliter(s).");
    }
}
```

This program prints out:

```
I see:
    0.75 gallon(s),
    173.2 cubic inch(es),
    2839.0 milliliter(s).
```

Many of the examples (and some of the challenges) that lie ahead use the **UnitConstants** units to create and to apply various fireworks measurements.

## Class and Object Adapters

The designs in Figures 3.1 and 3.2 are *class adapters,* which adapt through subclassing. When you need to apply ADAPTER, you may not be able to subclass the class whose methods you need to adapt. In some cases, you may need to create an adapter that adapts information from more than one object. You may also find that the interface you need to adapt to is not a Java interface but rather an **abstract class** that you must subclass. In such cases, you need to create an *object adapter*—an adapter that uses delegation rather than subclassing.

A good example of a class that requires you to write an object adapter is the JTable class in javax.swing. This class creates a **GUI (graphical user interface)** table component filled with the information that your adapter feeds to it. To display data from your domain, JTable provides constructors that accept an instance of the TableModel defined in javax.swing.table and shown in Figure 3.4.

Many of the methods in TableModel suggest the possibility of a default implementation. Happily, the **JDK (Java Development Kit)** supplies an abstract class that provides default implementations of all but the most domain-specific methods in TableModel. Figure 3.5 shows this class.

**FIGURE 3.4:** The JTable class is a Swing component that lifts data from an implementation of TableModel into a GUI table.

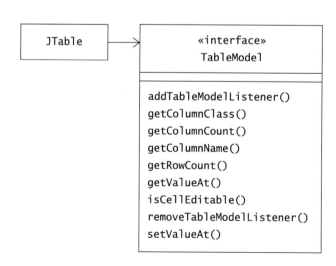

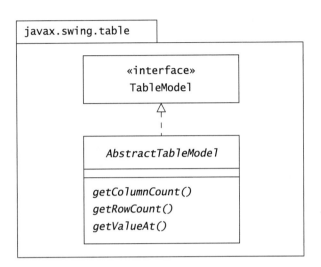

**FIGURE 3.5:** The `AbstractTableModel` class provides defaults for all but a few of the methods in `TableModel`.

Suppose that you want to show a few rockets in a table, using a Swing user interface. As Figure 3.6 shows, you can create a `RocketTable` class that adapts an array of rockets to the interface that `TableModel` and `AbstractTableModel` expect.

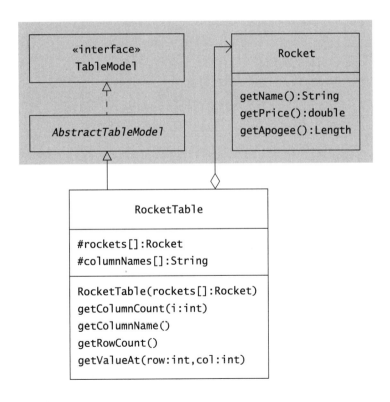

**FIGURE 3.6:** The RocketTable class adapts the `TableModel` interface to the Rocket class from the Oozinoz domain.

The `RocketTable` class has to subclass `AbstractTableModel` because
`AbstractTableModel` is a class, not an interface. Whenever the interface
you are adapting to is supported with an abstract class, you must use an
object adapter. In this example, though, there is a second reason you cannot use a class adapter. A `RocketTable` is not a kind or a subtype of
`Rocket`. When an adapter class must draw on information from more
than one object, you have to implement the adapter as an object adapter.

When you create the `RocketTable` class, you can easily display information about rockets in a Swing `JTable` object, as Figure 3.7 shows. To
create the application that Figure 3.7 shows, you have to develop the
`RocketTable` class and before writing an application that shows the table:

```
package com.oozinoz.applications;
import javax.swing.table.*;
import com.oozinoz.fireworks.*;
public class RocketTable extends AbstractTableModel
{
    protected Rocket[] rockets;
    protected String[] columnNames =
        new String[] { "Name", "Price", "Apogee" };

    public RocketTable(Rocket[] rockets)
    {
        this.rockets = rockets;
    }

    public int getColumnCount()
    {
        // challenge!
    }

    public String getColumnName(int i)
    {
        // challenge!
    }
```

```
        public int getRowCount()
        {
            // challenge!
        }
        public Object getValueAt(int row, int col)
        {
            // challenge!

        }
    }
```

---

**CHALLENGE 3.2**

Fill in the code for the RocketTable methods that adapt an array of Rocket objects to serve as a TableModel.

*Solutions appear on page 363.*

---

To launch the display that Figure 3.7 shows, you can create a couple of example Rocket objects, place them in an array, construct an instance of RocketTable from the array, and use Swing classes to display the table. The ShowRocketTable class provides an example:

```
        package com.oozinoz.applications;
        import java.awt.*;
        import javax.swing.*;
        import java.awt.event.*;
        import com.oozinoz.fireworks.*;
        import com.oozinoz.units.*;
        public class ShowRocketTable implements UnitConstants
        {
            //....
        }
```

The main() method of ShowRocketTable sets up default table fonts, creates a Swing table, and displays it:

```
public static void main(String[] args)
{
    setFonts();
    JTable t = new JTable(getRocketTable());
    t.setRowHeight(36);
    JScrollPane jsp = new JScrollPane(t);
    jsp.setPreferredSize(
        new java.awt.Dimension(300, 100));
    display(jsp, " Rockets");
}
```

The setFonts() methods establishes the fonts to use for table cells and column headers:

```
private static void setFonts()
{
    Font f = new Font("Dialog", Font.PLAIN, 18);
    UIManager.put("Table.font", f);
    UIManager.put("TableHeader.font", f);
}
```

The getRocketTable() method returns a RocketTable object that fulfills the role of a TableModel. Essentially, the RocketTable object adapts a (row, column) request into a (rocket, attribute) request:

```
private static RocketTable getRocketTable()
{
    Rocket r1 = new Rocket(
        "Shooter", 3.95, (Length) METER.times(50));
    Rocket r2 = new Rocket(
        "Orbit", 29.95, (Length) METER.times(5000));
    return new RocketTable(new Rocket[] { r1, r2 });
}
```

The display() method contains reusable code:

```
public static void display(Component c, String title)
{
    JFrame f = new JFrame(title);
    f.getContentPane().add(c);
    f.addWindowListener
        (
            new WindowAdapter()
            {
                public void windowClosing(WindowEvent e)
```

```
                    {
                        System.exit(0);
                    }
                }
            );
        f.pack();
        f.setVisible(true);
    }
```

In Chapter 4, FACADE, you will port this code to a utility class. With fewer than 20 statements of its own, the ShowRocketTable class sits above hundreds or thousands of statements that collaborate to produce a table component within a GUI framework. The JTable class can handle nearly every aspect of displaying a table, but it can't know in advance what data you will want to present. To let you supply the data it needs, the JTable class sets you up to apply ADAPTER. To use JTable, you implement the TableModel interface that JTable expects, along with a class that provides the data you want to display.

It's easy to use JTable because this class is designed for adaptation. In practice, when you need to adapt an existing class to meet a client's needs, you may find that the client code designers have not foreseen this possibility and have not provided an interface to adapt to.

## Unforeseen Adaptation

Suppose that an existing application at Oozinoz issues warnings and prints out other messages to System.out. The commonly used expression System.out is an instance of PrintStream. Noting this and foreseeing that you might want to redirect the message output, the application's designers have built in a setOutput() method. It would be better if these designers had defined the interface they required for displaying messages. That would have let you provide an implementation for just the PrintStream methods that the application uses. But at least the setOutput() method lets you supply a different instance of PrintStream as the message channel.

Suppose that you want to redirect the messages to appear in a JText-Area object. Inspecting the application, you note that the only call it makes to the PrintStream object you supply is print(), with an Object

**FIGURE 3.8:** A `MessageAdapter` object is a `PrintStream` object that forwards messages to a `JTextArea` object's `append()` method.

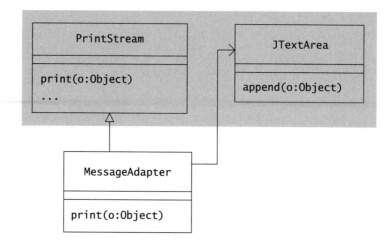

argument. To redirect these `print()` calls to a `JTextArea` object, you might design the `MessageAdapter` class as shown in Figure 3.8.

Suppose that you implement this design and pass a `MessageAdapter` object to the application's `setOutput()` method. Although you may find that all your tests pass, this design is fragile.

---

**CHALLENGE 3.3**

Write down a comment explaining what might go wrong with this approach to adaptation.

*A solution appears on page 364.*

---

You could try making `MessageAdapter` more robust by overriding every method in `PrintStream`, but this is difficult and relies on your ability to translate every `PrintStream` behavior to a meaningful counterpart in `JTextArea`. A better solution would specify the interface that the application can use. If you have access to the developers of the client code, you can ask for support on their end.

---

**CHALLENGE 3.4**

You'd like to narrow the responsibility of the MessageAdapter class with a specification of the calls the client might make to it. What request should you make?

*A solution appears on page 365.*

---

## Recognizing ADAPTER

Adapters are healthier when a Java interface narrows the responsibility that the adapter class bears to the client. The JTable class, for example, specifies the exact interface it needs with the TableModel interface. By comparison, the MessageAdapter class has no contract with the application it plugs into that the application won't expand its use of a PrintStream object's behavior. In fact, although the word *adapter* appears in the name of the MessageAdapter class, you might question whether MessageAdapter is an instance of the ADAPTER pattern.

---

**CHALLENGE 3.5**

Provide an argument that MessageAdapter, as it appears in Figure 3.8, is or is not an example of ADAPTER.

*A solution appears on page 365.*

---

In answering Challenge 2.4, you explained the value of the WindowAdapter class. The MouseAdapter class, as Figure 3.9 shows, is another example of a class that stubs out the requirements of a registration interface.

**FIGURE 3.9:** The MouseAdapter class stubs out the requirements of the MouseListener interface.

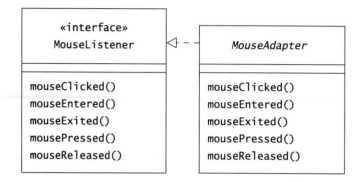

---

## CHALLENGE 3.6

Provide an argument that you are applying the ADAPTER pattern when you use the MouseAdapter class. Alternatively, argue that this is not the case.

*A solution appears on page 366.*

---

### Summary

The JTable component in Swing is a good example of a class whose developers applied the ADAPTER pattern. A JTable component sets itself up as a client that needs table information as defined by the TableModel interface. This makes it easy for you to write an adapter that feeds the table data from domain objects, such as instances of the Rocket class.

To use JTable, you need to write an *object* adapter that delegates calls to instances of an existing class. Two aspects of JTable prevent you from using a *class* adapter. First, you will usually create your table adapter as a subclass of AbstractTableModel, so you can't also subclass your existing class. Second, the JTable class requires a collection of objects, and only an object adapter can adapt information from more than one object.

A class adapter produces a single object that is the adapter. This avoids forwarding calls from an adapter object to instance(s) of the class that it adapts. A class adapter object simply translates method names, forwarding calls to itself.

The relative advantages of class and object adapters are small in comparison to the advantage of having a Java interface that defines the client's needs. In the absence of such an interface, your adapter object poses as an instance of the client's required type, with no contract defining the client's needs. In a situation like this you should, if possible, ask the client developers to build in an interface to which you can adapt.

# 4

# FACADE

A GREAT ADVANTAGE of object-oriented (OO) programming is that it helps keep applications from becoming monolithic programs with hopelessly interwoven pieces. An "application" in an OO system is a minimal class that knits together the behaviors from reusable toolkits of other classes. A toolkit or subsystem developer often creates packages of well-designed classes without providing any applications that tie the classes together. The packages in the JDK are generally like this; they are toolkits from which you can weave an endless variety of domain-specific applications.

The reusability of toolkits comes with a problem: The diverse applicability of classes in an OO subsystem may offer an oppressive variety of options. A developer who wants to use the toolkit may not know where to begin. This is especially a problem when a developer wants to apply a normal, no-frills, *vanilla* usage of the classes in a package. The FACADE pattern addresses this need. A facade is a class with a level of functionality that lies between a toolkit and a complete application, offering a vanilla usage of the classes in a package or a subsystem. The intent of the FACADE pattern is to provide an interface that makes a subsystem easy to use.

## Refactoring to FACADE

A facade provides an interface, but it does not use a Java interface. Rather, a facade is a class with methods that make it easy to use the classes in a subsystem.

Consider an example from the early days at Oozinoz, when there were not yet standards for GUI development. Suppose that you come across an

**FIGURE 4.1:** The
`FlightPanel_1` class
displays the flight path
of an unexploded shell.

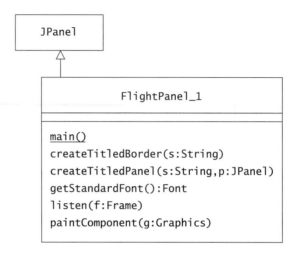

**FIGURE 4.1:** The
`FlightPanel_1` class
displays the flight path
of an unexploded shell.

application that a developer has created to show the flight path of an unexploded shell. Figure 4.1 shows this class. As before, the underscore in the name of the `FlightPanel_1` class is a hint that this class, from `com.oozinoz.applications`, needs refactoring.

Aerial shells are designed to explode high in the sky, with spectacular results. But occasionally, a shell does not explode at all; it is a **dud**. If a shell does not explode, its return to Earth becomes interesting. A shell, unlike a rocket, is unpowered, so if you ignore the effects of wind and air resistance, the flight path of a dud is a simple parabola. Figure 4.2 shows a screen shot of the window that appears when you execute `Flight-Panel_1.main()`.

**FIGURE 4.2:** The
`FlightPanel_1`
application shows
where a dud may land.

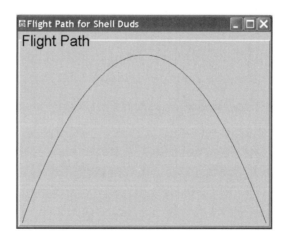

There is a problem with the FlightPanel_1 class: It intermingles three purposes. Its primary purpose is to act as a panel that displays a flight path. A second purpose of this class is to calculate a parabolic flight path. The FlightPanel_1 class currently performs this calculation in its paintComponent() code:

```
public void paintComponent(Graphics g)
{
    super.paintComponent(g); // paint the background
    int nPoint = 101;
    double w = getWidth() - 1;
    double h = getHeight() - 1;
    int[] x = new int[nPoint];
    int[] y = new int[nPoint];

    for (int i = 0; i < nPoint; i++)
    {
        // t goes 0 to 1
        double t = ((double) i) / (nPoint - 1);
        // x goes 0 to w
        x[i] = (int) (t * w);
        // y is h at t = 0 and t = 1, and
        // y is 0 at t = .5
        y[i] = (int) (4 * h * (t - .5) * (t - .5));
    }
    g.drawPolyline(x, y, nPoint);
}
```

See the sidebar Parametric Equations on page 40 for an explanation of how this code establishes the *x* and *y* values of the dud's path.

The third purpose that FlightPanel_1 fulfills is to act as a complete application, wrapping the flight path panel in a titled border and displaying it. This code appears in the main() routine:

```
public static void main(String[] args)
{
    FlightPanel_1 fp = new FlightPanel_1();
    fp.setPreferredSize(new Dimension(300, 200));
    JPanel fp_titled = createTitledPanel("Flight Path", fp);
    //
    JFrame frame = new JFrame("Flight Path for Shell Duds");
    frame.getContentPane().add(fp_titled);
```

```
frame.addWindowListener
    (
        new WindowAdapter()
        {
            public void windowClosing(WindowEvent e)
            {
                System.exit(0);
            }
        }
    );
frame.pack();
frame.setVisible(true);
}
```

## Parametric Equations

When you need to plot a curve, it can be difficult to describe the *y* values as functions of *x* values. **Parametric equations** let you define both *x* and *y* in terms of a third parameter that you introduce. Specifically, you can define that time t goes from 0 to 1 as the curve is drawn, and you can define *x* and *y* as functions of the parameter t.

For example, suppose that you want the parabolic flight of a nonexploding shell to stretch across the width, *w*, of a `Graphics` object. Then a parametric equation for *x* is easy:

```
x = w * t
```

The *y* values for a parabola must vary with the square of the value of t. *Y* values increase going down the screen. For a parabolic flight, *y* should be 0 at time t = 0.5:

```
y = k * (t - 0.5) * (t - 0.5)
```

Here, *k* represents a constant that we still need to determine. The equation provides for *y* to be 0 at t = 0.5 and provides for *y* to have the same value at t = 0 and t = 1. At those two times, *y* should be *h*, so with a little algebraic manipulation, you can find the complete equation for *y*:

```
y = 4 * h * (t - 0.5) * (t - 0.5)
```

Figure 4.2 shows the equations for a parabola in action.

Another advantage of parametric equations is that there is no problem drawing curves that have more than one *y* value for a given *x* value. Consider drawing a circle. The equation for a circle with a radius of 1 is:

$$x^2 + y^2 = r^2$$

or

$$y = +- \text{ sqrt } (r^2 - x^2)$$

Handling the fact that two *y* values emerge for every *x* value is complicated. It's also difficult to adjust these values to plot correctly within a **Graphics** object's height and width. Polar coordinates make the function for a circle simpler:

```
x = r * cos(theta)
y = r * sin(theta)
```

These formulas are parametric equations that show *x* and *y* as functions of a new parameter, theta. Theta represents the sweep of an arc that varies from 0 to 2 pi as a circle is drawn. You can set the radius of a circle so that it will fit within the height *h* and width *w* of a **Graphics** object. A handful of parametric equations suffice to plot a circle within the bounds of a **Graphics** object:

```
theta = 2 * pi * t
r = min(w, h)/2
x = w/2 + r * cos(theta)
y = h/2 - r * sin(theta)
```

Translating these equations into Java produces the circle shown in Figure 4.3.

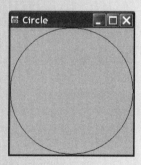

**FIGURE 4.3:** Parametric equations simplify the modeling of curves where *y* is not a single-valued function of *x*.

The code that draws a circle is a fairly direct translation of the mathematical formulas. One subtlety is that the code reduces the height and width of the `Graphics` object because the pixels are numbered from 0 to height −1 and from 0 to width −1:

```java
package com.oozinoz.applications;
import javax.swing.*;
import java.awt.*;
import com.oozinoz.ui.SwingFacade;
public class ShowCircle extends JPanel
{
    public static void main(String[] args)
    {
        ShowCircle sc = new ShowCircle();
        sc.setPreferredSize(new Dimension(300, 300));
        SwingFacade.launch(sc, " Circle");
    }
    protected void paintComponent(Graphics g)
    {
        super.paintComponent(g);
        int nPoint = 101;
        double w = getWidth() - 1;
        double h = getHeight() - 1;
        double r = Math.min(w, h) / 2.0;
        int[] x = new int[nPoint];
        int[] y = new int[nPoint];
        for (int i = 0; i < nPoint; i++)
        {
            double t = ((double) i) / (nPoint - 1);
            double theta = Math.PI * 2.0 * t;
            x[i] = (int) (w / 2 + r * Math.cos(theta));
            y[i] = (int) (h / 2 - r * Math.sin(theta));
        }
        g.drawPolyline(x, y, nPoint);
    }
}
```

Defining *x* and *y* functions in terms of t lets you divide the tasks of determining *x* values and *y* values. This is often simpler than defining *y* in terms of *x* and often facilitates the mapping of *x* and *y* onto a `Graphics` object's coordinates. Parametric equations also simplify the plotting of curves where *y* is not a single-valued function of *x*.

---

## CHALLENGE 4.1

Complete the diagram in Figure 4.4 to show the code for FlightPanel_1 refactored into three classes: a FlightPath class, a reduced FlightPanel class that draws a flight path, and a SwingFacade class. Provide the facade with the utility methods that appeared in the initial FlightPanel_1 class. Also provide the facade with a method to launch a frame.

*A solution appears on page 366.*

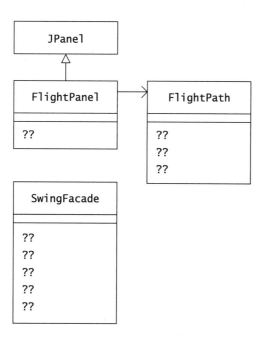

**FIGURE 4.4:** This diagram shows the flight path application refactored into classes that each have one job.

After refactoring, the FlightPanel class is much simpler:

```
package com.oozinoz.applications;
import javax.swing.*;
import java.awt.*;
import com.oozinoz.simulation.FlightPath;
public class FlightPanel extends JPanel
{
    public void paintComponent(Graphics g)
    {
```

```
            super.paintComponent(g); // paint the background
            int nPoint = 101;
            FlightPath fp =
                new FlightPath(
                    getWidth() - 1, getHeight() - 1);
            g.drawPolyline(
                fp.getX(nPoint),
                fp.getY(nPoint),
                nPoint);
        }
    }
```

The FlightPath class provides the parabolic flight path of a dud:

```
package com.oozinoz.simulation;
public class FlightPath
{
    protected double distance;
    protected double apogee;

    public FlightPath(double distance, double apogee)
    {
        this.distance = distance;
        this.apogee = apogee;
    }

    public int[] getX(int nPoint)
    {
        int[] x = new int[nPoint];
        for (int i = 0; i < nPoint; i++)
        {
            // t goes 0 to 1
            double t = ((double) i) / (nPoint - 1);
            // x goes 0 to distance
            x[i] = (int) (t * distance);
        }
        return x;
    }

    public int[] getY(int nPoint)
    {
        int[] y = new int[nPoint];
        for (int i = 0; i < nPoint; i++)
        {
            // t goes 0 to 1
```

```
            double t = ((double) i) / (nPoint - 1);
            // y is apogee at t = 0 and t = 1,
            // and y is 0 at t = .5
            y[i] = (int) (4 * apogee * (t - .5) * (t - .5));
        }
        return y;
    }
}
```

Most of the code of the `main()` routine of the initial `FlightPanel` class migrates to **static methods** in the `SwingFacade` class:

```java
package com.oozinoz.ui;
import javax.swing.*;
import javax.swing.border.*;
import java.awt.*;
import java.awt.event.*;
public class SwingFacade
{
    public static TitledBorder createTitledBorder(
        String title)
    {
        TitledBorder tb =
            BorderFactory.createTitledBorder(
                BorderFactory.createBevelBorder(
                    BevelBorder.RAISED),
                title,
                TitledBorder.LEFT,
                TitledBorder.TOP);
        tb.setTitleColor(Color.black);
        tb.setTitleFont(getStandardFont());
        return tb;
    }

    public static JPanel createTitledPanel(
        String title,
        JPanel in)
    {
        JPanel out = new JPanel();
        out.add(in);
        out.setBorder(createTitledBorder(title));
        return out;
    }
```

```
public static Font getStandardFont()
{
    return new Font("Dialog", Font.PLAIN, 18);
}

public static JFrame launch(
    Component c,
    String title)
{
    JFrame frame = new JFrame(title);
    frame.getContentPane().add(c);
    listen(frame);
    frame.pack();
    frame.setVisible(true);
    return frame;
}

public static void listen(Frame f)
{
    f.addWindowListener
        (
            new WindowAdapter()
            {
                public void windowClosing(WindowEvent e)
                {
                    System.exit(0);
                }
            }
        );
    }
}
```

You may have found that refactoring FlightPanel_1 made the application disappear, with no main() method appearing anywhere. It often happens that refactoring a monolithic application produces a facade and eliminates the presence of a main() method on any of the new classes. To achieve the results of the original application in this example, you can create a standalone class with just one method:

```
package com.oozinoz.applications;
import java.awt.Dimension;
import javax.swing.*;
```

```
import com.oozinoz.ui.SwingFacade;
public class ShowFlightPanel
{
    public static void main(String[] args)
    {
        FlightPanel fp = new FlightPanel();
        fp.setPreferredSize(new Dimension(300, 200));
        JPanel p =
            SwingFacade.createTitledPanel("Flight Path", fp);
        SwingFacade.launch(p, "Flight Path for Shell Duds");
    }
}
```

Running this class produces exactly the same results as the main() in the original FlightPanel class. But now, you have a more reusable toolkit and a Swing facade that provides standard components and simplifies launching Swing applications.

## Facades, Utilities, and Demos

A facade class may have all static methods, as is the case with the SwingFacade class provided in the solutions. Such a class is called a **utility** in UML (Booch, Rumbaugh, and Jacobson 1999). A **demo** is an example that shows how to use a class or a subsystem. As such, demos provide much of the same value as facades.

---

**CHALLENGE 4.2**

Write down two differences between a demo and a facade.

*A solution appears on page 367.*

---

The javax.swing package contains JOptionPane, a class that "makes it easy to pop up a standard dialog box," according to the class comment.

**FIGURE 4.5:** The
JOptionPane class
makes it easy to display
dialogs such as this one.

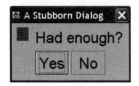

For example, the following code displays and redisplays a dialog until the
user clicks the Yes button (see Figure 4.5):

```
package com.oozinoz.applications;
import javax.swing.*;
public class ShowOptionPane
{
    public static void main(String[] args)
    {
        int option;
        do
        {
            option =
                JOptionPane.showConfirmDialog(
                    null,
                    "Had enough?",
                    " A Stubborn Dialog",
                    JOptionPane.YES_NO_OPTION);
        }
        while (option == JOptionPane.NO_OPTION);
    }
}
```

**CHALLENGE 4.3**

The JOptionPane does in fact make it easy to display a dialog. State whether this class is a
facade, a utility, or a demo, and justify your answer.

*A solution appears on page 367.*

---

**CHALLENGE 4.4**

Few facades appear in the Java class libraries. Why is that?

*A solution appears on page 367.*

---

## Summary

Ordinarily, you should refactor the classes in a subsystem until each class has a well-defined purpose. This will make your code easier to maintain, but it can also make it difficult for a user of your subsystem to know where to begin. To help the developer who is using your code, you can supply demos or facades that go with your subsystem. A demo is usually a stand-alone, nonreusable application that shows one way to apply a subsystem. A facade is usually a configurable, reusable class with a higher-level interface that makes the subsystem easier to use.

# 5

# COMPOSITE

A COMPOSITE is a group of objects in which some objects may contain others; thus, one object may represent groups, and another may represent an individual item, or **leaf**. When you model a composite, two powerful concepts emerge. One important modeling idea is to design groups so that they can contain either individual items or other groups. (A common error is to define groups so that they can contain only leaves.) A second powerful concept is to define common behaviors for individual objects and for compositions. You can bring these ideas together by defining a common type for groups and items and by modeling groups as containing a collection of objects of this type. This fulfills the intent of the COMPOSITE pattern: COMPOSITE lets clients treat individual objects and compositions of objects uniformly.

## An Ordinary Composite

Figure 5.1 shows an ordinary composite structure. The Leaf and Composite classes share a common interface that Component abstracts, and a Composite object retains a collection of other Composite and Leaf objects. Note that the Component class in Figure 5.1 is an abstract class with no concrete operations, so you could define it as an interface that Leaf and Composite implement.

**FIGURE 5.1:** The key ideas of COMPOSITE are that composites can contain other composites—not just leaves—and that composite and leaf nodes share a common interface.

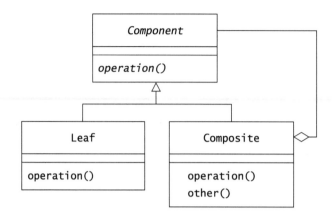

## CHALLENGE 5.1

Give two reasons why the interface that Leaf and Composite share usually appears in an abstract class rather than in an interface.

*A solution appears on page 368.*

## Recursive Behavior in Composites

Engineers at Oozinoz perceive a natural composition in the processing machines they use to produce fireworks. The factory is composed of bays; each bay has one or more manufacturing lines; a line is a collection of machines that collaboratively produce material to meet a schedule. The developers at Oozinoz have modeled this composition from the problem domain with the class structure shown in Figure 5.2. As the figure shows, the getMachineCount() behavior applies to both individual machines and collections of machines and returns the number of machines in any given component.

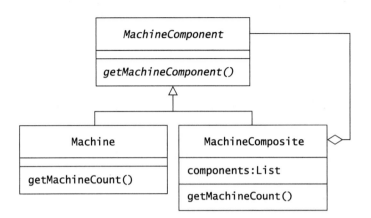

**FIGURE 5.2:** The getMachineCount() method is an appropriate behavior for both individual machines and composites.

---

**CHALLENGE 5.2**

Write the code for the getMachineCount() methods implemented by Machine and by MachineComposite.

*Example solutions appear on page 368.*

---

Suppose that MachineComponent also needs the following methods:

| Method | Behavior |
|---|---|
| isCompletelyUp() | Indicates whether all the machines in a component are in an "up" state |
| stopAll() | Directs all the machines in a component to stop processing |
| getOwners() | Returns a set of process engineers responsible for the machines in a component |
| getMaterial() | Return all the in-process material in a machine component |

The definition and operation of each method in MachineComponent is recursive. For example, the count of machines in a composite is the sum of the counts of machines in its components.

---

**CHALLENGE 5.3**

For each method declared by MachineComponent, give recursive definitions for MachineComposite and nonrecursive definitions for Machine.

| Method | Class | Definition |
|---|---|---|
| getMachineCount() | MachineComposite | Return the sum of the counts for each component in components. |
|  | Machine | Return 1. |
| isCompletelyUp() | MachineComposite | ?? |
|  | Machine | ?? |
| stopAll() | MachineComposite | ?? |
|  | Machine | ?? |
| getOwners() | MachineComposite | ?? |
|  | Machine | ?? |
| getMaterial() | MachineComposite | ?? |
|  | Machine | ?? |

*A solution appears on page 369.*

---

## Trees in Graph Theory

In a composite structure, we can say that a node that holds references to other nodes is a **tree**. However, this definition is a bit loose. To be more precise, we can apply a few terms from **graph theory** to object modeling.

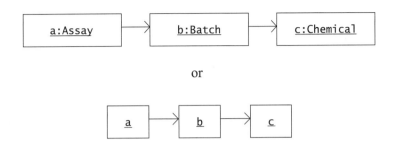

**FIGURE 5.3:** The two UML diagrams here show alternative representations of the same information: Object a refers to object b, and object b refers to object c.

We can start by drawing an object model as a **graph**—a collection of nodes and edges—with objects as nodes and object references as edges.

Consider an object model of an **assay**, or analysis, of a batch of a chemical. The Assay class has a batch attribute of type Batch, and the Batch class has a chemical attribute of type Chemical. Suppose that a particular Assay object a has a batch attribute that refers to a Batch object b. Suppose too that the chemical attribute of the Batch object b refers to a Chemical c. Figure 5.3 shows two alternative diagrams for this object model.

There is a **path**—a series of object references—from a to c because a refers to b and b refers to c. A **cycle** is a path in which a node appears twice. There would be a cycle of references in this object model if the c Chemical object referred back to the a:Assay object.

Object models are **directed graphs**: An object reference has a direction. Graph theory usually applies the term *tree* to refer to undirected graphs. However, a directed graph may be called a *tree* if it

- Has a **root** node that has no references to it
- Has exactly one edge, or reference, to all other nodes

We can also express the second rule by saying that each node except the root has exactly one *parent*—the node that refers to it.

The object model that Figure 5.3 depicts is a tree. For larger object models, it can be difficult to tell whether the model is a tree. Figure 5.4 shows the object model of a factory, called plant, that is a MachineComposite object. This plant contains a bay that has three machines: m, n, and o. The object model also shows that the plant object's list of machine components contains a direct reference to machine m.

**FIGURE 5.4:** An object model of a small fire-works factory

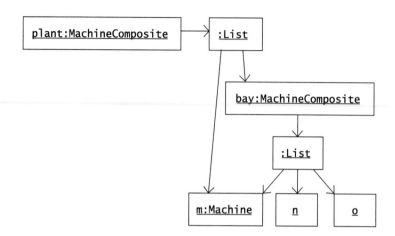

The plant object in Figure 5.4 does not contain a cycle, but note that it is not a tree, because two objects refer to the Machine object m. The bay object model, viewed in isolation from the plant object, *is* a tree.

Methods that work on composites may have defects if they assume that a composite is a tree. Challenge 5.2 asked for a definition of a getMachineCount() operation. The Machine class implementation of this operation as given in the solution to this challenge is arguably correct:

```
public int getMachineCount()
{
    return 1;
}
```

The MachineComposite class also correctly implements getMachineCount(), returning the sum of the counts for each of a composite's components:

```
public int getMachineCount()
{
    int count = 0;
    Iterator i = components.iterator();
    while (i.hasNext())
    {
        MachineComponent mc = (MachineComponent) i.next();
        count += mc.getMachineCount();
    }
    return count;
}
```

These methods are correct so long as MachineComponent objects are trees. It can happen, though, that a composite that you suppose is a tree suddenly becomes not a tree. This is especially likely to occur when users can edit the composition. Consider an example that might occur at Oozinoz.

The fireworks engineers at Oozinoz use a GUI application to record and to update the composition of machinery in the factory. One day, they report a defect regarding the number of machines that are reported to exist in the factory. You reproduce their object model with a `plant()` method on an `OozinozFactory` class:

```
public static MachineComposite plant()
{
    MachineComposite plant = new MachineComposite(100);
    MachineComposite bay = new MachineComposite(101);

    Machine m = new Mixer(102);
    Machine n = new Mixer(103);
    Machine o = new Mixer(104);
    bay.add(m);
    bay.add(n);
    bay.add(o);

    plant.add(m);
    plant.add(bay);
    return plant;
}
```

This code produces the `plant` object shown in Figure 5.4.

---

## CHALLENGE 5.4

What does the following program print out?

```
package com.oozinoz.machine;
public class ShowPlant
{
    public static void main(String[] args)
    {
        MachineComponent c = OozinozFactory.plant();
        System.out.println(c.getMachineCount());
    }
}
```

A solution appears on page 369.

**FIGURE 5.5:** An
isTree() method can
detect whether a com-
posite is in fact a tree.

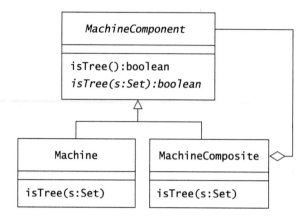

The GUI application that Oozinoz uses to let engineers build object models of a factory's machinery should check whether a node already exists in
a component tree before adding it a second time. A simple way to do this
is to maintain a set of existing nodes. You may not, however, always have
control over how a composite is formed. In this case, you can write an
isTree() method to check whether a composite is a tree.

An object model is a tree if an algorithm can traverse its references
without encountering the same node twice. You can implement an
isTree() method on the abstract class MachineComponent so that it delegates to an isTree() method that maintains a set of visited nodes. The
MachineComponent class can leave the implementation of the parameter-
ized isTree(s:Set) method abstract. Figure 5.5 shows the placement of
the isTree() methods.

The MachineComponent code delegates an isTree() call to its abstract
isTree(s:Set) method:

```
public boolean isTree()
{
    return isTree(new HashSet());
}


public abstract boolean isTree(Set s);
```

The implementation of isTree() for Machine reflects the fact that individual machines are always trees:

```
protected boolean isTree(Set visited)
{
    visited.add(this);
    return true;
}
```

The `MachineComposite` implementation of `isTree()` should add the receiving object (`this`) to the visited set and then iterate over the composite's components. The method can return `false` if any component has been previously visited or if any component is not itself a tree. Otherwise, the method can return `true`.

---

**CHALLENGE 5.5**

Write the code for `MachineComposite.isTree(Set s)`.

*A solution appears on page 370.*

---

With some care, you can guarantee that an object model is a tree by refusing changes that would make `isTree()` false. On the other hand, you may need to allow composites that are not trees, particularly when the problem domain that you are modeling contains cycles.

## Composites with Cycles

The nontree composite that Challenge 5.4 refers to was an accident. For physical objects, you may want to disallow the notion that an object is contained by more than one other object. Physical objects also usually cannot appear in cyclic models, in which an object ultimately contains itself. However, a problem domain can have nonphysical elements where cycles of containment make sense. This occurs frequently when modeling process flows.

Consider the construction of aerial shells such as the one that Figure 5.6 depicts. We launch a shell from a mortar by igniting the lifting charge of black powder that is seated beneath the core charge. The secondary

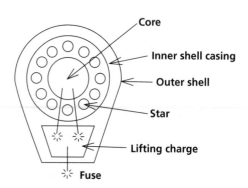

fuses burn while the shell in the air, eventually reaching the core. When the shell core explodes its stars ignite, creating the visual effects of aerial fireworks.

The process flow for making an aerial shell consists of building an inner shell, having it inspected, and then either reworking it or finishing its assembly. To make the inner shell, an operator uses a shell assembler to place some stars in a hemispherical casing, insert a black powder core, attach more stars on top of the core, and seal this subassembly with another hemispherical casing.

An inspector verifies that the inner shell meets safety and quality standards. If it doesn't, the operator disassembles the inner shell and, grumbling, makes it again. When an inner shell passes inspection, the operator finishes the shell, using a fuser to connect a lifting charge to the inner shell with fusing. Finally, the operator manually wraps the complete aerial shell.

As with machine composites, Oozinoz engineers have a GUI that lets them describe the composition of a process. Figure 5.7 shows the class structure that supports process modeling.

Figure 5.8 shows the objects that represent the process flow for making an aerial shell. The make process is a sequence of the buildInner step, the inspect step, and the reworkOrFinish subprocess. The reworkOrFinish subprocess takes one of two alternate paths. It may require a disassemble step followed by the make process, or it may require just the finish step.

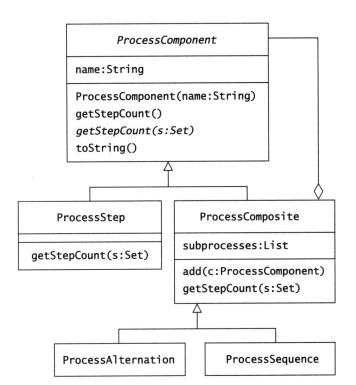

**FIGURE 5.7:** The process for manufacturing fireworks includes some steps that are alternations, or sequences, of other steps.

## CHALLENGE 5.6

Figure 5.8 shows the objects in a model of the shell assembly process. A complete object diagram would show links between any objects that refer to each other. For example, the diagram shows the references that the make object retains. Your challenge is to fill in the missing links in the diagram.

*A solution appears on page 370.*

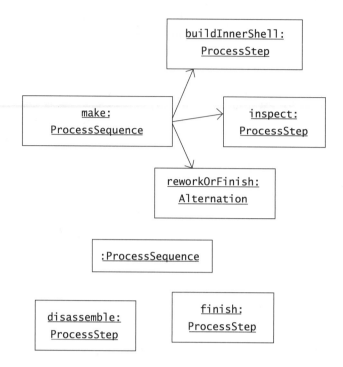

The getStepCount() operation in the ProcessComponent hierarchy counts the number of steps in a process flow. This method has to be careful to count each step only once and to not enter an infinite loop when a process contains a cycle. The ProcessComponent class implements the getStep-Count() method so that it relies on a companion method that passes along a set of visited nodes:

```
public int getStepCount()
{
    return getStepCount(new HashSet());
}


public abstract int getStepCount(Set visited);
```

The ProcessComposite class takes care in its implementation of the getStepCount() method not to visit a previously visited node:

```
public int getStepCount(Set visited)
{
    visited.add(this);
    int count = 0;
```

```
        Iterator i = subprocesses.iterator();
        while (i.hasNext())
        {
            ProcessComponent pc = (ProcessComponent) i.next();
            if (!visited.contains(pc))
            {
                count += pc.getStepCount(visited);
            }
        }
        return count;
    }
```

The `ProcessStep` class implementation of `getStepCount()` is simple:

```
    public int getStepCount(Set visited)
    {
        visited.add(this);
        return 1;
    }
```

The `com.oozinoz.process` package contains a `ShellProcess` class that has a `make()` method that returns the make object that Figure 5.8 depicts. (The code for this method appears on page 320, although the point here is that the make process contains four steps.) The `process` package also has a `TestProcess` class that provides automated tests of various types of process graphs. For example, this class includes a method that tests that the `getStepCount()` operation correctly counts the number of steps in the cyclic make process:

```
    public void testShell()
    {
        assertEquals(4, ShellProcess.make().getStepCount());
    }
```

This test runs and passes within the **JUnit** testing framework. See www.junit.org for more information about JUnit.


## Consequences of Cycles

Most operations on a composite, such as counting its number of leaf nodes, make sense even if the composite is not a tree. Usually, the only difference that nontree composites introduce is that you have to be careful to not operate on a given node twice. However, some operations become meaningless if the composite contains a cycle.

Operations that don't make sense if a composite contains cycles include any behavior that depends on the length of a path in the composite. For example, the *height* of a tree is the length of the longest path from the root to a leaf. This concept does not apply when cycles appear in a composite, as there is no limit to the length of some paths. In the fireworks process example, there is no "height" of the process composite. This mirrors the fact that there is no limit to the number of times an aerial shell may be reworked.

Another result of allowing composites that are not trees is that you lose the ability to assume that each node has a single parent. If a composite is not a tree, a node may have more than one parent. For example, the process that Figure 5.8 models might have several composite steps that use the inspect step, giving the inspect object multiple parents. There is no inherent problem in a node's having multiple parents, but a problem may arise if you create a model that insists otherwise.

## Summary

COMPOSITE contains two powerful, related concepts. One concept is that a group can contain either individual items or other groups. Related to this concept is the idea that groups and individual items may share a common interface. These ideas come together in object modeling, whereby you can create an abstract class or a Java interface that defines the behaviors that are common to groups and to individual objects.

Modeling composites often leads to recursive definition of methods on composite nodes. When recursion is present, a danger exists of writing code that produces an infinite loop. To avoid such problems, you can take steps to guarantee that your composites are always trees. Alternatively, you can allow cycles to occur in a composite, but you have to modify your algorithms to watch for recursion. You can handle cycles in composites by maintaining a collection of observed nodes.

# 6

## BRIDGE

The BRIDGE PATTERN focuses on the implementation of an **abstraction**. *Design Patterns* (Gamma et al. 1995) uses the word *abstraction* to refer to a class that relies on a set of abstract operations, where several implementations of the set of abstract operations are possible.

The ordinary way to implement an abstraction is to create a class hierarchy, with an abstract class at the top that defines the abstract operations; each subclass in the hierarchy provides a different implementation of the set of abstract operations. This approach becomes insufficient when you need to subclass the hierarchy for another reason. It can also happen that the abstract operations need to be defined and implemented in advance of abstractions that will use them.

You can create a *bridge* by moving the set of abstract operations to an interface, so that an abstraction will depend on an implementation of the interface. The intent of the BRIDGE pattern is to decouple an abstraction from the implementation of its abstract operations, so that the abstraction and its implementation can vary independently.

### A Classic Example of BRIDGE: Drivers

A common use of BRIDGE occurs when an application uses a driver. A **driver** is an object that operates a computer system or an external device according to a well-specified interface. Applications that use drivers are *abstractions*: The effect of running the application depends on which driver is in place. Each driver is an instance of the ADAPTER pattern, providing the interface a client expects, using the services of a class with a

**65**

different interface. An overall design that uses drivers is an instance of BRIDGE. The design separates application development from the development of the drivers that implement the abstract operations on which the applications rely.

An everyday example of applications using drivers to operate computer systems appears in database access. Database connectivity in Java usually depends on **JDBC**. ("JDBC" is a trademarked name, not an acronym.) A good resource that explains how to apply JDBC is *JDBC Database Access with Java™* (Hamilton, Cattell, and Fisher 1997). In short, JDBC is an **application programming interface (API)** for executing **structured query language (SQL)** statements. Classes that implement the interface are JDBC drivers, and applications that rely on these drivers are abstractions that can work with any database for which a JDBC driver exists. The JDBC architecture decouples an abstraction from its implementation so that the two can vary independently—an excellent example of BRIDGE.

To use a JDBC driver, you load it, connect to a database, and create a Statement object:

```
Class.forName(driverName);
Connection c =
    DriverManager.getConnection(url, user, passwd);
Statement s = c.createStatement();
```

A discussion of how the DriverManager class works is outside the scope of a discussion on BRIDGE. The point here is that the variable s is a Statement object, capable of issuing SQL queries that return result sets:

```
ResultSet r = s.executeQuery(
    "select name, apogee from firework");
while(r.next())
{
    String name = r.getString("name");
    int apogee = r.getInt("apogee");
    System.out.println(name + ", " + apogee);
}
```

**CHALLENGE 6.1**

Figure 6.1 shows a UML sequence diagram that illustrates the message flow in a typical JDBC application. Fill in the missing type names and the missing message name in this illustration.

*A solution appears on page 371.*

Figure 6.1 is a **sequence diagram**. You can use a **class diagram** to show the relationship of the application to the driver it applies. Figure 6.2 shows the general form of an abstraction and its implementation in an application of the Bridge pattern. This figure brings out the separation of an abstraction and its implementation. The effect of calling the opera-tion() method depends on which implementation of the Implementor interface is in place.

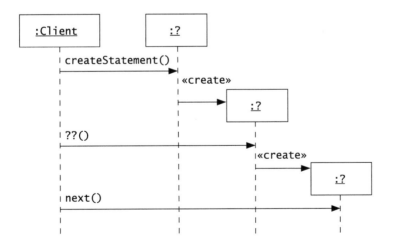

**FIGURE 6.1:** This diagram shows most of the typical message flow in a JDBC application.

**FIGURE 6.2:** A BRIDGE structure moves the abstract operations that an abstraction relies on into a separate interface.

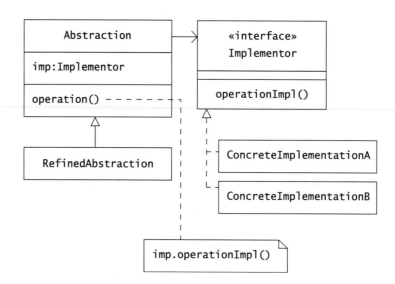

It can be challenging to see how the classes in a JDBC application align with the BRIDGE structure that Figure 6.2 shows. The questions to answer are: Which classes are abstractions? Which classes are "implementations"?

Consider the JDBCAdapter class that Sun Microsystems packages in the JDK as a demonstration of how to display data from a database table. This class implements the TableModel interface as shown in Figure 6.3.

The JDBCAdapter class constructor establishes a database connection and creates a Statement object. The adapter passes queries to the Statement object and makes the results available in a GUI component.

The JDBCAdapter class assumes that a client will call executeQuery() before making calls to extract data from the query. The results of not providing a query are somewhat unpredictable. Noticing this, suppose that you decide to subclass JDBCAdapter with an OzJDBCAdapter class that throws a NoQuery exception if a client forgets to issue a query before asking for data.

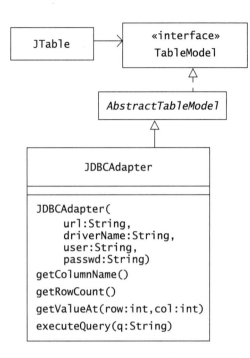

FIGURE 6.3: The JDBCAdapter class adapts information in a database table to appear in Swing JTable component.

**CHALLENGE 6.2**

Draw a diagram that shows the relationships among the classes JDBCAdapter, OzJDBCAdapter, NoQuery, and Statement.

*A solution appears on page 371.*

The JDBC architecture clearly divides the roles of the driver writer and the application writer. In some cases, this division will not exist in advance, even if you are using drivers. You may be able to set up drivers as sub-classes of an abstract superclass, with each subclass driving a different subsystem. In such a case, you can be forced to set up a BRIDGE when you need more flexibility.

## Refactoring to BRIDGE

Sometimes, you have to refactor an abstract class into a BRIDGE to gain more flexibility in the abstraction. Consider the MachineController hierarchy at Oozinoz. Other than database drivers, the most common application of drivers is to operate external devices. These devices may be peripherals, such as printers and pen plotters, or any machine capable of communicating with computers. Applications at Oozinoz control most of the machines on the factory floor with the drivers, or controllers, that Figure 6.4 shows.

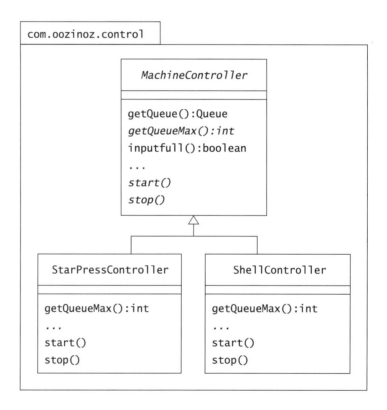

**FIGURE 6.4:** Instances of classes in the MachineController hierarchy drive machines in the Oozinoz factory.

The MachineController class defines the interface for an object that controls a machine. Subclasses provide different implementations of the methods that drive a machine. Most of the methods that Machine-Controller declares are abstract, but it does have concrete methods that depend on its **abstract methods**. For example, the inputFull() method is concrete, but its effects depend on how subclasses implement getQueueMax():

```
public boolean inputFull()
{
    return getQueueMax() >= getQueue().size();
}
```

The MachineController class is an abstraction whose implementation occurs in its subclasses, and we can consider separating the abstraction from its implementation. The motivation to separate an abstraction from its implementation usually occurs when a new reason for subclassing emerges. For example, suppose that you want to differentiate normal controllers from testing controllers. A testing controller has new methods that test or stress machines, such as an overflow() method that dispatches material to a machine until the input queue overflows and the machines signals an alarm. Figure 6.5 shows a design that provides for testing classes.

Introducing a TestController class turns out to force you to create three new classes, as test controllers for star presses and shell assemblers implement getQueueMax() differently. This is a problem because you'd like to be able to add new classes individually. The problem arises because the hierarchy is factored according to two principles: Each machine needs its own controller, and different types of controllers are used for normal operation and for testing. You really need a class for every combination of machine type and controller type—a maintenance nightmare. You can solve the problem by separating the MachineController abstraction from its implementation.

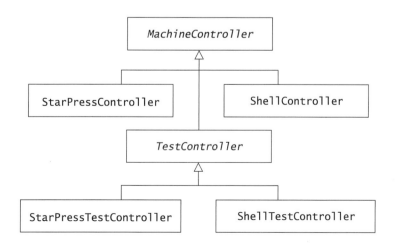

**FIGURE 6.5:** In this factoring, subclasses of MachineController exist for various types of machines and for various types of controllers.

To refactor a hierarchy with an abstract class at its top into a bridge, do the following.

1. Move the abstract operations in the superclass into an interface.
2. Define implementation classes that provide different implementations of the interface.
3. Redefine the remaining operations in the abstract class as operations on an instance of the new interface.

## CHALLENGE 6.3

Figure 6.6 shows the MachineController hierarchy refactored into a bridge. Fill in the missing labels.

*A solution appears on page 373.*

**FIGURE 6.6:** This diagram, when complete, will show the results of refactoring MachineController to apply BRIDGE.

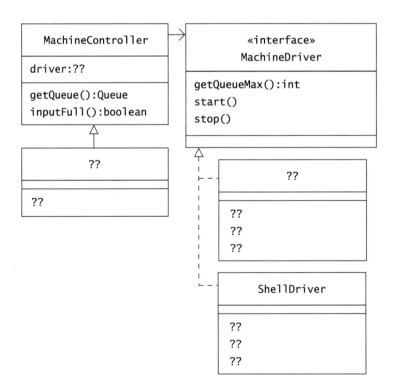

After this type of refactoring, you can usually change the declaration of the abstract superclass to be a **concrete class**. Note, however, that the class is still an *abstraction* in that its operations depend on the implementation of abstract operations defined in the interface.

## A Bridge Using the List Interface

Drivers offer good examples of the BRIDGE pattern, but you can apply BRIDGE in other situations, too. Whenever you separate an abstraction—a class that relies on a set of abstract operations—from the implementation of its abstract operations, you have applied BRIDGE.

Consider the Queue class in use at Oozinoz. When using a list to model a conveyor, you have discovered that it is easy to get confused about which end of the list applies to which end of a conveyor. To avoid this confusion, Oozinoz developers always define the ends of the conveyor as the conveyor's tail and head and define that the belt moves from the tail toward the head. Placing material on the tail of a conveyor *enqueues* the material on the conveyor; removing material from the head *dequeues* the material from the conveyor. Figure 6.7 shows the Queue class. The add() method adds an object to the tail of a list, and a call to remove(0) removes the head of a list.

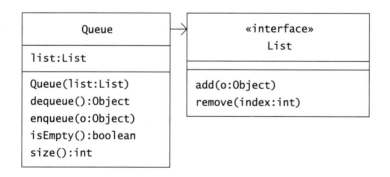

**FIGURE 6.7:** The Queue class defines operations that rely on an abstract List object.

**CHALLENGE 6.4**

Write the code for dequeue() and enqueue().

*A solution appears on page 373.*

## Summary

A common example of BRIDGE occurs in drivers. An application that uses a driver is an abstraction—the choice of driver determines what happens when the application runs. The interface between applications and drivers lets you vary either side independently. You can create new applications that use the drivers without changing the drivers. You can also add new drivers without changing existing applications. That is the intent of BRIDGE.

You may encounter abstractions that are not decoupled from their implementation but rather are arranged as an abstract class whose concrete subclasses provide various implementations. In such a case, you can apply BRIDGE if you want to factor the hierarchy along another line. Moving the implementations out lets each implementation become a new class that implements a standard interface. This lets you add new subclasses to the abstraction, regardless of which implementation of the interface you will use. This move also lets you add new implementations of the interface without affecting the abstraction hierarchy. The BRIDGE pattern decouples an abstraction from its implementation so that the two can vary independently.

# PART II

# RESPONSIBILITY PATTERNS

# 7

# INTRODUCING RESPONSIBILITY

THE RESPONSIBILITY of an object is comparable to the responsibility of a representative in the Oozinoz call center. When you order fireworks from Oozinoz, the person you speak to is a representative for the company—a proxy. He or she performs foreseeable tasks, usually by delegating tasks to other systems and people. Sometimes, the representative will delegate a request to a single, central authority who will mediate the situation or will escalate problems up a chain of responsibility.

Like call center representatives, ordinary objects have the information and methods they need to operate independently. Sometimes, however, you need to centralize responsibility, diverting from the normal independent operation of objects. Several design patterns address this need. Other patterns let objects escalate requests and isolate an object from other objects that depend on it. Responsibility-oriented patterns provide techniques for centralizing, escalating, and limiting ordinary object responsibility.

## Ordinary Responsibility

You probably have a strong sense of how attributes and responsibilities should come together in a well-formed class, although it can be challenging to explain your views.

## CHALLENGE 7.1

The class structure shown in Figure 7.1 has at least ten questionable assignments of responsibility. Circle as many problems as you can find; for four of these points, write a statement of what is wrong.

*Solutions appear on page 374.*

Looking at all the oddities in Figure 7.1 may loosen up your thinking about appropriate object modeling. This is a good frame of mind to be in when you set out to define terms, such as *class*. The value of defining terms increases as it helps people communicate and decreases as it becomes a goal in itself and a source of conflict. In this spirit, take the following difficult challenge.

**FIGURE 7.1:** What's wrong with this picture?

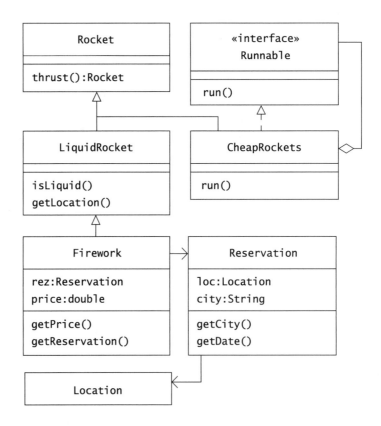

---

**CHALLENGE 7.2**

Define the qualities of an effective, useful class.

*Points to consider appear on page 375.*

---

One feature that makes a class easier to use is that its method names suggest, accurately, what the methods do. However, you have seen some exceptions to this principle in challenges from earlier chapters.

---

**CHALLENGE 7.3**

Give an example of when the effect of calling a method differs from the behavior implied by the method's name.

*Some solutions appear on page 375.*

---

Establishing principles for the proper assignment of responsibility in object-oriented systems seems to be an area ripe for progress in computer science. A system in which every class and method clearly defines its responsibilities and bears them correctly is a strong system, probably stronger than most systems we encounter today.

It is common to speak of classes and methods as bearing various responsibilities. In practice, this usually translates into *your* bearing responsibility for the solid design and proper functioning of your code. Fortunately, Java offers some relief. You can limit the visibility of your classes, fields, and methods and thereby limit your responsibility to developers who use your code.

## Controlling Responsibility with Visibility

Consider the `SolidRocket` simulation class shown in Figure 7.2. This class's constructor requires four parameters that establish a rocket's thrust. (The figure shows only the burn rate parameter; the other parameters are the specific impulse, propellant density, and burn area of the rocket.) Suppose that you own the `simulation` package and have a habit of declaring instance variables with the `protected` modifier. This policy lets other classes in your package access a `SolidRocket` instance's fields without having to call `get-` methods. This is somewhat risky, as you have to understand, for example, that changing the burn rate in a simulation means that you have to recalculate a rocket's thrust.

One day, you notice that another developer has subclassed your `SolidRocket` class with a class she calls `Burrow`. In this class, she has

**FIGURE 7.2:** Protected visibility lets classes outside your package access your code in ways that may be inappropriate.

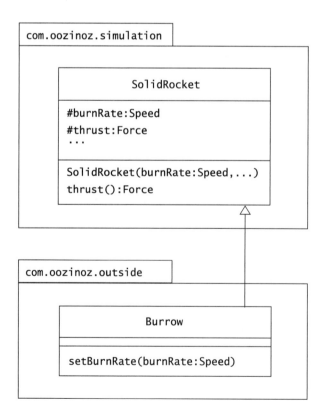

added a `setBurnRate()` method that updates the burn rate attribute. She needs it because she wants to plot a graph showing several burn rates and the corresponding rocket thrust. You don't have this method in `Solid-Rocket`. *Her approach fails because you calculate thrust only in the constructor, when you first receive the burn rate.* This situation comes to your attention when she calls to ask why the thrust doesn't change after she updates the burn rate.

---

**CHALLENGE 7.4**

In this situation, how could you prevent other developers from taking advantage of `protected` fields by subclassing into classes in your package?

*Some solutions appear on page 376.*

---

## Summary

As a Java developer, you take on responsibility for creating classes that form a logical collection of attributes and associated behaviors. You are also responsible for ensuring that your methods perform the services implied by their names. You can limit your responsibility with the proper use of visibility, but to be a developer implies that some of your code must be available to other developers.

## ■ BEYOND ORDINARY RESPONSIBILITY

Like developers, objects have certain responsibilities but in a different sense. Objects cannot bear a moral, ethical, or professional responsibility, but we do say that object-oriented development distributes responsibility to individual objects. This is primarily a way of characterizing *encapsulation*, the idea that an object works on its own data. Object-oriented development ordinarily distributes responsibility as far as it will go, meaning that each object does its own work.

Distributed responsibility is the norm, but several design patterns oppose this and move responsibility to an intermediary or to a particular object. A central figure may absorb certain responsibilities, or you may also need policies for escalating requests to other authorities. And, although objects are normally highly responsible, you may want to observe their behavior without their knowing it. You can think of the intent of the OBSERVER pattern and several other patterns as exceptions to the ordinary rule of distributed responsibility.

| If you intend to | Apply the pattern |
| --- | --- |
| • Centralize responsibility in a single instance of a class | SINGLETON (Chapter 8) |
| • Decouple an object from awareness of which other objects depend on it | OBSERVER (Chapter 9) |
| • Centralize responsibility in a class that oversees how a set of other objects interact | MEDIATOR (Chapter 10) |
| • Let an object act on behalf of another object | PROXY (Chapter 11) |
| • Allow a request to escalate up a chain of objects until one handles it | CHAIN OF RESPONSIBILITY (Chapter 12) |
| • Centralize responsibility in shared, fine-grained objects | FLYWEIGHT (Chapter 13) |

The intent of each design pattern is to solve a problem in a context. Responsibility-oriented patterns address contexts in which you need to deviate from the normal rule that responsibility should be distributed as far as possible. For example, when you need to centralize responsibility in a single instance of a class, you can apply the SINGLETON pattern.

# 8

# SINGLETON

OBJECTS CAN USUALLY act responsibly just by performing their own work on their own attributes, without incurring obligations beyond self-consistency. Some objects, though, take on further responsibilities, such as modeling real-world entities, coordinating work, or modeling the overall state of a system. When a particular object in a system bears a responsibility on which other objects rely, you need a way of finding the responsible object. For example, you might need to find an object that represents a particular machine or a customer object that can construct itself from data in a database or an object that initiates system memory recovery.

When you need to find a responsible object, the object that you need will, in some cases, be the only instance of its class. For example, at Oozinoz, there is at present only one factory and only one `Factory` object. In this case, you need SINGLETON. The intent of the SINGLETON pattern is to ensure that a class has only one instance and to provide a global point of access to it.

## SINGLETON Mechanics

The mechanics of SINGLETON are more memorable than its intent. It is easier to explain *how* to ensure that a class has only one instance than it is to say *why* you might want this restriction. You might categorize SINGLETON as a "creational" pattern, as *Design Patterns* (Gamma et al. 1995) does. You should, of course, think of patterns in whatever way helps you remember, recognize, and apply them. But the *intent* of the SINGLETON pattern implies that a specific object bears a responsibility on which other objects rely.

You have some options about how you create an object that takes on a unique role. But regardless of how you create a singleton, you have to ensure that other developers don't create new instances of the class you intend to limit.

---

**CHALLENGE 8.1**

How can you prevent other developers from constructing new instances of your class?

*A solution appears on page 376.*

---

When you design a singleton class, you need to decide when to instantiate the single object that will represent the class. One choice is to create this instance as a static field in the class. For example, the `Runtime` class in `java.lang` includes the line:

```
private static Runtime currentRuntime = new Runtime();
```

This class makes its unique instance available through its public, static `getRuntime()` method.

Rather than creating a singleton instance ahead of time, you might wait until the instance is first needed, or **lazy-initialize** it. For example, a Factory class might make its single instance available with:

```
public static Factory getFactory()
{
    if (factory == null)
    {
        factory = new Factory();
        // ...
    }
    return factory;
}
```

**CHALLENGE 8.2**

Why might you decide to lazy-initialize a singleton instance rather than initialize it in its field declaration?

*A solution appears on page 376.*

## Singletons and Threads

If you want to lazy-initialize a singleton in a multithreaded environment, you have to take care to prevent multiple threads from initializing the singleton. In a multithreaded environment, a method is not guaranteed to run to completion before a method in another thread starts running. This opens the possibility, for example, that two threads will try to initialize a singleton at roughly the same time. Suppose that a method finds that a singleton is null. If another thread begins executing at that moment, it will also find that the singleton is null. Then both methods will proceed to initialize the singleton. To prevent this sort of contention, you need a locking ability to help coordinate methods running in different threads.

The Java language and class libraries include good support for multithreaded development. In particular, Java supplies every object with a **monitor**—a lockable aspect that represents possession of the object by a thread. To ensure that only one thread initializes a singleton, you can synchronize the initialization on the monitor of a suitable object. Other methods that require exclusive access to the singleton can synchronize on the same monitor. *Concurrent Programming in Java™* (Lea 2000) suggests synchronizing on the monitor that belongs to the class itself:

```
package com.oozinoz.machine;
public class Factory_2 {
```

```
private static Factory_2 factory;
private static final Object
    classLock = Factory_2.class;
private long wipMoves;

private Factory_2()
{
    wipMoves = 0;
}

public static Factory_2 getFactory()
{
    synchronized (classLock)
    {
        if (factory == null)
        {
            factory = new Factory_2();
        }
        return factory;
    }
}

public void recordWipMove()
{
    // challenge!
}
// ...
}
```

The `getFactory()` code ensures that if a second thread begins to
lazy-initialize the singleton after another thread has begun the same initialization, the second thread will wait to obtain the `classLock` object's
monitor. When it obtains the monitor, the second thread will find that the
singleton is no longer null.

The `wipMoves` variable records the number of times that **work in process (WIP)** advances. Every time a bin moves onto a new machine, the
subsystem that causes or records the move must call the factory singleton's `recordWipMove()` method.

**CHALLENGE 8.3**

Write the code for the `recordWipMove()` method of the `Factory_2` class.

*A solution appears on page 377.*

## Recognizing SINGLETON

Unique objects are not uncommon. In fact, most objects in an application bear a unique responsibility; why would you create two objects with identical responsibilities? Similarly, nearly every class has a unique role. Why would you develop the same class twice? On the other hand, singleton classes—classes that allow only a single instance—are relatively rare. The fact that an object or a class is unique does not imply that the SINGLETON pattern is at work. Consider the classes in Figure 8.1.

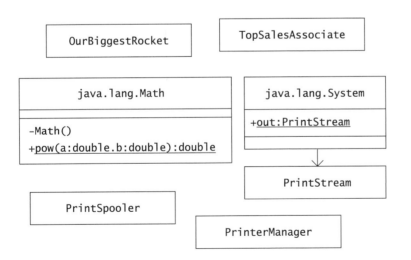

**FIGURE 8.1:** Which classes appear to apply SINGLETON?

**CHALLENGE 8.4**

For each class in Figure 8.1, say whether it appears to be a singleton class, and why.

*Solutions appear on page 377.*

## Summary

Code that supports SINGLETON ensures that a class has only one instance and provides a global point of access to it. A common way to achieve this is through lazy-initialization of a singleton object, instantiating it only when the singleton is first needed. In a multithreaded environment, you must take care to manage the collaboration of threads that may access a singleton's methods and data at approximately the same time. Regardless of the mechanics that you apply, the value of SINGLETON lies in centralizing authority in a single object.

# 9

# OBSERVER

CLIENTS ORDINARILY gather information from an interesting object by calling its methods. But when an interesting object changes, a problem arises: How do clients that depend on the object's information know that the information has changed?

You may encounter designs that make an object responsible for informing clients when an interesting aspect of the object changes. The problem with this is that the knowledge of which attributes about an object are interesting lies with the client. The interesting object shouldn't accept responsibility for updating the client.

One solution is to arrange for clients to be informed when the object changes and leave it to the clients to follow up with interrogations about the object's new state. The intent of the OBSERVER pattern is to define a one-to-many dependency such that when one object changes state, all its dependents are notified and updated automatically.

## A Classic Example: OBSERVER in Swing

The most common case in which clients depend on changing objects occurs in graphical user interfaces. Whenever a user clicks a button or adjusts a slider, many objects in the application may need to react to the change. Java Swing anticipates that you will be interested in knowing when a user changes a Swing component, and the OBSERVER pattern is evident throughout Swing. Swing refers to interested clients as "listeners" and lets you register as many listeners as you like to be notified of a component's events.

**FIGURE 9.1:** The curves shown change in real time as the user adjusts the tPeak variable with the slider.

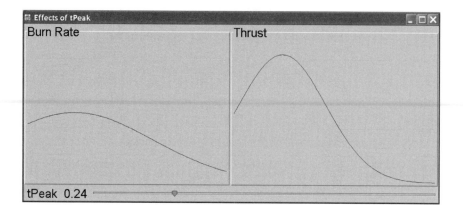

Consider a typical Oozinoz application with a Swing GUI, such as the one that Figure 9.1 shows. This application lets a fireworks engineer experiment visually with parameters that determine the relationship between a rocket's thrust and the surface area of its fuel.

When a solid rocket engine ignites, the part of its fuel that is exposed to air burns, producing thrust. From ignition to maximum burn rate, the burn area increases from the initial ignition area to the full surface area of the fuel. This maximum rate occurs at time $t_{peak}$. As fuel burns off, the surface area reduces again until the fuel is consumed.

Suppose that the burn rate and thrust equations are:

$$rate = 25^{-(t - t_{peak})^2}$$
$$thrust = 1.7 \cdot \left(\frac{rate}{0.6}\right)^{1/0.3}$$

The application in Figure 9.1 shows how $t_{peak}$ affects the burn rate and thrust of a rocket. As a user moves the slider, the value of $t_{peak}$ changes, and the curves take on new shapes. Figure 9.2 shows the primary classes that make up the application. The ShowBallistics_1 class and the

BallisticsPanel_1 class are members of the com.oozinoz.applications package. The BallisticsFunction interface is a member of the com.oozinoz.ballistics package. That package also contains a Ballistics utility class that provides that instances of BallisticsFunction that define the burn rate and thrust curves.

When the ballistics application initializes the slider, the application registers itself to receive slider events. When the slider changes, the application updates the panels that show the curves and updates the label that shows the value of $t_{peak}$.

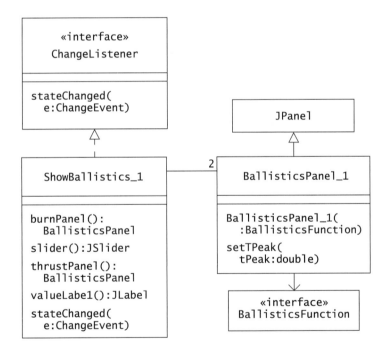

**FIGURE 9.2:** The ballistics application registers itself to receive slider events.

**CHALLENGE 9.1**

Complete the `slider()` and `stateChanged()` methods for `ShowBallistics_1` so that the ballistics panels and the $t_{peak}$ label reflect the slider's value.

```
public JSlider slider()
{
    if (slider == null)
    {
        slider = new JSlider();
        sliderMax = slider.getMaximum();
        sliderMin = slider.getMinimum();
        slider.addChangeListener( ?? );
        slider.setValue(slider.getMinimum());
    }
    return slider;
}

public void stateChanged(ChangeEvent e)
{
    double val = slider.getValue();
    double tp = (val - sliderMin) / (sliderMax - sliderMin);
    burnPanel().?? ( ?? );
    thrustPanel().?? ( ?? );
    valueLabel().?? ( ?? );
}
```

*A solution appears on page 378.*

The `ShowBallistics_1` class updates the burn panel, thrust panel, and value label objects that depend on the slider's value. This is not uncommon and not necessarily bad code, but note: This code completely undoes the intent of OBSERVER! Swing applies OBSERVER so that the slider is not responsible for knowing which clients are interested in it. The `ShowBallistics_1` code registers a single dependent object—itself—that dispatches changes to interested objects. This object takes on responsibility for knowing which clients depend on the slider, instead of letting each dependent object register itself.

To be consistent with OBSERVER, you can make a few changes in the code to let each interested component register itself to receive the slider's change events.

---

**CHALLENGE 9.2**

Provide a new class diagram showing a design that lets each interested object register for slider events. Be sure to account for the label that shows the slider's value.

*A solution appears on page 379.*

---

In this design, you can move the calls to addChangeListener() out of the slider() method and into the constructors of the dependent components:

```
public BallisticsPanel_2(
    BallisticsFunction func,
    JSlider slider)
{
    this.func = func;
    this.slider = slider;
    slider.addChangeListener(this);
}
```

When the slider changes, the BallisticsPanel_2 object is notified. The label recalculates its tPeak value and repaints itself:

```
public void stateChanged(ChangeEvent e)
{
    double val = slider.getValue();
    double max = slider.getMaximum();
    double min = slider.getMinimum();
    tPeak = (val - min) / (max - min);
    repaint();
}
```

A new problem emerges in this refactoring. The design adjusts responsibilities so that each interested object registers for and reacts to changes in the slider. The distribution of responsibility is good, but now each component that listens to the slider needs to recalculate the value of tPeak. In particular, if you use a BallisticsLabel_2 class, as the solution to Challenge 9.2 does, its stateChanged() method will be nearly identical to the stateChanged() method of BallisticsPanel_2. To consolidate this duplicated code, we can refactor again, extracting an underlying domain object from the current design.

## Model/View/Controller

As applications and systems grow, it is important to divide and redivide responsibility so that classes and packages stay small enough to maintain. The phrase **model/view/controller** (**MVC**) refers to separating an interesting object—the model—from GUI elements that portray it—the view and the controller. Java supports this separation of responsibility with its OBSERVER mechanics.

The initial versions of the ShowBallistics application combine intelligence about an application GUI with information about ballistics. You can refactor this code, following MVC to divide this application's responsibilities. In this refactoring, the revised ShowBallistics class should retain the views and controllers in its GUI elements.

The creators of MVC envisioned that the look of a component—its "view"—might be separable from its feel—its "controller." In practice, the appearance of a GUI component and its support for user interaction are tightly coupled, and Swing does not divide views from controllers. The value of MVC is to push the "model" out of an application into its own domain.

When you divide GUI objects from **business objects**, you can create layers of code. A **layer** is a group of classes with similar responsibilities, often collected in a single Java package. Higher layers, such as a GUI layer, usually depend only on classes in equal or lower layers. Layering usually includes a clear definition of the interfaces between layers, such as a GUI and the business, or domain, objects it represents. This opens the possibility of arranging for different layers to execute on different computers. A layer that executes on a computer is a **tier** in an *n*-tier system. You can

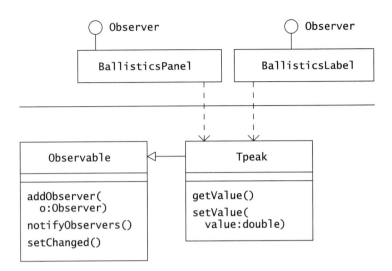

**FIGURE 9.3:** By creating an observable **Tpeak** class you can separate a business logic layer from a GUI layer.

reorganize the responsibilities of the ShowBallistics code, achieving a layered system, as Figure 9.3 shows.

The design that Figure 9.3 illustrates creates a Tpeak class to model the $t_{peak}$ value, the critical value in the ballistics equations that the application displays. The BallisticsPanel and BallisticsLabel classes *depend* on Tpeak. Rather than making a Tpeak object responsible for updating GUI elements, the design applies OBSERVER so that interested objects can register for notification when Tpeak changes. The Java class libraries supports this, providing an Observable class and an Observer interface in the java.util package. The Tpeak class can subclass Observable and can update its observers when its value changes.

```
public void setValue(double value)
{
    this.value = value;
    setChanged();
    notifyObservers();
}
```

Note that you have to call setChanged() so that the Observable code will broadcast the change. (It is questionable whether a design that requires two steps to notify observers is ideal.)

**FIGURE 9.4:** A `Ballis-ticsLabel` is an `Observer`; it can register its interest in an `Observable` object so that the label's `update()` method is called when the `Observable` object changes.

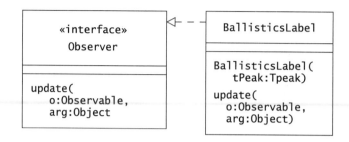

The `notifyObservers()` methods calls the `update()` method of each registered observer. The `update()` method is a requirement for implementers of the `Observer` interface, as Figure 9.4 shows.

A `BallisticsLabel` object need not retain a reference to the `Tpeak` object it observes. Rather, the `BallisticsLabel` constructor can register for updates when the `Tpeak` object changes. The label's `update()` method will receive the `Tpeak` object as its `Observable` argument. The method can cast the argument to `Tpeak`, extract the new value, change the label's text, and repaint.

---

### CHALLENGE 9.3

Write the complete code for `BallisticsLabel.java`.

*A solution appears on page 379.*

---

The new design of the ballistics application separates a business object from the GUI elements that represent it. Two requirements must be met for this design to work.

1. Implementations of `Observer` must register their interest and must update themselves appropriately, often including repainting themselves.
2. Subclasses of `Observable` must remember to notify observers when their values change.

These two steps set up most of the wiring you need across layers in the ballistics application. You also need to arrange for a Tpeak object to change when the application's slider changes. You can achieve this without writing a class, by instantiating an anonymous subclass of ChangeListener.

---

**CHALLENGE 9.4**

Suppose that tPeak is an instance of Tpeak and an attribute of the ShowBallistics class. Complete the code for ShowBallistics.slider() so that the slider's changes update tPeak.

```
public JSlider slider()
{
    if (slider == null)
    {
        slider = new JSlider();
        sliderMax = slider.getMaximum();
        sliderMin = slider.getMinimum();
        slider.addChangeListener
            (
                new ChangeListener()
                {

                    ??

                }
            );
        slider.setValue(slider.getMinimum());
    }
    return slider;
}
```

*A solution appears on page 380.*

---

When you apply MVC, the flow of events may seem indirect. Slider movement in the ballistics application causes a ChangeListener to update a Tpeak object. In turn, a change in the Tpeak object notifies the application's label and panels, and these objects repaint themselves. Change propagates from the GUI layer to the business layer and back up to the GUI layer.

**CHALLENGE 9.5**

Fill in the messages in Figure 9.5.

*A solution appears on page 380.*

**FIGURE 9.5:** MVC causes calls to pass from a GUI layer into a business layer and back into the GUI layer.

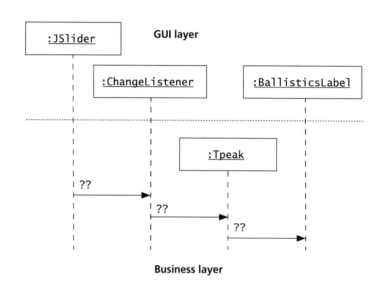

The payback for a layered design is in the value of the interface and in the independence that you get between the layers. The layering of code is a layering of responsibility, which makes the code easier to maintain. For example, in the ballistics example, you can add a second GUI, perhaps for a handheld device, without having to change classes in the business object layer. In the business object layer, you might add a new source of change that updates a Tpeak object. In this case, the OBSERVER mechanics you have in place will automatically update objects in the GUI layer.

Another advantage of layering code is that layering supports a move to an *n*-tier architecture, with layers executing as tiers on different computers. This minimizes the amount of code that must execute on a user's desktop. It also lets you make changes in business classes without updating software on user machines, greatly simplifying deployment.

In short, OBSERVER supports MVC. MVC supports *n*-tier computing, which brings many practical advantages to software development and deployment.

## Maintaining an Observable Object

You may not always be able to make the class you want to observe a subclass of Observable. In particular, your class may already be a subclass of something other than Object. In this case, you can provide your class with an Observable object and have your class forward key method calls to it. The Component class in java.awt uses this approach, although it uses a PropertyChangeSupport object instead of an Observable object.

The PropertyChangeSupport class is quite similar to the Observable class but is part of the java.beans package. The JavaBeans API exists to support the creation of reusable components. This API has found its greatest applicability to GUI components, but you can certainly apply it elsewhere. The Component class uses a PropertyChangeSupport object to let interested observers register for notification of changes in the properties of labels, panels, and other GUI components. Figure 9.6 shows the relationship between the Component class from java.awt and the PropertyChangeSupport class.

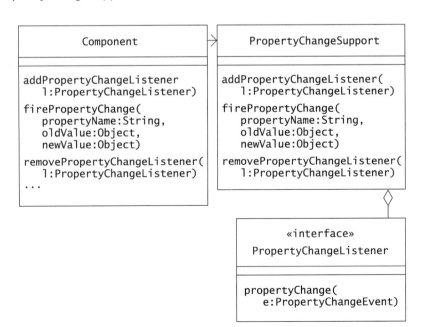

**FIGURE 9.6:** A Component object maintains a PropertyChangeSupport object that maintains a collection of listeners.

The Component class duplicates part of the interface of the PropertyChangeSupport class. These methods in Component each forward the message call to an instance of the PropertyChangeSupport class.

**CHALLENGE 9.6**

Complete the class diagram in Figure 9.7 to show Tpeak using a PropertyChangeSupport object to manage listeners.

*A solution appears on page 381.*

**FIGURE 9.7:** A Tpeak business object can delegate calls that affect listeners to a **Property-ChangeSupport** object.

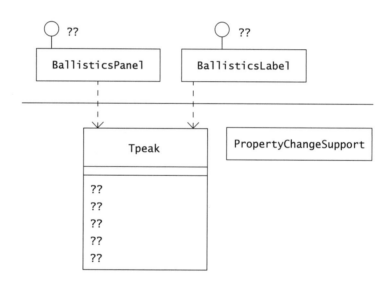

Whether you use Observer, PropertyChangeSupport, or another class to establish the OBSERVER pattern, the point is to define a one-to-many dependency among objects. When one object changes state, all its dependents are notified and updated automatically. This limits the responsibility and eases maintenance of both interesting objects and their interested observers.

## Summary

The OBSERVER pattern appears most frequently in GUI applications and is a fundamental aspect of Java's Swing architecture. With Swing, you never have to change or subclass a component class just to communicate its events to an interested object. For small applications, a common practice is to register a single object to receive all the events in a GUI. Doing so has no inherent problem, but you should recognize that it reverses the distribution of responsibility that OBSERVER intends. For a large GUI, consider letting each interested object register for events rather than introducing a mediator.

OBSERVER lets you delineate the responsibility between business objects and a GUI, which allows you to establish an MVC design. MVC lets you create loosely coupled layers than can change independently and that may execute on different machines.

When you decide to apply OBSERVER, you can write the registration and listening mechanisms yourself, but Java includes two packages with classes that have these mechanics. You can use the `Observable` class and the `Observer` interface in `java.util`. Alternatively, you can use the `PropertyChangeSupport` class and `PropertyChangeListener` in `java.beans`. The mechanics of these class/interface pairs are similar. In particular, you can use either an `Observable` object or a `PropertyChangeSupport` object when your interesting class needs to implement OBSERVER through delegation instead of subclassing.

The value of OBSERVER remains the same whether you effect it through subclassing or delegation and regardless of the classes you use to support it. OBSERVER lets clients know when an interesting object changes, at the same time minimizing the responsibility of the interesting object.

# 10

# MEDIATOR

ORDINARY OBJECT-ORIENTED development distributes responsibility as far as it will go, with each object doing its own work independently. The OBSERVER pattern supports this distribution by minimizing the responsibility of an object that other objects find interesting. The SINGLETON pattern resists the distribution of responsibility to let you centralize responsibility in particular objects that clients locate and reuse. The MEDIATOR pattern too centralizes responsibility but for a particular set of objects rather than for all the clients in a system.

Providing a central authority for a group of objects is useful when the interactions the objects gravitate toward the complex condition in which every object is aware of every other object in the group. Centralization of responsibility is also useful when the logic surrounding the interactions of the related objects is independent of the other behavior of the objects. The MEDIATOR pattern defines an object that encapsulates how a set of objects interact. This promotes loose coupling, keeping the objects from referring to one another explicitly, and lets you vary their interaction independently.

## A Classic Example: GUI Mediators

You will probably most often encounter the MEDIATOR pattern when you develop an application with a GUI. Such applications tend to become *thick*, gathering code that you can refactor into other classes. The FlightPanel class in Chapter 4, FACADE, initially performed three roles.

Before you refactored it, this class acted as a display panel, as a complete GUI application, and as a flight path calculator. After refactoring, the application that launches the flight panel display became simple, containing just a few lines of code. Large applications, however, can remain complex after this type of refactoring, even when they contain just the logic that creates components and that arranges for the components' interaction.

Consider the application in Figure 10.1. Oozinoz stores chemical batches in rubber tubs supplied by the Dubdub Rubber Tub company. Machines at Oozinoz read bar codes on the tubs to keep track of where tubs are in the factory. Sometimes, though, a manual override is necessary, particularly when humans move a tub instead of waiting for a robot to transfer it. In this case, the application in Figure 10.1 lets a user specify the machine at which a tub is located. The user types in the tub ID, chooses a machine from a list, and clicks Ok! to make the association. Figure 10.2 shows the application class.

**FIGURE 10.1:** This application lets its user manually update the location of a tub of chemicals.

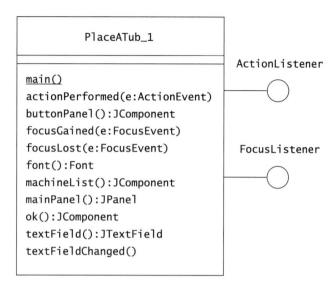

**FIGURE 10.2:** The PlaceATub_1 class has a mix of component-building and event-handling methods.

About half of the methods in PlaceATub_1 exist to lazy-initialize variables that contain the application's components. The textField() method is typical:

```
public JTextField textField()
{
    if (textField == null)
    {
        textField = new JTextField();
        textField.setFont(font());
        textField.addActionListener(this);
        textField.addFocusListener(this);
    }
    return textField;
}
```

Most of the remaining methods in `PlaceATub` contain logic that handles the application's events. The `focusGained()` and `focusLost()` methods, for example, manage the effects of the user's tabbing in and out of the text field:

```
public void focusGained(FocusEvent e)
{
    textField.selectAll();
}

public void focusLost(FocusEvent e)
{
    textFieldChanged();
}
```

The `textFieldChanged()` method updates the affected machine and tub objects.

Note that the Mediator pattern is at work in this class. Components don't update one another directly; rather, they issue events that a class can register for and react to. A `PlaceATub_1` object encapsulates how the components in a GUI interact. The mechanics of Swing nudge you into using a mediator, although nothing in Swing suggests that an application must be its own mediator.

Instead of mingling component-creation methods with event-handling methods in one class, you can move all event handling into a separate mediator class. This refactoring results in a pair of simpler classes, with two specializations: component creation and event handling.

---

**CHALLENGE 10.1**

Complete the diagram in Figure 10.3 to show a refactoring of `PlaceATub_1`, introducing a new `PlaceATubMediator` class to receive the events of the `PlaceATub` GUI.

*A solution appears on page 382.*

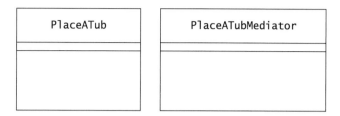

**FIGURE 10.3:** Separate the component-building and event-handling parts of the application.

The refactoring consolidates the mediator into a separate class, letting you develop it and focus on it separately. Now when the `PlaceATub` application runs, components pass events to a `PlaceATubMediator` object. This object may call back components in the GUI: for example, to select all the text in the text field when the user tabs into it. The mediator may also call domain objects: for example, calling a `Tub` object's `setMachine()` method when the user clicks the Ok! button.

---

**CHALLENGE 10.2**

Draw a diagram that shows what happens when the user clicks the Ok! button. Show the button, the mediator, the affected tub, and the sequence of messages that pass among these objects.

*A solution appears on page 383.*

---

Java Swing components apply the MEDIATOR pattern as a matter of course, notifying a mediator when events occur rather than taking responsibility for updating other components directly. Swing applications give rise to perhaps the most common application of the MEDIATOR pattern, but you may want to introduce a mediator in other cases as well.

Whenever the interaction of a set of objects is complex, you can centralize the responsibility for this interaction in a mediator object that stands outside the interacting group. This promotes **loose coupling**—a reduction in the responsibility that the interacting objects bear to one another. Managing the interaction of objects in an independent class also has the advantage of simplifying and standardizing the interaction rules. One example of the value of a mediator occurs when you need to manage relational integrity.

---

### Relational Integrity

An object model is *relationally consistent* if every time object **a** points to object **b**, object **b** points to object **a**. For a more rigorous definition, consider two classes: `Alpha` and `Beta`. Let $A$ represent the set of objects in the model that are instances of class `Alpha`, and let $B$ represent the set of objects that are instances of class `Beta`. Let **a** and **b** denote members of $A$ and $B$, and let the *ordered pair* (a, b) denote that object $a \in A$ has a reference to object $b \in B$. This reference may be either a direct reference or one of a set of references, as when object **a** has a `List` object that includes **b**.

The *Cartesian product* $A \times B$ is the set of all possible ordered pairs (a, b) with $a \in A$ and $b \in B$. The sets $A$ and $B$ allow the two Cartesian products $A \times B$ and $B \times A$. An *object model relation* on $A$ and $B$ is the subset of $A \times B$ that exists in an object model. Let $AB$ denote this subset, and let $BA$ denote the subset of $B \times A$ that exists in the model.

Any binary relation $R \subseteq A \times B$ has an *inverse* $R^{-1} \subseteq B \times A$ defined by:

```
(b, a) ∈ R⁻¹ if and only if (a, b) ∈ R
```

The inverse of $AB$ provides the set of references that must occur from instances of $B$ to instances of $A$ if the object model is consistent. In other words, instances of classes `Alpha` and `Beta` are relationally consistent if and only if $BA$ is the inverse of $AB$.

---

## Relational Integrity Mediators

Part of the strength of the object-oriented paradigm is that it lets you easily map connections between Java objects and objects in the real world. However, a Java object model's ability to reflect the real world has at least two fundamental deficits. First, objects in the real world vary with time, but no support for this is built into Java. For example, assignment statements obliterate any previous value instead of remembering it, as a human would. Second, in the real world, relations are as important as objects, but relations receive little support in today's object-oriented languages, including Java. For example, there is no built-in support for the

**TABLE 10.1:** Modeling a Relationship

| TUB | MACHINE |
|-----|---------|
| T305 | StarPress-2402 |
| T308 | StarPress-2402 |
| T377 | ShellAssembler-2301 |
| T379 | ShellAssembler-2301 |
| T389 | ShellAssembler-2301 |
| T001 | Fuser-2101 |
| T002 | Fuser-2101 |

fact that if Star Press 2402 is in bay 1, bay 1 must contain Star Press 2402. In fact, it is quite possible for such relations to go awry in Java, which in turn invites the application of the MEDIATOR pattern.

Consider the rubber tubs of chemicals at Oozinoz. Tubs are always assigned to a particular machine. You can model this relationship with a table, as Table 10.1 shows. Recording relational information in a table lets you preserve relational integrity. In Table 10.1, keeping the Tub column unique guarantees that no tub can appear on two machines at once.

Table 10.1 shows the **relation** of tubs and machines—the way in which they stand with regard to each other. Mathematically, a relation is a subset of all ordered pairs of objects, so there is a relation of tubs to machines and a relation of machines to tubs. See the sidebar Relational Integrity on page 108 for a more strict definition of relational consistency in an object model.

When you record tub and machine relational information in a table, you can guarantee that each tub is on only one machine by enforcing the restriction that each tub occurs only once in the Tub column. The most common way to do this is to make the Tub column the primary key of the table in a relational database. With this model, as in reality, a tub cannot appear on two machines at once. In an object model, such a guarantee is more difficult to make, because the relation information is distributed to the modeled objects, as Figure 10.4 shows.

**FIGURE 10.4:** An object model distributes information about relations.

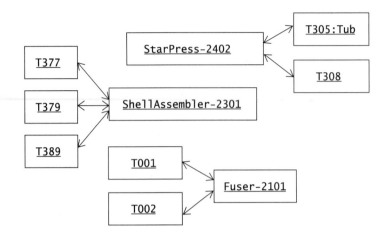

The arrowheads in Figure 10.4 emphasize that tubs know about machines and that machines know about tubs. In a typical implementation, each `Tub` object would have a `Machine` attribute to indicate its current location, and each `Machine` object would have a list of `Tub` objects representing tubs located at the modeled machine. The distribution of the tub/machine relationship makes the management of the relationship more difficult and makes this management a candidate for application of the MEDIATOR pattern.

Consider a defect that occurred at Oozinoz when a developer began modeling a new machine that included a bar code reader for identifying tubs. After scanning a tub for its ID, the developer set the location of tub b to machine m with the following code:

```
//tell tub about machine, and machine about tub
t.setMachine(m);
m.addTub(t);
```

**CHALLENGE 10.3**

Suppose that the object t represents tub T308 and that the object m represents the machine Fuser-2101. Complete the object diagram in Figure 10.5, showing the effects of the code that updates the tub's location. What defect does this reveal?

*A solution appears on page 383.*

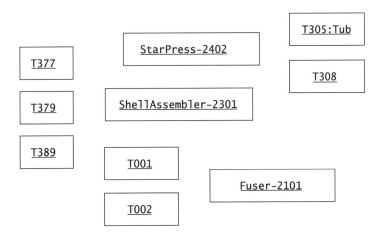

**FIGURE 10.5:** When completed, this diagram will show the flaw in a developer's code that updates a tub's location.

The easiest way to guarantee relational consistency is to pull the relational information back into a single table managed by a mediating object. Instead of having tubs know about machines and machines know about tubs, you can give all these objects a reference to a mediator that keeps a single table of tubs and machines. The java.util package provides the Map interface, along with several implementing classes, to store

**FIGURE 10.6:** The MEDIATOR pattern lets you define an object that encapsulates how tubs and machines interact.

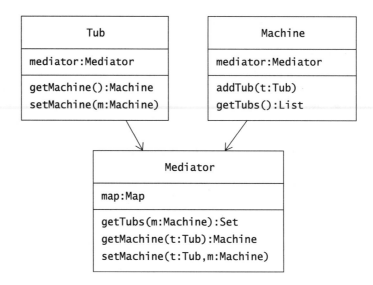

key/value pairs. Figure 10.6 shows a class diagram with a mediator in place. The `Mediator` class uses a `Map` object to store the tub/machine relationship:

```
package com.oozinoz.machine;
import java.util.*;
import com.oozinoz.chemical.Tub;
public class Mediator
{
    protected Map tubToMachine = new HashMap();

    public Machine getMachine(Tub t)
    {
        return (Machine) tubToMachine.get(t);
    }

    public Set getTubs(Machine m)
    {
        Set set = new HashSet();
        Iterator i = tubToMachine.entrySet().iterator();
        while (i.hasNext())
        {
            Map.Entry e = (Map.Entry) i.next();
            if (e.getValue().equals(m))
            {
                set.add(e.getKey());
            }
```

```
        }
        return set;
    }
    public void set(Tub t, Machine m)
    {
        tubToMachine.put(t, m);
    }
}
```

---

**CHALLENGE 10.4**

Write the code for the Tub methods getMachine() and setMachine().

*A solution appears on page 384.*

---

When you have an object model that is not tied to a relational database, you can use mediators to sustain the relational integrity of your model. Move the logic that gets and sets relations between objects into mediator classes. Such classes can specialize in maintaining relational integrity and can apply tablelike data structures that naturally guarantee integrity.

---

**CHALLENGE 10.5**

With respect to factoring logic out of a class, MEDIATOR is similar to other patterns. List two patterns that may involve moving an aspect of behavior out of an existing class or hierarchy.

*A solution appears on page 385.*

## Summary

The MEDIATOR pattern promotes loose coupling, keeping related objects from referring to one another explicitly. MEDIATOR shows up most often in GUI application development, in which you don't want to manage the complexity of individual widgets' updating one another. The architecture of Swing guides you in this direction, encouraging you to define objects that register for GUI events. If you are developing with Swing, you are probably applying MEDIATOR.

Swing nudges you into using MEDIATOR, but Swing does not force you to move this mediation outside an application class. Doing so can simplify your code. You can let a mediator class concentrate on the interaction between objects and let an application class concentrate on component construction.

There are other cases in which you can benefit from introducing a mediator object. For example, you might need a mediator to centralize responsibility for maintaining the relational integrity in an object model. You can apply MEDIATOR whenever you need to define an object that encapsulates how a set of objects interact.

## 11

# PROXY

An ordinary object does its own work in support of the public interface that it advertises. It can happen, though, that a legitimate object cannot live up to this ordinary responsibility. This occurs most frequently when an object takes a long time to load or when the object is running on another computer. In these cases, a proxy object can take the responsibility that a client expects and forward the request appropriately to an underlying target object. The intent of the PROXY pattern is to provide a surrogate, or placeholder, for another object to control access to it.

## A Classic Example: Image Proxies

While conducting plant tours, the Oozinoz public relations manager wants to pause at one point to show images of previous exhibitions. Your design team decides to satisfy this requirement with a PC-based Java application with a Swing GUI. You might convert to a browser-based thin-client design in the future, but in any case, you can rely on Java's extensive support for loading, manipulating, and displaying images.

As you start constructing the application, realize that you will want to load some images only on demand. You might make clickable, thumbnail versions of larger images, but in the first pass, you decide to show prebuilt Absent and Loading… images. Figure 11.1 shows three screen shots of the system you intend to construct. (The code that displays the windows that Figure 11.1 shows is in the ShowProxy class in the `com.oozinoz.applications` package. The underlying code that supports the application is in the `com.oozinoz.imaging` package.)

**115**

**FIGURE 11.1:** Three screen shots show a mini-application before, during, and after loading a large image. (Photo courtesy of Corbis, Inc.)

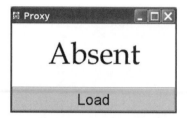 

Paul Katz/Index Stock Imagery, Inc.

The user interface displays one of three images: one indicating that loading has not begun, one indicating that the real image is loading, or the real image. When the application starts, it shows Absent, a JPEG image that you have built in an image-processing tool. When the user clicks Load, the image changes almost instantly to another prebuilt image, Loading... . After a few moments, the desired image appears.

An easy way to display a image saved in, say, a JPEG file is to use an `ImageIcon` object as an argument to a "label" that will show the image:

```
ImageIcon i = new ImageIcon("Fest.jpg");
JLabel l = new JLabel(i);
```

In the application that you are building, you want to pass into `JLabel` a proxy that will forward painting requests to Absent, Loading..., or the desired image. The message flow might look like the sequence diagram in Figure 11.2.

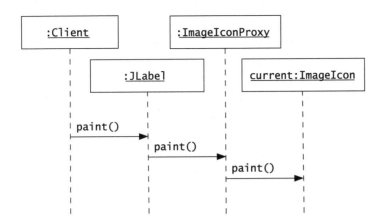

**FIGURE 11.2:** An `ImageIconProxy` object forwards `paint()` requests to the current `ImageIcon` object.

When the user clicks Load, your code will cause the `ImageIconProxy` object to change its current image to be the Loading... image. The proxy will also begin loading the desired image. When the desired image is completely loaded, the `ImageIconProxy` object will change its current image to be the desired image.

To set up a proxy, you can create a subclass of `ImageIcon`, as Figure 11.3 shows. The code for `ImageIconProxy` defines two static variables that contain the Absent and Loading... images:

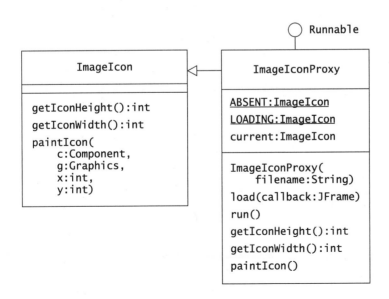

**FIGURE 11.3:** An `ImageIconProxy` object can stand in for an `ImageIcon` object because an `ImageIcon-Proxy` object *is* an `ImageIcon` object.

```
static final ImageIcon ABSENT =
    new ImageIcon("absent.jpg");

static final ImageIcon LOADING =
    new ImageIcon("loading.jpg");
```

The constructor for ImageIconProxy accepts the name of an image file to eventually load. When an ImageIconProxy object's load() method is called, it sets the image to LOADING and starts a separate thread to load the image. Using a separate thread keeps the application from hanging while the images loads. The load() method accepts a JFrame object that the run() method calls back once the desired image is loaded. The almost-complete code for ImageIconProxy.java is:

```
pacakage com.oozinoz.imaging;
import java.awt.*;
import javax.swing.*;
public class ImageIconProxy extends ImageIcon
implements Runnable
{
    static final ImageIcon ABSENT =
        new ImageIcon("absent.jpg");

    static final ImageIcon LOADING =
        new ImageIcon("loading.jpg");

    ImageIcon current = ABSENT;
    protected String filename;
    protected JFrame callbackFrame;

    public ImageIconProxy(String filename)
    {
        super(ABSENT.getImage());
        this.filename = filename;
    }

    public void load(JFrame callbackFrame)
    {
        this.callbackFrame = callbackFrame;
        current = LOADING;
        callbackFrame.repaint();
        new Thread(this).start();
    }
```

```
public void run()
{
    current = new ImageIcon(filename);
    callbackFrame.pack();
}

public int getIconHeight()
{
    // challenge!
}

public int getIconWidth()
{
    // challenge!
}

public synchronized void paintIcon(
    Component c, Graphics g, int x, int y)
{
    // challenge!
}
}
```

### CHALLENGE 11.1

An ImageIconProxy object accepts three image display calls that it must pass on to the current image. Write the code for getIconHeight(), getIconWidth(), and paintIcon() for the ImageIconProxy class.

*A solution appears on page 385.*

Suppose that you get the code working for this small demonstration application. Before you build the real application, which has more than just a Load button, you hold a design review, and the fragility of your design comes to light.

As with many proxies, there is a dangerous dependency between Image-Icon and ImageIconProxy. The current design assumes that you have correctly ascertained, or guessed, the right methods to override. Even if you have, the ImageIcon class can change in a future release and break your code. You and the design review team decide to rework your approach.

## Image Proxies Reconsidered

At this point, you might ask whether design patterns have helped you. You faithfully implemented a pattern, and now you're looking at tearing it out. In fact, this is natural and healthy, although it appears more often in applied development than in books. An author, with the help of his or her reviewers, can rethink and replace an inferior design before any reader sees it. In practice, a design pattern can help you get an application running and can facilitate the discussion of your design. In the ImageIconProxy example at Oozinoz, the pattern has served its purpose, even though it is much simpler to achieve the effect you desire without a literal implementation of a proxy.

The ImageIcon class operates on an Image object. Rather than forwarding painting requests to a separate ImageIcon object, it is easier to operate on the Image object that ImageIcon wraps. Figure 11.4 shows an Image-IconLoader class, from com.oozinoz.imaging, that has just two methods beyond its constructor: load() and run().

**FIGURE 11.4:** The ImageIconLoader class works by switching the Image object that it holds.

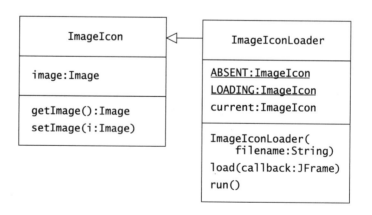

The load() method in this revised class still receives a JFrame object to call back after the desired image is loaded. When load() executes, it calls setImage() with the image held by LOADING, repaints the frame, and starts a separate thread for itself. The run() method, executing in a separate thread, creates a new ImageIcon object for the file named in the constructor, calls setImage() with the image held by this object, and repacks the frame. The almost-complete code for ImageIconLoader.java is:

```java
import java.awt.*;
import javax.swing.*;
public class ImageIconLoader extends ImageIcon
implements Runnable
{
    static final ImageIcon ABSENT =
        new ImageIcon("absent.jpg");

    static final ImageIcon LOADING =
        new ImageIcon("loading.jpg");

    protected String filename;
    protected JFrame callbackFrame;

    public ImageIconLoader(String filename)
    {
        super(ABSENT.getImage());
        this.filename = filename;
    }

    public void load(JFrame callbackFrame)
    {
        // challenge!
    }

    public void run()
    {
        // challenge!
    }
}
```

**CHALLENGE 11.2**

Fill in the code for `load()` and `run()` in `ImageIconLoader`.

*A solution appears on page 386.*

The revised code is less coupled to the design of `ImageIcon`, relying primarily on `getImage()` and `setImage()` rather than on the mechanics of which methods to forward. In fact, no forwarding exists: `ImageIcon-Loader` is a proxy in spirit but not in structure.

## Remote Proxies

The idea of a proxy is that one object intelligently forwards calls to another object. This can become complex and fragile, as in the case of `ImageIcon`, where it is difficult to know which calls to forward. Even if you forward every call, your code may break if the class of the proxied object changes. When you encounter the PROXY pattern in a design, you should question whether the benefit justifies the accompanying fragility of code. There *are* cases in which applying PROXY is well justified, as when an object and its proxy are active on different computers.

If the object whose method you want to call is running on another computer, you must find a way to communicate with the remote object other than calling it directly. You could open a socket on the remote machine and devise a protocol to pass messages to the remote object. Ideally, such a scheme would let you pass messages in almost the same way as if the object were local. You should be able to call methods on a proxy object that forwards the calls to the real object on the remote machine. In fact, such schemes have been realized, notably in the **common object request broker architecture (CORBA)** and in Java's **remote method invocation (RMI)**.

RMI makes it about as easy as possible for a client to obtain a proxy object that forwards calls to a desired object that is active on another computer. It is well worth learning about RMI, as RMI is part of the underpinning of the **Enterprise JavaBeans (EJB)** specification, an important emerging industry standard. Regardless of how industry standards evolve, the role of PROXY in distributed computing will continue into the foreseeable future, and RMI provides a good example of this pattern in action.

To experiment with RMI, you will need a good reference on this topic, such as *Java™ Enterprise in a Nutshell* (Flanagan et al. 1999). The following example is not a tutorial on RMI but merely points out the presence and value of PROXY within RMI applications.

Suppose that you decide to explore the workings of RMI, making an object's methods available to a Java program running on another computer. The initial development step is to create an interface for the class that you want to provide remote access to. As an experimental project, suppose that you create a Rocket interface that is independent of existing code at Oozinoz:

```
package com.oozinoz.remote;
import java.rmi.*;
public interface Rocket extends Remote
{
    void boost(double factor) throws RemoteException;
    double getApogee() throws RemoteException;
    double getPrice() throws RemoteException;
}
```

The Rocket interface extends Remote, and the methods in the interface all declare that they throw RemoteException. The reasons for these aspects of the interface lie outside the scope of this book, but any book that teaches RMI should cover them. Your RMI source should also explain that, to act as a server, the implementation of your remote interface can subclass UnicastRemoteObject, as Figure 11.5 shows.

---

**FIGURE 11.5:** To use RMI, you can define the interface you want for messages that pass between computers and create a subclass of `UnicastRemoteObject` that implements it.

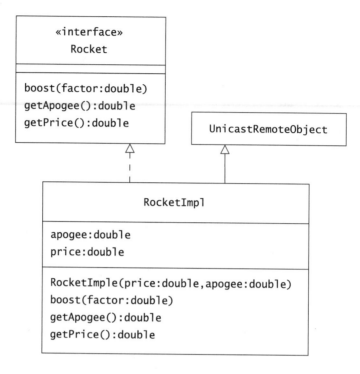

Your plan is for `RocketImpl` objects to be active on a server and to be available through a proxy that is active on a client. The code for RocketImpl is simple:

```java
package com.oozinoz.remote;
import java.rmi.*;
import java.rmi.server.UnicastRemoteObject;
public class RocketImpl
    extends UnicastRemoteObject
    implements Rocket
{
    protected double price;
    protected double apogee;

    public RocketImpl(double price, double apogee)
    throws RemoteException
    {
        this.price = price;
        this.apogee = apogee;
    }

    public void boost(double factor)
    {
```

```
        apogee *= factor;
    }
    public double getApogee()
    {
        return apogee;
    }
    public double getPrice()
    {
        return price;
    }
}
```

An instance of `RocketImpl` can be active on one machine and can be accessed by a Java program running on another machine. For this to work, a client needs a proxy for the `RocketImpl` object. This proxy needs to implement the `Rocket` interface and must have the additional features required to communicate with a remote object.

A great benefit of RMI is that it *automates* the construction of this proxy. To generate the proxy, place the `RocketImpl.java` file and the `Rocket.java` interface file below the directory in which you will run the RMI registry:

```
c:\rmi> dir com\oozinoz\remote
Rocket.java
RocketImpl.java
```

To create the `RocketImpl` stub that facilitates remote communication, run the RMI compiler that comes with the JDK:

```
c:\rmi> rmic -v1.2 com.oozinoz.remote.RocketImpl
```

Note that the `rmic` executable takes a class name, not the file name, as an argument. Earlier versions of the JDK constructed separate files for use on the client and the server machines. As of version 1.2, the RMI compiler creates a single stub file that both the client and the server machines need. The `rmic` command forces the compilation of the classes it needs and creates a `RocketImpl_Stub` class:

```
c:\rmi> dir com\oozinoz\remote
RocketImpl.java
Rocket.java
RocketImpl.class
```

```
Rocket.class
RocketImpl_Stub.class
```

To make an object active, you must register it with an RMI registry running on the server. The `rmiregistry` executable comes as part of the JDK. When you run the registry, specify the port that the registry will listen to:

```
c:\rmi> rmiregistry 5000
```

With the registry running on the server machine, you can create and register a `RocketImpl` object:

```
package com.oozinoz.remote;
import java.rmi.*;
public class RegisterRocket
{
    public static void main(String[] args)
    {
        try
        {
            // challenge!
            Naming.rebind(
                "rmi://localhost:5000/Biggie", biggie);
            System.out.println("Registered biggie");
        }
        catch (Exception e)
        {
            e.printStackTrace();
        }
    }
}
```

If you copy this code to the same directory that the other files reside in, you can compile and run it. The program displays a confirmation that the rocket is registered:

```
c:\rmi> javac com\oozinoz\remote\RegisterRocket.java
c:\rmi> java com.oozinoz.remote.RegisterRocket
Registered biggie
```

You need to replace the `//challenge!` line in the `RegisterRocket` class with code that creates a `biggie` object that models a rocket. The remaining code in the `main()` method registers this object. A description of the mechanics of the `Naming` class is outside the scope of this discussion.

However, you should have enough information to create the `biggie` object that this code registers.

---

**CHALLENGE 11.3**

Replace the `//challenge!` line with a declaration and instantiation of the `biggie` object. Define `biggie` to model a rocket with a price of $29.95 and an apogee of 820 meters.

*A solution appears on page 386.*

---

Running the `RegisterRocket` program makes a `RocketImpl` object, specifically `biggie`, available on a server. A client that runs on another machine can access `biggie` if the client has access to the `Rocket` interface and the `RocketImpl_Stub` class. If you are working on a single machine, you can still test out RMI, accessing the server on `localhost` rather than another host:

```
package com.oozinoz.remote;
import java.rmi.*;
public class ShowRocketClient
{
    public static void main(String[] args)
    {
        try
        {
            Object o = Naming.lookup(
                "rmi://localhost:5000/Biggie");
            Rocket biggie = (Rocket) o;
            System.out.println(biggie.getApogee());
        }
        catch (Exception e)
        {
            System.out.println(
                "Exception while looking up a rocket:");
            e.printStackTrace();
        }
    }
}
```

When this program runs, it looks up an object with the registered name of "Biggie." The class that is serving this name is RocketImpl, and the object o that lookup() returns will be an instance of RocketImpl_Stub class. The RocketImpl_Stub class implements the Rocket interface, so it is legal to cast the object o as an instance of the Rocket interface. The Rocket_Impl class subclasses a RemoteStub class that lets the object communicate with a server.

To see the ShowRocketClient program in action, copy the Rocket and RocketImpl_Stub classes to a client area:

```
d:\client> dir com\oozinoz\remote
Rocket.class
RocketImpl_Stub.class
ShowRocketClient.java
```

Running the ShowRocketClient program prints out the apogee of a "Biggie" rocket:

```
d:\client> javac com\oozinoz\remote\ShowRocketClient.java
d:\client> java com.oozinoz.remote.ShowRocketClient
820.0
```

Through a proxy, the getApogee() call is forwarded to an implementation of the Rocket interface that is active on a server.

## CHALLENGE 11.4

Figure 11.6 shows the getApogee() call being forwarded. The rightmost object appears in a bold outline, indicating that it is active outside the ShowRocketClient program. Fill in the class names of the unlabeled objects in this figure.

*A solution appears on page 386.*

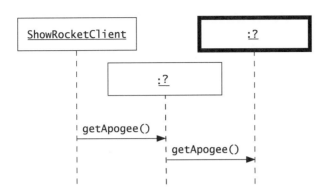

**FIGURE 11.6:** When completed, this diagram will show the flow of messages in an RMI-based distributed application.

The benefit of RMI is that it lets client programs interact with a local object that is a proxy for a remote object. You define the interface for the object that you want clients and servers to share. RMI supplies the communication mechanics and isolates both server and client from the knowledge that two implementations of Rocket are collaborating to provide nearly seamless interprocess communication.

## Summary

Implementations of the PROXY pattern establish a placeholder object that manages access to a target object. A proxy object can isolate clients from shifts in state of a desired object, as when loading an image endures a discernible duration. The problem with PROXY is that by its nature, it relies on a tight coupling between the placeholder and the proxied object.

Nowhere is this coupling more justified than in remote computing. Here, the PROXY pattern represents the ideal form of intercomputer communication. Rather than relying on another protocol, distributed computing schemes, such as RMI, establish communication with remote objects as normal-looking method calls. This lets a client communicate with a remote object through a proxy as if the remote object were local. The role of PROXY in distributed computing appears to be a permanent advance in object-oriented computing.

# 12

# CHAIN OF RESPONSIBILITY

O BJECT-ORIENTED DEVELOPERS strive to keep objects loosely coupled, keeping the responsibility between objects specific and minimal. This lets you introduce change more easily and with less risk of introducing defects. To a degree, decoupling occurs naturally in Java. Clients see only an object's visible interface and remain isolated from the details of the object's implementation. This arrangement, however, leaves in place the fundamental coupling that the client knows which object has the method the client needs to call.

An opportunity to loosen the restriction that a client must know which object to use occurs when you can arrange the objects in chains. In such a case, you can provide these objects with an operation that each object either performs or passes along the chain. The intent of the CHAIN OF RESPONSIBILITY pattern is to avoid coupling the sender of a request to its receiver by giving more than one object a chance to handle the request. To apply this pattern, chain the receiving objects and pass the request along the chain until an object handles it.

## Varieties of Lookup

In CHAIN OF RESPONSIBILITY, an object model takes on the job of finding which object can satisfy a client's request. This approach goes beyond the two lookup mechanisms that are built into Java: exception handling and method lookup.

When an exception is thrown, the Java interpreter looks back up the call stack to find a method called from a block enclosed in a try/catch

**131**

statement. If this try/catch statement does not catch an exception of the type thrown, the Java interpreter keeps looking. This can propagate up to the main() method. If the exception is not handled there, the Java interpreter prints out an error message and stack trace and then exits.

The more common case of lookup in Java is **method lookup**—the algorithm for deciding which definition of a method to use when a client calls an object's method. For example, if you call an object's toString() method, Java will use the method's implementation that appears lowest in the object's class hierarchy. When the compiler cannot make this determination in advance, the Java interpreter looks up the right method to invoke, at runtime.

---

**CHALLENGE 12.1**

How does the Chain of Responsibility pattern differ from ordinary method lookup?

*A solution appears on page 387.*

---

### Refactoring to Chain of Responsibility

The Oozinoz application suite includes a visualization that shows machines on the factory floor. The visualization includes the ability to select multiple items and to pop up a menu of various requests. One item on the pop-up menu displays a list of the engineers who are responsible for the selected equipment. The simulated items include machines, machine composites, tools, and tool carts. Tools are always assigned to tool carts, and tool carts have a responsible engineer. In determining who is responsible for the machine, machines may have a responsible engineer or may defer to the line they are part of or to the factory itself. Figure 12.1 shows the classes involved in finding the engineers who are responsible for selected equipment.

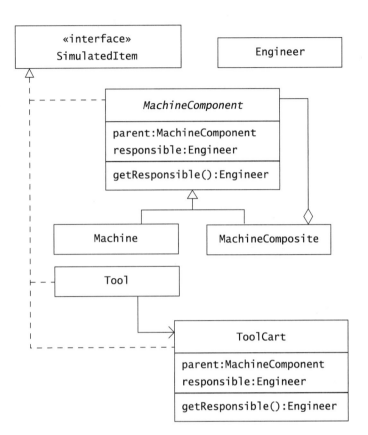

**FIGURE 12.1:** Items in a simulation include machines, machine composites, tools, and tool carts.

The menu code that finds the engineer responsible for a given machine uses a series of if statements and instanceof operators. These traits are signs that refactoring can improve the code.

```
package com.oozinoz.applications;
import com.oozinoz.machine.*;
public class AmbitiousMenu
{
    public Engineer getResponsible(SimulatedItem item)
    {
        if (item instanceof Tool)
        {
            Tool t = (Tool) item;
            return t.getToolCart().getResponsible();
        }

        if (item instanceof MachineComponent)
        {
```

```
                        MachineComponent c = (MachineComponent) item;
                        if (c.getResponsible() == null)
                        {
                            if (c.getParent() != null)
                            {
                                return c.getParent().getResponsible();
                            }
                        }
                    }
                    return null;
                }
            }
```

You can clean up this code by applying the CHAIN OF RESPONSIBILITY
pattern.

---

**CHALLENGE 12.2**

Redraw the diagram in Figure 12.1, moving getResponsible() to SimulatedItem and adding
this behavior to Tool.

*A solution appears on page 387.*

---

The client code is a lot simpler if it can ask any selectable item for its
responsible engineer:

```
        public Engineer getResponsible(SimulatedItem item)
        {
            return item.getResponsible();
        }
```

The implementation of getResponsible() for each item is simpler, too.

Sample solutions appear on page 388.

**CHALLENGE 12.3**

Write getResponsible() for:

A. MachineComponent
B. Tool
C. ToolCart

## Anchoring a Chain

When you write the getResponsible() method for MachineComponent, you have to consider that a MachineComponent object's parent might be null. Alternatively, you can tighten up your object model, insisting that MachineComponent objects have a non-null parent. To achieve this, add a parent argument to the constructor for MachineComponent. (You may want to throw an exception if the supplied object is null.) Also consider that an object will be the *root*—a distinguished object that has no parent. A reasonable approach is to create a MachineRoot class as a subclass of MachineComposite (not MachineComponent). Then you can guarantee that a MachineComponent object always has a responsible engineer if

- The constructor(s) for MachineRoot require an Engineer object
- The constructor(s) for MachineComponent require a non-null parent object that is itself a MachineComponent

**CHALLENGE 12.4**

Fill in the constructors in Figure 12.2 to support a design that ensures that every MachineComponent object has a responsible engineer.

A solution appears on page 388.

**FIGURE 12.2:** How can constructors ensure that every `MachineComponent` object has a responsible engineer?

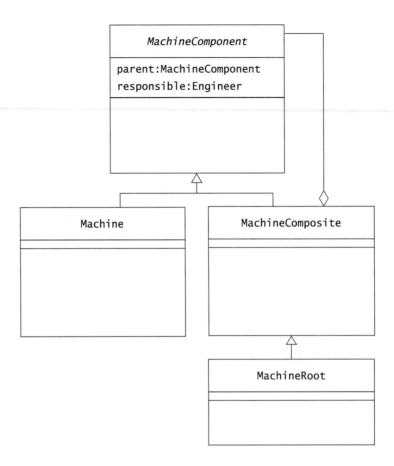

By anchoring a chain of responsibility, you strengthen the object model and simplify the code. Now you can implement the getResponsible() method of MachineComponent as:

```
public Engineer getResponsible()
{
    if (responsible != null)
    {
        return responsible;
    }
    return parent.getResponsible();
}
```

## CHAIN OF RESPONSIBILITY without COMPOSITE

CHAIN OF RESPONSIBILITY requires a strategy for ordering the search for an object that can handle a request. Usually, the order to follow will depend on an underlying aspect in the modeled domain. This frequently occurs when there is composition, as in the Oozinoz machine hierarchy. However, this pattern can apply outside object models that are composites.

---

**CHALLENGE 12.5**

Cite an example when the CHAIN OF RESPONSIBILITY pattern might occur if the chained objects do not form a composite.

*A solution appears on page 389.*

---

## Summary

When you apply the CHAIN OF RESPONSIBILITY pattern, you relieve a client from having to know which object in a collection supports a given behavior. By setting up the search for responsibility to occur across objects, you decouple the client from any specific object in the chain.

The CHAIN OF RESPONSIBILITY pattern occurs occasionally when an arbitrary chain of objects can apply a series of different strategies to tackling a problem, such as parsing a user's input. More frequently this pattern occurs in aggregations, in which a containment hierarchy provides a natural ordering for a chain of objects. CHAIN OF RESPONSIBILITY leads to simpler code in both the hierarchy and the client, which is the main advantage of this pattern.

# 13

# FLYWEIGHT

T HE FLYWEIGHT PATTERN addresses sharing, relying on an object's ability to be responsible to more than a single client. An ordinary object doesn't have to worry much about shared responsibility. Often, only one client will hold a reference to an object at any one time. When the object's state changes, it's because the client changed it, and the object does not have any responsibility to inform any other clients. Sometimes, though, you will want to arrange for multiple clients to share access to an object.

One incentive for sharing an object among multiple clients occurs when you must manage thousands or tens of thousands of small objects, such as the characters in an online version of a book. In such a case, you may have a performance incentive to share these fine-grained objects among many clients. A book needs only one A object, although it needs a way to model where different As appear.

In any application having a large number of small objects, you may need to provide a way for clients to safely share the common elements of these objects. The intent of the FLYWEIGHT pattern is to use sharing to support large numbers of fine-grained objects efficiently.

## Recognizing FLYWEIGHT

To provide for the sharing of flyweight objects, you need a class with a method other than a constructor that returns the object to be shared. This lets you control flyweight creation, ensuring that only one instance of any particular flyweight exists. There is an example of a flyweight factory in a Swing class that is a factory for Swing components. This class comment says, "wherever possible, this factory will hand out references to shared ... instances." We used this class in Chapter 4, FACADE, and in Chapter 9, OBSERVER.

---

**CHALLENGE 13.1**

Name a Swing class that provides an example of FLYWEIGHT.

*A solution appears on page 390.*

---

## Immutability

When a client changes the state of an object, the state changes for every client that has access to the object. This is no problem when there is only a single client, which is the most ordinary case. When multiple clients will share access to an object, the easiest and most common way to keep clients from affecting one another is to restrict clients from introducing any state changes in the shared object. You can achieve this by making an object **immutable** so that once created, the object cannot change. The most common immutable objects in Java are instances of the String class. Once you create a string, neither you nor any client with access to the string can change its characters.

---

**CHALLENGE 13.2**

Either justify why the creators of Java made String objects immutable or argue that this was an unwise restriction.

*A solution appears on page 390.*

When you have large numbers of similar objects, you may want to arrange for shared access to these objects, but they may not be immutable. In this case, a preliminary step in applying the FLYWEIGHT pattern is to extract the immutable part of an object so that this part can be shared.

## Extracting the Immutable Part of a Flyweight

Around Oozinoz, chemicals are as prevalent as characters in a document. The purchasing, engineering, manufacturing, and safety departments are all concerned with directing the flow of thousands of chemicals through the factory. Batches of chemicals are often modeled with instances of the Substance_1 class, as shown in Figure 13.1.

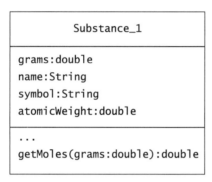

**FIGURE 13.1:** A Substance_1 object models a physical batch of chemical material.

The Substance_1 class has get- methods for its attributes and also has a getMoles() method that returns the number of **moles**—a count of molecules—in the substance. For example, 32 grams of sulfur contains 1 mole of sulfur atoms, as the atomic weight of sulfur is 32. The getMoles() method of the Substance_1 class returns the number of moles that a particular Substance_1 instance represents.

The Substance_1 class uses the atomic weight of a chemical when it calculates the number of moles of a modeled quantity of substance. For example, 10 grams of sulfur contains 10/32 moles:

```
public double getMoles()
{
    return grams / atomicWeight;
}
```

The **molality** of a substance combines information about the mass of a particular batch and the immutable atomic weight of the substance. To support the calculation of molality, developers at Oozinoz have placed mass and atomic weight together in the Substance_1 class. The molality of substances, combined with an understanding of chemical reactions, determines the amount of each substance that must appear in a chemical mixture. (For example, two moles of hydrogen and one mole of oxygen can make a mole of $H_2O$—water.)

At Oozinoz, no mixture is more common than the black powder that is part of most fireworks. Figure 13.2 shows an object diagram of a batch of black powder.

Given the proliferation of chemicals at Oozinoz, you might decide to model chemicals with shared, flyweight objects. As a first step, suppose that you decide to refactor the Substance_1 class, extracting its immutable part into a Chemical_1 class.

**FIGURE 13.2:** A batch of black powder contains saltpeter, sulfur, and carbon.

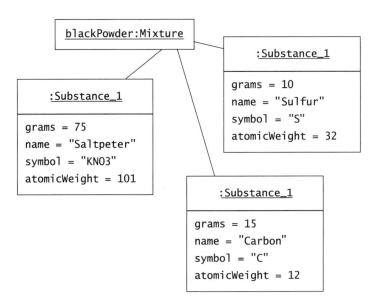

**CHALLENGE 13.3**

Complete the class diagram in Figure 13.3 to show a refactored Substance class and a new, immutable Chemical_1 class. Include a getMoles() method in the Chemical_1 class, so that classes other than Substance can check a chemical batch's molality.

*A solution appears on page 391.*

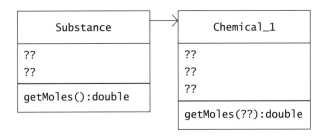

**FIGURE 13.3:** Complete this diagram to extract the immutable aspects of Substance into the Chemical_1 class.

## Sharing Flyweights

Extracting the immutable part of an object is half the battle in applying the FLYWEIGHT pattern. The remaining work includes creating a flyweight factory that instantiates flyweights and that arranges for clients to share them. You also have to ensure that clients will use your factory instead of constructing instances of the flyweight class themselves.

To make chemicals flyweights, you need a factory, perhaps a Chemical-Factory_1 class, with a static method that returns a chemical given its name. You might store chemicals in a hash map, creating known chemicals as part of the factory's initialization. Figure 13.4 shows a design for a ChemicalFactory_1. The code for ChemicalFactory_1 can use a static initializer to store Chemical_1 objects in a hash map:

**FIGURE 13.4:** The
`ChemicalFactory_1`
class is a flyweight fac-
tory that returns
`Chemical` objects.

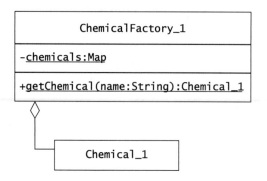

```
package com.oozinoz.chemical;
import java.util.*;
public class ChemicalFactory_1
{
    private static Map chemicals = new HashMap();
    static
    {
        chemicals.put(
            "carbon",
            new Chemical_1("Carbon", "C", 12));
        chemicals.put(
            "sulfur",
            new Chemical_1("Sulfur", "S", 32));
        chemicals.put(
            "saltpeter",
            new Chemical_1("Saltpeter", "KNO3", 101));
        //...
    }

    public static Chemical getChemical(String name)
    {
        return (Chemical) chemicals.get(name.toLowerCase());
    }
}
```

Having created a factory for chemicals, you now have to take steps to ensure that other developers use this factory instead of instantiating the `Chemical_1` class themselves. A simple approach is to rely on the visibility of the `Chemical_1` class.

> **CHALLENGE 13.4**
>
> How can you use the visibility of the Chemical_1 class to discourage other developers from instantiating Chemical_1 objects?
>
> *A solution appears on page 392.*

Visibility modifiers do not supply the complete control over instantiation that you might want. You might like to ensure that ChemicalFactory is absolutely the only class that can create new Chemical instances. To achieve this level of control, you can apply an *inner* class, defining the Chemical class within ChemicalFactory. *Java™ in a Nutshell* (Flanagan 1999b) has a good description of the various types of inner classes that Java provides.

For ChemicalFactory, you can declare Chemical as a static member class. This indicates that Chemical need not reference any instance variables in ChemicalFactory. You might want to name the inner class ChemicalImpl and use the name Chemical for an interface. This lets clients refer to Chemical objects rather than ChemicalFactory.Chemical objects. Clients will never reference the inner class directly, so you can make it private, ensuring that only ChemicalFactory has access to it:

```
package com.oozinoz.chemical;
import java.util.*;
public class ChemicalFactory
{
    private static Map chemicals = new HashMap();
    static
    {
        chemicals.put(
            "carbon",
            new ChemicalImpl("Carbon", "C", 12));
        //... these puts are all here, but elided for space
    }
```

```java
private static class ChemicalImpl implements Chemical
{
    ?? (declare instance variables) ??

    private ChemicalImpl(        ??        )
    {

        ??

    }
    public double getMoles(double grams)
    {
        return ??
    }
    public String getName()
    {
        return name;
    }
    public String getSymbol()
    {
        return symbol;
    }
    public double getAtomicWeight()
    {
        return atomicWeight;
    }
}

public static Chemical getChemical(String name)
{
    return ??
}
}
```

---

**CHALLENGE 13.5**

Complete the Java code for a ChemicalFactory version that defines ChemicalImpl as a private, static member class. The inner class implements a Chemical interface, and the getChemical() method of ChemicalFactory returns an object of type Chemical.

*A solution appears on page 392.*

## Summary

The FLYWEIGHT pattern lets you share access to objects, such as characters, chemicals, and borders, that may appear in large quantities. The flyweight objects must be immutable, a feature you can establish by extracting the immutable part of the class that you want to share. To ensure that your flyweight objects are shared, you have to provide a factory in which clients can find flyweights, and you have to enforce the use of this factory. Visibility modifiers give you some control over how other developers access your code. Inner classes take this further, letting you guarantee that a class is accessible by only its containing class. By ensuring that clients use your flyweight factory properly, you can provide safe, shared access to what would otherwise be a multitude of fine-grained objects.

# PART III

# CONSTRUCTION PATTERNS

## 14

# INTRODUCING CONSTRUCTION

WHEN YOU CREATE a Java class, you normally provide for the creation of objects of your class by supplying class constructors. In many regards, constructors are like any other methods, but Java has numerous rules that specifically govern the use of constructors. In particular, constructors have special abilities to collaborate with one another.

## Ordinary Construction

Java constructors are special methods. In many respects, including visibility modifiers and exception handling, constructors are like ordinary methods. On the other hand, a significant number of syntactic and semantic rules govern the use and behavior of constructors. These extra rules emerge because classes are significantly different from other objects in Java. In Smalltalk, by comparison, classes are objects that are responsible for providing constructors. There is no special syntax for constructors, a simplification that helps keep Smalltalk syntax small.

---

**CHALLENGE 14.1**

List three or four rules that govern the use and behavior of constructors in Java.

*A solution appears on page 393.*

---

Smalltalk's simple syntax for constructors is not proof per se of Smalltalk's superiority. In fact, Smalltalk's organization of the class of a class of a class is mind-numbingly difficult to comprehend for most developers. The point of comparing Java to other languages is not to determine superiority but rather for us to deepen our understanding of the design choices built into Java and how they affect us as developers. One aspect of Java constructors that is important to understand is the collaboration that you can orchestrate among constructors.

## Superclass Collaboration

Eventually, a constructor always collaborates with one of its superclass's constructors. If a class has no declared constructor, Java supplies a default one equivalent to a constructor with no arguments and no statements. If the first statement in a constructor is anything other than a specific invocation of another constructor, Java inserts a call to super(), the superclass's constructor with no arguments. This causes a compilation error if the superclass does not provide a constructor with no arguments.

In Figure 14.1, for example the classes capture the idea that a fountain is one type of firework. (A **fountain** is a ground-based firework that emits a spray of sparks.) Suppose that at an early stage of development, we have no constructors defined. In this case, Java supplies a default constructor—one that accepts no arguments—for both classes. It is legal to instantiate these objects with such lines as:

```
Fountain f = new Fountain();
```

A problem arises if we add a constructor to the superclass. Suppose that we add a name attribute to Firework and a constructor that accepts it:

**FIGURE 14.1:** In certain conditions, Java will provide default constructors and default constructor collaboration.

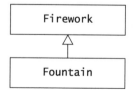

```
public Firework(String name)
{
    this.name = name;
}
```

After this change to `Firework`, the `Fountain` class will suddenly fail to compile. The `Fountain` class defines no constructor, so Java will supply a default constructor. This constructor makes a default call to `super()`, the superclass's default constructor. However, this constructor no longer exists. Java supplies a default constructor only if the class has no other constructor. By creating a constructor for `Firework`, we eliminate this class's default constructor and thereby break the `Fountain` class.

---

**CHALLENGE 14.2**

Write a constructor for the `Fountain` class that allows it to successfully compile.

*A solution appears on page 394.*

---

Java will not always insert a call to `super()` in a constructor. A constructor can avoid this default behavior by explicitly invoking a superclass constructor or by invoking another constructor of the current class with a call to `this()`. When a class has several constructors, they usually apply calls to `this()` to collaborate with one another.

## Collaboration within a Class

The constructors of a well-designed class usually interact. Consider what happens when we need to add a classification attribute to the `Firework` class so that each firework is classified as a consumer firework or as a display-type firework. Figure 14.2 shows the `Firework` class picking up firework classification constants from the `ClassificationConstants` interface and adding a `Classification` attribute.

**FIGURE 14.2:** The
`Firework` class
"inherits" classification
constants by implement-
ing the `Classifica-
tionConstants`
interface.

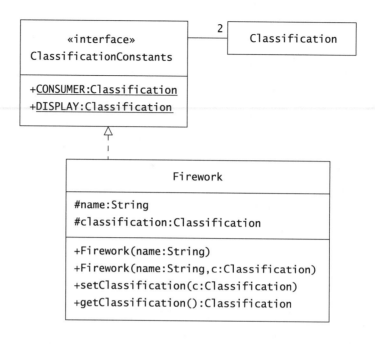

## CHALLENGE 14.3

Suppose that you want to use constructors to establish the default classification of a firework
as DISPLAY. Write constructors for `Firework` that ensure this, and make them collaborate so
that the one-parameter constructor uses the two-parameter constructor.

*A solution appears on page 394.*

Changing the constructors for the `Firework` class forces us to consider
changing the constructors for its subclass, `Fountain`.

---

**CHALLENGE 14.4**

Suppose that you want the Fountain class to abide by the decision that the default classification of a firework is DISPLAY. It is better not have this decision appear twice in the code. Write the constructors for Fountain so that they collaborate effectively with the superclass constructors, including observance of the superclass's ideas about defaults.

*A solution appears on page 395.*

## Summary

Ordinarily, you will furnish classes that you develop with constructors to provide a means for instantiating the class. These constructors may form a collaborating suite, and every call to a constructor will ultimately also invoke a superclass constructor.

## ■ BEYOND ORDINARY CONSTRUCTION

Java's constructor features provide many alternatives when you design a new class. However, constructors are effective only if the user of your class knows which class to instantiate and knows the required fields for instantiating an object. For example, the choice of which user interface component to compose may depend on whether the program is running on a handheld device or on a larger display. It can also happen that a developer knows which class to instantiate but does not have all the necessary initial values or has them in the wrong format. For example, the developer may need to create an object from a dormant or a textual version of an object. In such circumstances, you need to go beyond the use of ordinary Java constructors and apply a design pattern.

The following principles describe the intent of patterns that facilitate construction.

| If you intend to | Apply the pattern |
| --- | --- |
| • Gather the information for an object gradually before requesting its construction | BUILDER (Chapter 15) |
| • Defer the decision of which class to instantiate | FACTORY METHOD (Chapter 16) |
| • Construct a family of objects that share a trait | ABSTRACT FACTORY (Chapter 17) |
| • Specify an object to create by giving an example | PROTOTYPE (Chapter 18) |
| • Reconstruct an object from a dormant version that contains just the object's internal state | MEMENTO (Chapter 19) |

The intent of each design pattern is to solve a problem in a context. Construction-oriented patterns are designs that let a client construct a new object through a means other than calling a class constructor. For example, when you find the initial values for an object gradually, you may want to follow the BUILDER pattern.

## 15

# BUILDER

THE BUILDER PATTERN moves the construction logic for an object outside the class to instantiate. Making this move might be useful for several reasons. You might simply want to reduce the size of a class that has many methods. You may also want to allow step-by-step construction of a target object. This occurs when you acquire the parameters for a constructor gradually, as happens with parsers and may happen with a user interface.

## Building from a Parser

In addition to manufacturing fireworks, Oozinoz puts on fireworks displays. Travel agencies e-mail their reservation requests in the form

```
Date, November 5, Headcount, 250, City, Springfield,
DollarsPerHead, 9.95, HasSite, No
```

As you might guess, this protocol originated in the days before **XML** (**Extensible Markup Language**), but it has thus far proved sufficient. The request tells when a potential customer wants to see a display and in what city. The request also specifies the minimum headcount that the customer will guarantee and the amount of money per guest that the customer will pay. The customer in this example wants to put on a show for 250 guests and is willing to pay $9.95 per guest, or a total of $2,487.50. The travel agent has also indicated that the customer does not have a site in mind for the display.

The task at hand is to parse the textual request and create a Reservation object that represents it. We might approach this task by creating an

**157**

empty Reservation object and setting its parameters as our parser encounters them. This causes the problem that a given Reservation object may or may not represent a valid request. For example, we might finish reading the text of a request and then realize that it lacks a date.

To ensure that Reservation objects are always valid requests, we can use a ReservationBuilder class. The ReservationBuilder object can store a reservation request's attributes as a parser finds them and then build a Reservation object, verifying its validity. Figure 15.1 shows the classes we need for this design.

The classes that Figure 15.1 shows appear in the com.oozinoz.reservation package. The ReservationBuilder class is abstract, as is its build() method. We will create concrete subclasses of ReservationBuilder shortly. First, though, note that the constructor for Reservation is protected.

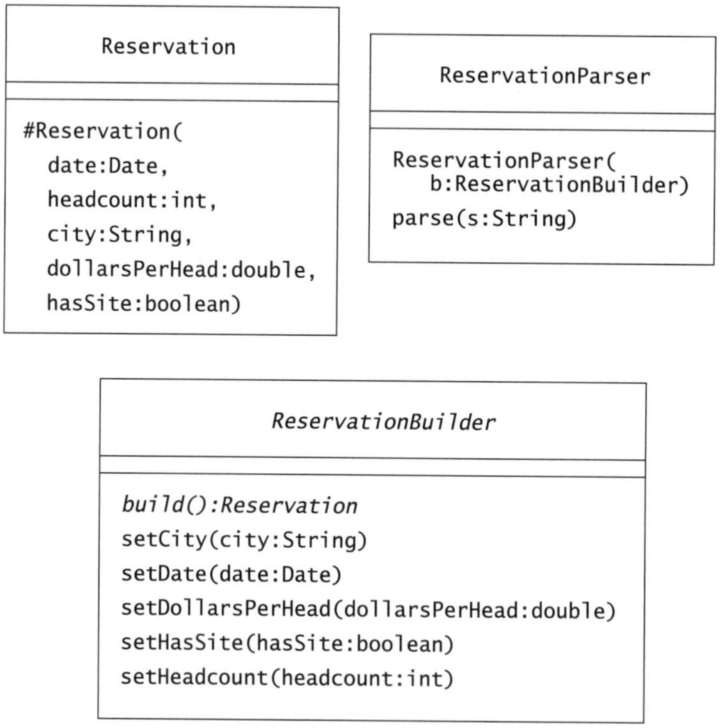

**FIGURE 15.1:** A builder class offloads construction logic from a domain class and can accept initialization parameters gradually, as a parser discovers them.

```
Reservation

#Reservation(
   date:Date,
   headcount:int,
   city:String,
   dollarsPerHead:double,
   hasSite:boolean)
```

```
ReservationParser

ReservationParser(
   b:ReservationBuilder)
parse(s:String)
```

```
ReservationBuilder

build():Reservation
setCity(city:String)
setDate(date:Date)
setDollarsPerHead(dollarsPerHead:double)
setHasSite(hasSite:boolean)
setHeadcount(headcount:int)
```

---

**CHALLENGE 15.1**

The Reservation constructor has protected visibility. Explain either why this is ideal or why it would be better to give this constructor private, public, or package protection.

*A solution appears on page 395.*

---

## Building under Constraints

You want to ensure that invalid Reservation objects are never instantiated. Specifically, suppose that every reservation must have a non-null date and city. Further, suppose that a business rule states that Oozinoz will not perform for fewer than 25 people or for less than $495.95. To support this rule, you can create a ReservationConstants interface:

```
public interface ReservationConstants
{
    public static final int MINHEAD = 25;
    public static final double MINTOTAL = 495.95;
}
```

A reservation for too small an audience or that generates too little income is invalid. To avoid creating an instance of Reservation when a request is invalid, you might place business logic checks and exception throwing in the constructor for Reservation or in an init() method that this constructor calls. But this logic is fairly independent of the normal function of a Reservation object once it is created.

Introducing a builder will make the Reservation class simpler, leaving it with methods that concentrate on behavior other than construction. Using a builder also creates an opportunity to validate the parameters of a Reservation object with different reactions to invalid parameters. Finally, by moving the construction job to a ReservationBuilder subclass, you allow construction to occur gradually, as the parser finds a reservation's attributes. Figure 15.2 shows concrete ReservationBuilder subclasses that differ in how forgiving they are of invalid parameters.

FIGURE 15.2: Builders can be forgiving or unforgiving as they try to create a valid object from a given set of parameters.

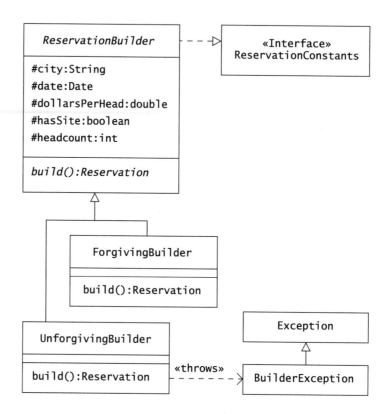

Code that uses a builder will look something like the following:

```
package com.oozinoz.applications;
import com.oozinoz.reservation.*;
public class ShowUnforgiving
{
    public static void main(String[] args)
    {
        String sample =
            "Date, November 5, Headcount, 250, "
                + "City, Springfield, DollarsPerHead, 9.95, "
                + "HasSite, No";

        ReservationBuilder b = new UnforgivingBuilder();
        new ReservationParser(b).parse(sample);

        try
        {
            Reservation r = b.build();
            System.out.println(r);
        }
```

```
            catch (BuilderException e)
            {
                System.out.println(e.getMessage());
            }
        }
    }
```

Running this program prints out a `Reservation` object:

```
    Date: Nov 5, 2001, Headcount: 250, City: Springfield,
    Dollars/Head: 9.95, Has Site: false
```

Given a reservation request string, the code instantiates a builder and a parser and asks the parser to parse the string. As it reads the string, the parser passes the reservation attributes to the builder, using the builder's set methods. (The parser is a bit off the topic of BUILDER, but its code is available at oozinoz.com.)

After parsing, the code asks the builder to build a valid reservation. This example just prints out an exception's message text rather than taking a more significant action as you would in a real application.

---

### CHALLENGE 15.2

The `build()` method of the `UnforgivingBuilder` class throws a `BuilderException` if the date or city is null, if the headcount is too low, or if the total cost of the proposed reservation is too low. Write the code for the `build()` method according to these specifications.

*A solution appears on page 396.*

---

## Building a Counteroffer

The `UnforgivingBuilder` class will reject requests that are anything less than fully formed. Suppose that the business decides that the software should make reasonable changes to requests that are missing certain details about the reservation. Specifically, suppose that an analyst asks you to set the headcount for an event to the minimum if this attribute is missing. Similarly, if the dollars/head value is missing, you are to set it to be high enough so that the total take is above the minimum. If you make either of these changes, you should mark the reservation as a counteroffer that the reservation system will confirm with the customer.

To meet this request, suppose that you add a Boolean `counteroffer` argument method to the `Reservation` constructor and develop a new `ForgivingBuilder` class. As you build a reservation in `ForgivingBuilder`, do the following.

1. If the reservation request specifies no headcount and no dollars/head, set the headcount to the minimum and set dollars/head to the minimum total divided by the headcount.
2. If there is no headcount but there is a dollars/head value, set the headcount to be at least the minimum attendance and at least enough to generate enough money for the event.
3. If there is a headcount but no dollars/head value, set the dollars/head value to be high enough to generate the minimum take.

As before, your code should throw an exception if the reservation fails to specify a city or a date, as there is no way to guess these values.

---

**CHALLENGE 15.3**

Write the code for the `build()` method of the `ForgivingBuilder` class.

*A solution appears on page 396.*

---

The classes `ForgivingBuilder` and `UnforgivingBuilder` let you guarantee that `Reservation` objects are always valid. Your design also gives you flexibility about what action to take when there is a problem in constructing a reservation.

## Summary

The BUILDER pattern separates the construction of a complex object from its representation. This has the immediate effect of making a complex target class simpler. It lets a builder class focus on the proper construction of an object, leaving the target class to focus on the operation of a valid instance. This is especially useful when you want to ensure the validity of an object before instantiating it and don't want the associated logic to appear in the target class's constructors. A builder also accommodates step-by-step construction, which occurs when you create an object by parsing text and may occur when you gather an object's parameters from a user interface.

# 16

# FACTORY METHOD

As a class developer, you will ordinarily provide class constructors to let users of your class instantiate it. Sometimes, however, a client that needs an object does not or should not know which of several possible classes to instantiate. The FACTORY METHOD pattern lets a class developer define the interface for creating an object while retaining control of which class to instantiate.

## Recognizing FACTORY METHOD

You might think any method that creates and returns a new object is a "factory" method. In object-oriented programming, however, methods that return new objects are common, and not every such method is an instance of the FACTORY METHOD pattern.

---

**CHALLENGE 16.1**

Name two commonly used Java methods that return a new object.

*A solution appears on page 398.*

---

The fact that a method creates a new object does not in itself mean that it is an example of the FACTORY METHOD pattern. The FACTORY METHOD pattern requires that an operation that creates an object also isolates its client from knowing which class to instantiate. In FACTORY METHOD, you will find several classes that implement the same operation, returning the same, abstract type but internally instantiating different classes that implement the type. To summarize, the signs that FACTORY METHOD is at work are that an operation:

- Creates a new object
- Returns a type that is an abstract class or an interface
- Is implemented by several classes

Table 16.1 shows a few methods from the Java class libraries; these methods have all or some of the characteristics of the FACTORY METHOD pattern. For example, the BorderFactory class has a variety of methods that create and return new objects. The class is a factory but is not an example of the FACTORY METHOD pattern.

**TABLE 16.1:** Characteristics of FACTORY METHOD

| METHOD | CREATES AN OBJECT | RETURNS ABSTRACT CLASS OR INTERFACE | IMPLEMENTED BY SEVERAL CLASSES | INSTANCE OF FACTORY METHOD |
|---|---|---|---|---|
| BorderFactory.createEtchedBorder() | x | | | |
| Arrays.asList() | x | x | | |
| toString() | x | | x | |
| iterator() | x | x | x | x |

---

**CHALLENGE 16.2**

Explain how the intent of FACTORY METHOD is different from the intent of the
BorderFactory class.

*A solution appears on page 398.*

---

You might feel that a method like `Arrays.asList()`, which instantiates
an object and has an interface return type, is an example of FACTORY
METHOD. After all, such methods do isolate a client from knowing which
class to instantiate. But the spirit of FACTORY METHOD is that the object
creator makes a choice about which of several possible classes to instantiate for the client. The `Arrays.asList()` method instantiates the same
type of object for every client, so this method does not fulfill the intent of
FACTORY METHOD.

Usually, you will find that several classes in a hierarchy implement
the FACTORY METHOD operation. Then the decision of which class to
instantiate depends on the class of the object that receives the call to
create. In other words, FACTORY METHOD lets subclasses decide which
class to instantiate.

Many classes, including those in hierarchies, implement the `toString()`
method. But the `toString()` method always returns a `String` object. The
classes that implement `toString()` do not determine which class to
instantiate, so this method is not an example of FACTORY METHOD.

## A Classic Example of FACTORY METHOD: Iterators

The ITERATOR pattern (see Chapter 28, ITERATOR) provides a way to access
the elements of collection sequentially. But `iterator()` methods themselves are usually good examples of the FACTORY METHOD pattern. An
`iterator()` method isolates its caller from knowing which class to instantiate. The Java JDK version 1.2 release introduced the `Collection` inter-

face, which includes the iterator() operation. All collections implement this operation.

An iterator() method creates an object that returns a sequence of the elements of a collection. For example, the following code creates and prints out the elements of a list:

```
package com.oozinoz.applications;
import java.util.*;
public class ShowIterator
{
    public static void main(String[] args)
    {
        List list =
            Arrays.asList(
                new String[] {
                    "fountain", "rocket", "sparkler" });
        Iterator i = list.iterator();
        while (i.hasNext())
        {
            System.out.println(i.next());
        }
    }
}
```

**CHALLENGE 16.3**

What class is the Iterator object in this code?

*A solution appears on page 399.*

The point of the FACTORY METHOD pattern, which the iterator() method exemplifies well, is that clients of the method need not know which class to instantiate.

## Taking Control of Which Class to Instantiate

As a client of, say, a List, you know when you need an iterator, but you don't know and don't want to know which class to instantiate to create the iterator. In this case, the service provider—the developers of the List class—know which class to instantiate when a client needs an iterator. This situation, in which the service provider has more knowledge than the client about which class to instantiate, also occurs frequently in application code.

Suppose that Oozinoz wants to start letting customers buy fireworks on credit. Early in the design of the credit authorization system, you accept responsibility for developing a CreditCheckOnline class that checks to see whether a customer can maintain a certain amount of credit with Oozinoz.

As you begin development, you realize that occasionally the credit agency will be offline. The analyst on the project determines that in this situation, the business wants you to bring up a dialog for the call center representative and to make a credit decision based on a few questions. To handle this, you create a CreditCheckOffline class and get it working to specification. Initially, you design the classes as shown in Figure 16.1. The creditLimit() method accepts a customer's identification number and returns that customer's credit limit.

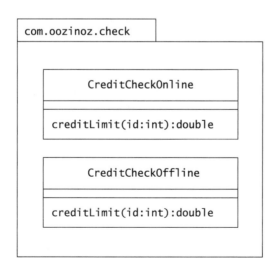

**FIGURE 16.1:** You can instantiate one of these classes to check a customer's credit, depending on whether the online credit agency is up.

With the classes in Figure 16.1 you can provide credit limit information whether or not the credit agency is online. The problem now is that the user of your classes needs to know which class to instantiate. But *you* are the one who knows whether the agency is up!

In this scenario, you need to commit to the interface for creating an object but keep control of which class to instantiate. One solution is to change both classes to implement a standard interface and to create a factory method that returns an object of that type. Specifically, you might

- Make `CreditCheck` a Java interface that includes the `creditLimit()` method
- Change both credit check classes to declare that they implement the `CreditCheck` interface
- Create a `CreditCheckFactory` class that provides a `createCreditCheck()` method that returns an object whose type is `CreditCheck`

When you implement `createCreditCheck()`, you will use your knowledge of the credit agency's status to decide which class to instantiate.

---

**CHALLENGE 16.4**

Draw a class diagram that establishes a way to create a credit-checking object while retaining control of which class to instantiate.

·

*A solution appears on page 399.*

---

By applying FACTORY METHOD, you let the user of your services call the `createCreditCheck()` method to get a credit-checking object that works regardless of whether the credit agency is online.

**CHALLENGE 16.5**

Assume that the `CreditCheckFactory` class has an `isAgencyUp()` method that tells whether the credit agency is available, and write the code for `createCreditCheck()`.

*A solution appears on page 400.*

## FACTORY METHOD in Parallel Hierarchies

The FACTORY METHOD pattern often appears when you use parallel hierarchies to model a problem domain. A **parallel hierarchy** is a pair of class hierarchies in which each class in one hierarchy has a corresponding class in the other hierarchy. Parallel hierarchies usually emerge when you decide to move a subset of behavior out of an existing hierarchy.

Consider the construction of aerial shells, as illustrated in Chapter 5, COMPOSITE. To build these shells, Oozinoz uses the machines modeled in Figure 16.2.

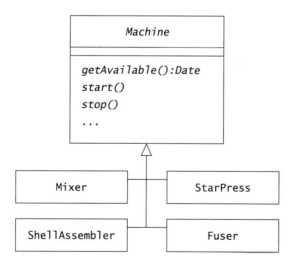

**FIGURE 16.2:** The `Machine` hierarchy contains logic for controlling physical machines and for planning.

To make a shell, we mix chemicals in a mixer and pass them to a star press, which extrudes individual stars. We pack stars into a shell around a core of black powder and place this over a lifting charge, using a shell assembler. We use a fuser to insert the fusing that will ignite both the lifting charge and the shell core.

Suppose that you need the `getAvailable()` method to forecast when a machine will complete its current processing and be available for more work. This method may require several supporting private methods, adding up to quite a bit of logic to add to each of our machine classes. Rather than adding the planning logic to the `Machine` hierarchy, you might prefer to have a separate `MachinePlanner` hierarchy. You need a separate planner class for most machine types, but mixers and fusers are always available for additional work. For these classes, you can use a `BasicPlanner` class.

---

**CHALLENGE 16.6**

Fill in the diagram of a `Machine`/`MachinePlanner` parallel hierarchy in Figure 16.3.

*A solution appears on page 401.*

---

**FIGURE 16.3:** Slim down the `Machine` hierarchy by moving planning logic to a parallel hierarchy.

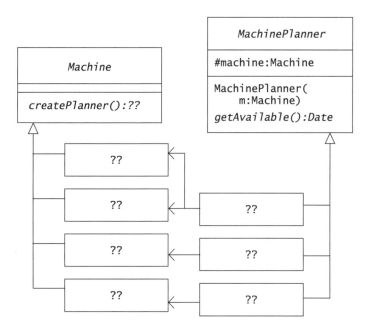

---

**CHALLENGE 16.7**

Suppose that you make the `Machine` class abstract and add an abstract method `createPlanner()`. Write a `createPlanner()` method for the `Fuser` and `StarPress` classes.

*A solution appears on page 402.*

---

## Summary

The intent of the FACTORY METHOD pattern is to define the interface for creating a new object so that a service provider decides which class to instantiate instead of clients. This pattern occurs in the Java class libraries and is common in application code.

You can also apply FACTORY METHOD when you want to introduce a parallel class hierarchy. This can help keep a set of classes from becoming bloated with many different aspects of behavior. FACTORY METHOD lets you connect parallel hierarchies by letting subclasses in one hierarchy determine which class to instantiate in the corresponding hierarchy.

# 17

# ABSTRACT FACTORY

SOMETIMES, YOU WANT to provide for object creation while retaining control of which class to instantiate. In such circumstances, you can apply the FACTORY METHOD pattern with a method that uses an outside factor to determine which class to instantiate. The outside factor can be anything. In Chapter 16, FACTORY METHOD, this factor was the status of an online credit agency. Sometimes, the factor that controls which object to instantiate can be thematic, running across several classes. The ABSTRACT FACTORY pattern addresses this situation. The intent of this pattern is to provide for the creation of a family of related, or dependent, objects.

## Abstract Factories for Families of Objects

To answer the challenges in Chapter 16, you designed a pair of classes to implement the CreditCheck interface. Your design isolates other developers from knowing whether the credit agency is up and running. Suppose that in supporting the verification of customer information, you add a couple of classes that check the status of a customer's billing and shipping addresses. Your package of checking services looks like Figure 17.1.

Now suppose that a requirements analyst tells you that Oozinoz wants to start servicing customers in Canada. To do business in Canada, you will use a different credit agency and different data sources to establish attributes of customer addresses, such as whether they incur tariffs or are residential. When a customer calls, the call center application needs a

**FIGURE 17.1:** Classes in this package check a customer's credit, shipping address, and billing address.

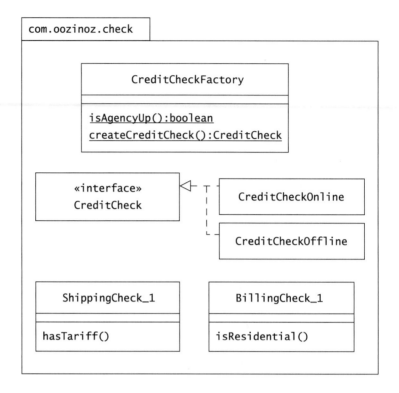

*family* of objects to perform a variety of checks. The family to use depends on whether the call is from Canada or from the United States. You can apply the ABSTRACT FACTORY pattern to provide for the creation of these object families.

Suppose that you decide to maintain three packages. Package com.oozinoz.check will contain three check interfaces and an abstract factory class. This class will have three create methods that create the three kinds of check objects. You will also put CreditCheckOffline in this package, as you can use this class for offline checks regardless of a call's origin. Figure 17.2 shows the new contents of com.oozinoz.check.

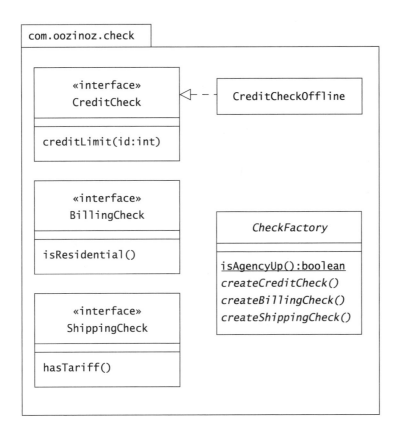

**FIGURE 17.2:** The revised package contains primarily interfaces and an abstract factory class.

To implement the interfaces in `com.oozinoz.check` with concrete classes, you can introduce two new packages: `com.oozinoz.check.canada` and `com.oozinoz.check.us`. Each of these packages can contain a concrete version of the factory class and classes to implement each of the interfaces in `com.oozinoz.check`.

---

**CHALLENGE 17.1**

Complete the diagram in Figure 17.3, which shows the classes in `com.oozinoz.check.canada` and their relation to classes and interfaces in `com.oozinoz.check`.

*A solution appears on page 402.*

**FIGURE 17.3:** Show the classes in the **canada** package and their relationships to classes in **com.oozinoz.check**.

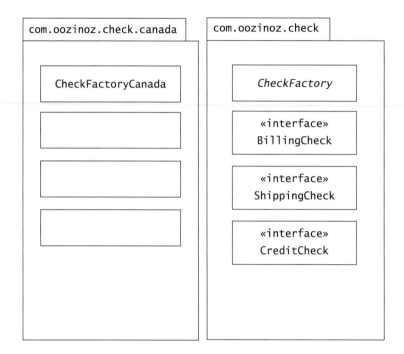

The concrete factory classes for Canadian and U.S. calls are fairly simple. The classes return the Canadian or U.S. versions of the check interfaces, with the exception that both concrete factories return a CreditCheck-Offline object if the local credit agency is offline. As in the previous chapter, the CheckFactory class has an isAgencyUp() method that tells whether the credit agency is available.

---

**CHALLENGE 17.2**

Complete the code for CheckFactoryCanada.java:

```
package com.oozinoz.check.canada;
import com.oozinoz.check.*;
public class CheckFactoryCanada extends CheckFactory
{

    // ??

}
```

*A solution appears on page 403.*

At this point, you have a solid design that applies the ABSTRACT FACTORY pattern to provide for the creation of families of objects that conduct checks of different kinds of customer information. You have one family for U.S. checks and one for Canada checks. A final step is to make your factories readily accessible.

---

**CHALLENGE 17.3**

Your system needs only one factory object for Canada checks and one for United States checks. Write CheckFactory.java, including static variables that make it easy for an application developer to access these factories:

```
package com.oozinoz.check;
import ??
import ??

public abstract class CheckFactory {
    public static final CheckFactory US = ??
    public static final CheckFactory ??

    public abstract ?? createBillingCheck ??

    public abstract ?? createCreditCheck ??

    public abstract ?? createShippingCheck ??
}
```

*A solution appears on page 404.*

---

## Packages and Abstract Factories

Speaking loosely, a package is usually a "family" of classes, and an abstract factory produces a "family" of objects. In the previous example, you used separate packages to support abstract factories for Canada and the United States, with a third package that provides common interfaces for the objects the factories produce.

---

**CHALLENGE 17.4**

Write down an argument supporting the decision to place each factory and its related classes in a separate package. Alternatively, argue that another approach is superior.

*A solution appears on page 405.*

---

## Abstract Factories for Look-and-Feel

Different operating systems have different standards about the look-and-feel—that is, the appearance and behavior—of user interface components. Java Swing comes with a platform-independent look-and-feel, as well as the ability to mimic the look-and-feel standards for Microsoft Windows and Motif. In application development, you can go well beyond these standards in specifying a look-and-feel for your application suite.

User environments that maintain consistent standards look more professional and are easier to use than systems that do not adhere to a standard. For example, you might want to standardize button sizes, fonts, background and foreground colors, border widths, and many other component attributes. Without a standard, user environments tend to take on an unpolished, crazy-quilt look that is difficult to navigate.

To provide a standard look-and-feel, you can establish a package of standard component classes. Figure 17.4 shows a user environment package for Oozinoz.

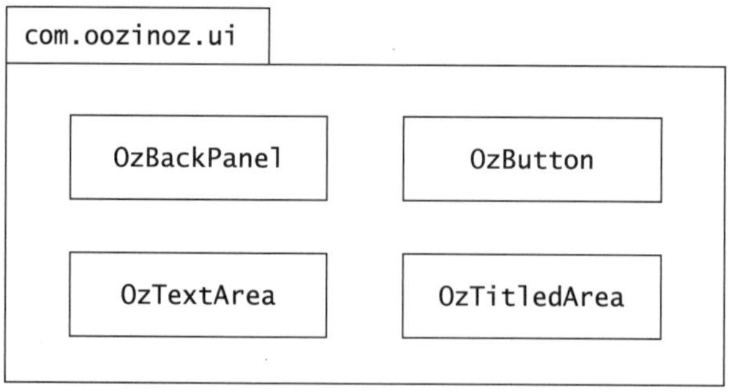

**FIGURE 17.4:** Oozinoz consistently uses subclasses of Swing components to achieve a sharp, uniform look.

com.oozinoz.ui

OzBackPanel    OzButton

OzTextArea    OzTitledArea

The current policy at Oozinoz requires developers to use these classes rather than corresponding Swing components. This policy helps to standardize the look-and-feel of Oozinoz applications. The problem may arise, however, that the business needs different look-and-feels in different situations.

---

**CHALLENGE 17.5**

Write down two reasons why Oozinoz might want to provide different look-and-feels in user environments.

*A solution appears on page 405.*

---

To allow for different look-and-feel standards to exist simultaneously, you can create an abstract class that returns the standard components. Concrete subclasses can then return families of components that are appropriate for a specific kind of user environment.

---

**CHALLENGE 17.6**

Draw a diagram of an abstract class that will create standard Oozinoz components.

*A solution appears on page 406.*

---

Concrete subclasses of your abstract class will work as factories. Each subclass will produce components that are appropriate to a specific type of display, such as handheld devices or full screens. For example, if you create HandheldKit as a subclass of your abstract factory, you will create HandheldKit.createButton() so that it creates and returns a small button with a small font size for its label. Each class that implements `createButton()` will return an `OzButton` object with attributes that are consistent with a look-and-feel.

*Design Patterns* (Gamma et al. 1995) says that the intent for ABSTRACT FACTORY is that clients can create families of objects "without specifying their concrete classes." A literal reading of this might exclude the hierarchy of user interface component factories because clients will in fact know the exact class for each type of object. However, the point of the ABSTRACT FACTORY pattern is that the factory classes isolate clients from knowing how to create objects.

With the user interface hierarchy, clients know which class to instantiate but do not know how to initialize each object. For example, clients will rely on the `HandheldKit` class to know how to initialize each component to be a reasonable size for a handheld device. Because the user interface hierarchy of factory classes isolates clients from knowing how to create objects, this hierarchy follows the intent of ABSTRACT FACTORY.

## Summary

The ABSTRACT FACTORY pattern lets you arrange for a client to create objects that are part of a family of related, or dependent, objects. The theme, or common trait of the family, such as which country the classes pertain to, may run across many classes. In this case, you may maintain parallel packages, perhaps placing each family in its own package. For GUI factories, you may not need more than one package if different "classes" of GUI components differ only in such attributes as text size and cursor type. However you organize your code, ABSTRACT FACTORY lets you provide a client with a factory that produces objects that are related by a common theme.

# 18

# PROTOTYPE

As a class developer, you ordinarily furnish your class with constructors to let client applications instantiate it. The construction-oriented patterns covered so far—BUILDER, FACTORY METHOD, and ABSTRACT FACTORY—isolate the user of an object from this constructor call. These patterns establish methods that instantiate an appropriate class on a client's behalf. The PROTOTYPE pattern also conceals object creation from clients but uses a different approach. Instead of bringing forth new, uninitialized instances of a class, the intent of the PROTOTYPE pattern is to provide new objects by copying an example.

## Prototypes as Factories

Suppose that you are using the ABSTRACT FACTORY pattern at Oozinoz to provide user interfaces for several contexts. Figure 18.1 shows the user interface factories you have in place.

The users at Oozinoz are thrilled with the productivity that results from applying the right user interface in the right context. The problem you face is that they want several more user interface kits, and it's becoming burdensome to create a new class for each context your users envision.

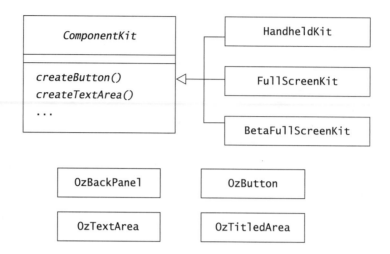

**FIGURE 18.1:** Three abstract factories, or kits, produce different user interface look-and-feels.

To halt the proliferation of user interface factory classes, you can replace them all with a single UIKit class that has prototypical objects in its instance variables. This class's creation methods will return copies of these prototypical objects. You haven't figured out yet how your copy methods will work or how you will set up your prototypical factories, but having a sketch of the class will give you a target to work toward.

---

**CHALLENGE 18.1**

Draw a diagram of a UIKit class, showing instance variables for prototypical button and text area objects and showing the creation methods that will return copies of these objects.

*A solution appears on page 406.*

---

Suppose that in the declarations of instance variables in UIKit, you initialize each object as follows:

```
protected OzButton button = new OzButton();
protected OzTextArea textArea = new OzTextArea();
//...
```

At present, the various user interfaces differ in the font and the cursor you use for each component. For full-screen components, you use the default cursor and the following font:

```
Font f = new Font("Dialog", Font.ITALIC, 18);
```

For handheld screen components you use the following cursor and font:

```
Cursor c = new Cursor(Cursor.HAND_CURSOR);
Font f = new Font("Dialog", Font.PLAIN, 8);
```

To create a factory for full-screen or handheld components, you create a UIKit object and set the cursor and font of this object's instance variables. A convenient place to do this work is in UIKit static methods that return instances of the appropriately tuned factories.

---

**CHALLENGE 18.2**

Write the code for UIKit.handheld(), a static method that returns a factory for handheld display components.

*A solution appears on page 407.*

---

## Prototyping with Clones

To complete the factory design, you have to establish how the prototypical instance variables in a UIKit object will copy themselves. You consider using clone(), a method that every class inherits from Object. However, this method must be used with caution; it does not provide foolproof copying of an object.

**CHALLENGE 18.3**

Consult the source code for Object.clone() and write down what this method does.

*A solution appears on page 407.*

Consider copying an OzTextArea object. When you investigate this class, you see that it is a subclass of JPanel, as Figure 18.2 shows.

Subclassing from JPanel lets OzTextArea objects uniformly wrap their contents in a scrolling panel and a standard border. This makes text panels in the GUI more appealing, but it also has the effect of giving OzText-Area objects a huge number of instance variables, including those that OzTextArea declares and all those that OzTextArea inherits from its superclasses.

A GUI object can easily have more than 100 instance variables. These attributes often include dependencies on other objects and on operating system resources that you cannot safely copy references to. Rather than

**FIGURE 18.2:** The OzTextArea class inherits a large number of methods and variables from its superclasses.

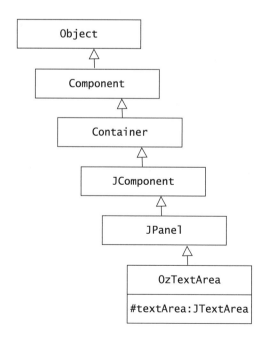

using `Object.clone()` to create a new GUI object, it is safer to instantiate the class you want and to set the new object's instance variables explicitly.

---

### CHALLENGE 18.4

Write `OzTextArea.clone()` so that it copies a text area without relying on a superclass implementation of `clone()`.

*A solution appears on page 407.*

---

After arranging for your prototypical GUI objects to copy themselves, your design is complete. You have replaced the complete `ComponentKit` hierarchy with a single class, `UIKit`. As with any abstract factory, you can create methods that build screens that are independent of the look-and-feel of a specific component set.

For example, the following class constructs and displays a panel with cross-sales instructions on a handheld device:

```
package com.oozinoz.ui;
import java.awt.*;
import javax.swing.*;
public class ShowKit
{
    public static JPanel crossSales(UIKit k)
    {
        JPanel p = new JPanel();
        p.setLayout(new BorderLayout());
        p.add(k.createButton("Clear"), "South");
        OzTextArea t = k.createTextArea();
        t.append(" 1) Consult the recommendation list.\n");
        t.append(" 2) Establish customer interest.\n");
        t.append(" 3) Close the sale.\n");
        p.add(t, "Center");
        return p;
    }
    public static void main(String[] args)
    {
```

```
            UIKit k = UIKit.handheld();
            JPanel p = ShowKit.crossSales(k);
            SwingFacade.launch(p, " Oozinoz Cross Sales");
        }
    }
```

This code launches a panel that is too tiny to show in this book. In practice, such an application will also set up an action listener to react to a user's screen clicks.

## Using Object.clone()

The Oozinoz application suite includes a visualization that shows users how material is flowing through machines on the factory floor. Now the business wants a simulation version of this screen to let the user experiment with releasing orders into the factory, changing machine attributes, and altering other aspects of the factory's operation. A particular feature your users want in the simulation is to be able to drag-and-drop a copy of a simulated machine. On this project, your job is to create the machine simulation objects, which you have completed as Figure 18.3 shows.

**FIGURE 18.3:** Machine simulations have at least a location and mean-time-between-failure for the machine.

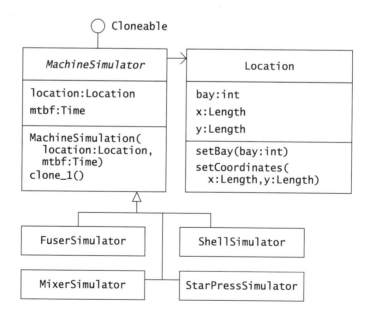

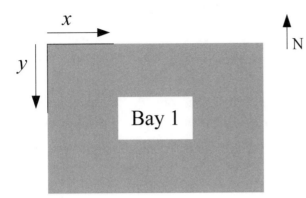

**FIGURE 18.4:** *X* and *Y* coordinates in a bay are measured as offsets from the northwest corner of the bay.

Every machine simulation object has a **mean-time-between-failure** (**MTBF**), a field that shows the average number of hours between the time a machine goes down and the time it comes up again. Each simulation also has a `Location` field. Note that in the simulation, bays are identified by number and are not treated as machine composites. The location of a machine is measured as the machine's distance, in any units, from the northwest corner of the bay that the machine is in. Figure 18.4 shows this coordinate system.

You have included a `clone_1()` method with `MachineSimulator`. (The underscore in the method name indicates that we will later alter this method.) The point of the method is that you can use `clone_1()` as a factory method, producing a new machine simulation object from a prototype the user clicks on. Your initial code for `MachineSimulator.clone_1()` is:

```
public Object clone_1()
{
    try
    {
        return super.clone();
    }
    catch (CloneNotSupportedException e)
    {
        // this shouldn't happen, since we are Cloneable
        throw new InternalError();
    }
}
```

This code makes the clone_1() method public, and we shall soon see that we need to modify this code to create a proper copy. First, though, note that MachineSimulator implements Cloneable. This interface is a marker that Object.clone() checks to ensure that the clone() method is appropriate for a subclass. Without this declaration, the clone_1() method would throw a CloneNotSupportedException when it called super.clone(). The possibility that this exception will be thrown forces you to enclose the call in a try/catch statement. However, you are confident that this exception will never be thrown; if it is thrown, you decide to throw in turn an InternalError error, which is what the frequently used ArrayList class does in this situation.

This code compiles and runs without throwing an exception. However, the code contains a defect that Challenge 18.5 brings out.

## CHALLENGE 18.5

The following lines of code create a simulation object of a mixer in bay 1 and a copy for bay 2:

```
package com.oozinoz.simulation;
import com.oozinoz.units.*;
public class ShowCloningProblem implements UnitConstants
{
    public static void main(String[] args)
    {
        // Mixer 1 is in bay 1, at coordinate(15m, 25m)
        Length x = (Length) METER.times(15);
        Length y = (Length) METER.times(25);
        Location loc = new Location(1, x, y);


        // 10 hours mean-time-between-failure
        MixerSimulator m1 =
            new MixerSimulator(loc, (Time) HOUR.times(10));
        MixerSimulator m2 = (MixerSimulator) m1.clone_1();
```

**CHALLENGE 18.5** *(Continued)*

```
    // Mixer 2 is in bay 2, at coordinate (20, 75)
            m2.location.setBay(2);
            m2.location.setCoordinates(
                (Length) METER.times(20),
                (Length) METER.times(75));
            System.out.println(m1.location.bay);
        }
    }
```

Draw a diagram of the objects created by this code. Also, write down the results of the `println()` statement.

*A solution appears on page 408.*

You might want to make `Location` objects immutable, removing the class's set methods, so that any number of clients could safely share a reference to the same location. At Oozinoz, however, machine locations do occasionally change. Rather than making `Location` objects immutable, you can fix the problem with `MachineSimulator.clone()` by making `Location` objects cloneable.

**CHALLENGE 18.6**

Suppose that you change the `Location` class to declare that it implements `Cloneable` and write a properly functioning `clone()` method for it. Now write a revised version of the `clone()` method for the `MachineSimulator` class.

*A solution appears on page 408.*

## Summary

The PROTOTYPE pattern lets a client create new objects by copying an example. A major difference between calling a constructor and copying an object is that a copy typically includes some of the state of the original object. You can use this to your advantage, particularly when different "classes" of objects differ only in their attributes, not in their behaviors. In such a case, you can create new classes at runtime by crafting prototypical objects for a client to copy.

When you need to create a copy, `Object.clone()` can help, but you must remember that this method creates a new object with the same fields. This object may not be a suitable clone, but any difficulties related to deep copying are your responsibility. If creating a deep copy is too complex or if a prototypical object has too many fields, you can create a copy by instantiating a new object and setting its fields to match just the aspects of original object that you need to copy.

## 19

# MEMENTO

SOMETIMES, YOU WANT to create an object that existed previously. This occurs when you want to let a user undo operations, revert to an earlier version of work, or resume work that he or she previously suspended. The intent of the MEMENTO pattern is to provide storage and restoration of an object's state.

## Memento Durability

A *memento* is a tiny repository that saves an object's state. You can create a memento by using another object, a string, or a file. The anticipated duration between the storage and the reconstruction of an object has an effect on the strategy that you can use in designing a memento. The time that elapses can be moments, hours, days, or years.

---

**CHALLENGE 19.1**

Write down two reasons that might drive you to saving a memento in a file rather than as an object.

*A solution appears on page 409.*

---

## Applying Memento

In the preceding chapter, you used the Prototype pattern to design a simulation that let users speculatively create new machine simulators from existing ones. Your users like the simulation, but they sometimes make changes that they wish they could undo.

You might consider using the javax.swing.undo package to support an undo operation. However, the undo package focuses its support on operations for textual Swing components. In this application, it is simpler to apply the Memento pattern to save and to restore the state of the simulation at key points.

- Each time the user adds or moves a machine in the visualization, your code will create a memento of the simulated factory and add it to a stack.
- Each time the user clicks the Undo button, your code will pop the most recent memento and then restore the simulation to the state stored at the top of the stack.

When your visualization starts up, you will stack an initial, empty memento and never pop it, to ensure that the top of the stack is always a valid memento. Any time the stack contains just one memento, you disable the Undo button. Figure 19.1 shows the visualization after the user has added and dragged several machines into place.

**FIGURE 19.1:** This visualization adds machines at the top left location of the panel and lets a user drag machines into place. Users can undo either drags or adds.

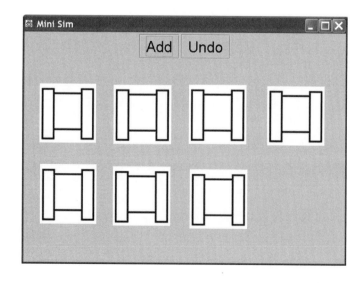

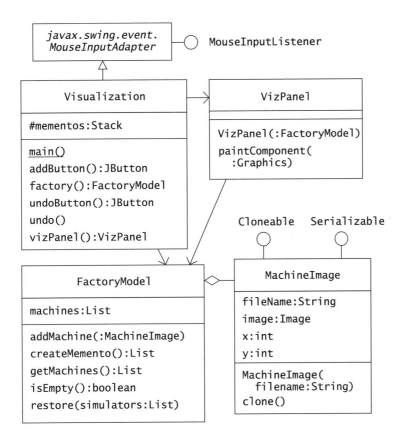

**FIGURE 19.2:** A Visualization object lets a user paint a picture of a prospective factory.

The com.oozinoz.visualization package contains the classes that support the visualization. An executable Visualization class subclasses from the MouseInputAdapter class, from java.swing.event, to simplify listening to mouse events. The Visualization class relies on a machine.gif file that must lie in its class path. Both this class and a VizPanel class rely on a FactoryModel object that contains the machine images and their locations. Figure 19.2 shows the classes in the visualization package.

When the user clicks Add or drags and releases a machine image, the Visualization object asks the FactoryModel object for a new memento. The Visualization object stacks this memento. When the user clicks Undo, the Visualization object pops a memento and calls the Factory-Model object's restore() method, passing in the memento at the new top of the stack. The FactoryModel object creates a memento by creating a list and populating it with clones of the current MachineImage objects in its machines list.

## CHALLENGE 19.2

Write the code for the `createMemento()` method of `FactoryModel` so that the method returns a `List` of clones of machine simulators.

*A solution appears on page 409.*

The counterpart to a `createMemento()` method is a `restore()` method that restores the state of the object according to the information in the memento. In this example, the memento is a list of machine simulators. The `restore()` method for `FactoryModel` takes this list as an argument and looks something like this:

```
public void restore(List memento)
{
    machines = new ArrayList();
    Iterator i = memento.iterator();
    while (i.hasNext())
    {
        MachineImage mi = (MachineImage) i.next();
        machines.add(mi.clone());
    }
}
```

When the user clicks the Undo button, the visualization's `undo()` method pops the most recent memento, discarding the state to undo. Then this method restores the simulation from the memento at the top of the stack. Finally, this method disables the Undo button if the stack contains only the initial memento.

## CHALLENGE 19.3

Write the code for the visualization's `undo()` method.

*A solution appears on page 410.*

In this example, a clone of a `MachineImage` object contains all the state information you need to later set the object back to that state. Furthermore, a `FactoryModel` object needs only a collection of clones of its machine images to store the state it needs to restore to in an `undo()` operation. When clones are available and they store the information you need to create a memento, you can apply MEMENTO using clones. In other cases, you may need to create a special class, such as `FactoryMemento`, to store the state of a factory model.

## Persisting Mementos across Sessions

A **session** occurs when a user runs a program, conducts transactions in the program, and exits. Suppose that your users want to be able to save a simulation in one session and restore it in another session. This ability is a matter normally referred to as **persistent storage**. Persistent storage fulfills the intent of the MEMENTO pattern and is a natural extension to the undo functionality you have already implemented.

Suppose that you subclass the `Visualization` class with a `Visualization2` class[1] that has a menu bar with a File menu. This menu offers Save and Load commands that you link to action methods:

```
protected void save() {
    int status = fc().showSaveDialog(null);
    if (status == JFileChooser.APPROVE_OPTION)
    {
        File f = fc.getSelectedFile();
        try
        {
            ObjectOutputStream out =
                new ObjectOutputStream(
                    new FileOutputStream(f));
            out.writeObject(/* ? */);
            out.flush();
            out.close();
        }
        catch (IOException e)
        {
```

---

1. The `Visualization2` class's name ends with a number but no underscore, to indicate that it is a revision but not a class that will be refactored.

```
                             // explain the problem and offer to try again
                         }
                     }
                 }

                 protected JFileChooser fc()
                 {
                     if (fc == null)
                     {
                         fc = new JFileChooser();
                     }
                     return fc;
                 }
```

The save() method uses a JFileChooser dialog to determine where the user wants to save the simulation state. The ObjectOutputStream class, from java.io, provides the ability to write an object to disk.

---

**CHALLENGE 19.4**

What object should the save() method write out?

*A solution appears on page 410.*

---

For the save() method to work correctly, the MachineImage class must implement the Serializable interface, and the class's persistent attributes must also be serializable. If you inspect the code in the visualization package, you will find that the MachineImage class marks its image attribute as transient. This causes a serialization of a MachineImage class to not save the image attribute. The class lazy-initializes its image from the image's file name, so when a MachineImage object is restored, the image is rebuilt from the original graphics file. (This requires that the image exist in the class path of the Visualization2 class.)

To allow users to restore a previously constructed simulation, the File menu offers a Load item that calls a load() method. The load() method is parallel in design to the save() method but uses the classes ObjectInputStream and FileInputStream instead of their Output counterparts to retrieve a visualization's prior state. The `load()` method empties the mementos stack, pushes the retrieved memento, disables the Undo button, and calls the `FactoryModel` class's `restore()` method:

```
protected void load()
{
    int dialogStatus = fc().showOpenDialog(null);
    if (dialogStatus == JFileChooser.APPROVE_OPTION)
    {
        File f = fc.getSelectedFile();
        try
        {
            ObjectInputStream in =
                new ObjectInputStream(
                    new FileInputStream(f));
            List m = (List) in.readObject();
            in.close();


            mementos.removeAllElements();
            mementos.push(m);
            factory().restore(m);
            undoButton().setEnabled(false);
            vizPanel().repaint();
        }
        catch (Exception e)
        {
            System.out.println(e);
        }
    }
}
```

For another complete example of applying serialization, see *Java™ Examples in a Nutshell* (Flanagan 1997).

## Using Strings as Mementos

Object serialization provides a simple means for a memento to persist across multiple sessions that occur, say, on a given day. If, on the other hand, your user wants to revive a simulation after a six-month sabbatical, he or she may find that various classes in the simulation package have evolved to new versions. The `java.io` package provides some support for deserializing an object when its class has changed since the serialization was written, but proper handling of object serialization across class versions is, in practice, problematic. To avoid this problem, you can "serialize" your object to text.

One way to provide persistent storage of an object is to write out a textual description of it. You can save an object's data as an XML file or in a proprietary language of your own design. When you read in such a file, it is comparatively easy to handle missing data or changes in class design that can occur when a class version changes while the data is in storage.

---

**CHALLENGE 19.5**

Write down at least one disadvantage of storing an object as text.

*A solution appears on page 410.*

---

*Design Patterns* (Gamma et al. 1995) states the intent of the MEMENTO pattern as, "Without violating encapsulation, capture and externalize an object's internal state so that the object can be restored to this state later" (p. 283). You might argue that this intent addresses online storage only: specifically, the storage of an object's data in another object. If you widen the meaning of memento to include offline storage, arguably every database row and every XML string that contains an object's state is a memento. Possibly for these reasons, *Design Patterns* does not provide any offline storage examples of MEMENTO.

On the other hand, MEMENTO and persistent storage both capture and externalize an object's internal state. An XML string may lie somewhere between an online memento and a database, placing an object's state in a machine-readable and human-readable form. If you say you create mementos by storing an object's data in an XML string, I will understand what you mean. And that's the point of design patterns: By using a common vocabulary, we can readily discuss design concepts and their application.

## Summary

The MEMENTO pattern lets you capture an object's state so you can restore the object later. The means of storage may depend on whether you need to be able to restore an object after a few clicks and keystrokes or after days or years. The most common reason for saving and restoring objects during an application session is the support of undo operations. In such a case, you can store an object's state in another object, possibly a clone. To let an object persist across sessions, you can save the memento either through object serialization or as text that you will parse to restore the object.

# PART IV

# OPERATION PATTERNS

## 20

# INTRODUCING OPERATIONS

WHEN YOU WRITE a Java method, you produce a fundamental unit of work that is a level up from writing a statement. Your methods have to participate in an overall design, architecture, and test plan, but no activity is more central to programming than writing methods. Ironically, despite the central role of methods, it is easy to get confused about what methods are and how they function. You need to be aware of a few syntactic subtleties in Java methods. But more confusing is the tendency of many developers and authors to slosh together the meaning of the words *method*, *operation*, and *algorithm*. By distinguishing the meanings of these terms, you can express important concepts that surface in many design patterns.

Having a clear understanding of what methods are will also help you understand several design patterns. In particular, STATE, STRATEGY, and INTERPRETER all work by implementing an operation in methods across several classes, but such observations are useful only if we agree on the meaning of method and operation.

## Operations, Methods, and Algorithms

It is useful to distinguish operation from method and to then discuss these concepts' relations to algorithm. Fortunately, the UML defines the difference between an operation and method (Booch, Rumbaugh, and Jacobson 1999, p. 128).

- An **operation** is a specification of a service that can be requested from an instance of a class.
- A **method** is an implementation of an operation.[1]

An operation specifies something that a class does and specifies the interface for calling on this service. Multiple classes may implement the same operation in different ways. For example, many classes implement the `toString()` operation. Every class that implements an operation implements it with a method, the code that makes the operation work for that class.

The definitions of *method* and *operation* help to clarify the structure of many design patterns. The meaning of *operation* is a level of abstraction up from the idea of *method*. Because design patterns are also a level up from classes and methods, it is no surprise that operations feature prominently in many patterns. For example, COMPOSITE arranges for operations to apply to both items and groups. PROXY lets an intermediary that has the same operations as a target object interpose itself to manage access to the target.

---

**CHALLENGE 20.1**

Explain how CHAIN OF RESPONSIBILITY implements an operation.

*A solution appears on page 411.*

---

If we agree on the UML definitions of these words, it is illuminating to say that a *method* is an implementation of an *operation*. How, then, do operations and methods come together to implement an algorithm? Before answering that, we should agree on what *algorithm* means. *Introduction to Algorithms* (Cormen, Leiserson, and Rivest 1990) says: "An *algorithm* is any well-defined computational procedure that takes some value, or set of

---

1. For definitions of the related terms *abstract method* and *static method*, see the Glossary.

values, as input and produces some value, or set of values, as output"
(p. 1).

An **algorithm** is a procedure—a sequence of instructions—that accepts
inputs and produces output. In this regard, an algorithm is similar to a
method. A method accepts inputs—its parameter list—and produces an
output—its return value. However, many algorithms require more than
one method to execute in an object-oriented program. For example, the
isTree() algorithm in Chapter 5, COMPOSITE, requires four methods, as
Figure 20.1 shows.

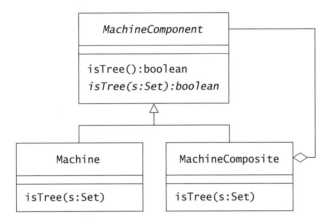

**FIGURE 20.1:** Four
isTree() methods
collaborate to effect the
algorithm for determin-
ing whether an instance
of MachineComponent is
a tree.

---

## CHALLENGE 20.2

How many algorithms, operations, and methods does Figure 20.1 depict?

*The answer appears on page 411.*

---

Algorithms get something done. They may appear as part of a method, or
they may involve many methods. Algorithms that require more than one
method often rely on *polymorphism* to allow multiple implementations of

a single operation. **Polymorphism** is the principle that method invocation depends on both the operation invoked and the class of the invocation receiver.

For example, you might ask which method executes when Java encounters the expression m.isTree(). The answer is, *it depends*. If m is an instance of Machine, Java will invoke Machine.isTree(). If m is an instance of MachineComposite, Java will invoke MachineComposite.isTree(). Informally, polymorphism means that the right method gets invoked for the right type of object. Many patterns use polymorphism, which in some cases ties directly to the intent of the pattern. But before we investigate those patterns, it is a good idea to have a solid understanding of the mechanics of Java methods.

## The Mechanics of Methods

When you write a method, it becomes available for invocation according to its **signature**. The *Java™ Language Specification* (Gosling et al. 2000) says: "The *signature* of a method consists of the name of the method and the number and types of formal parameters to the method" (p. 169).

Note that a method's signature does not include return type. However, if a method declaration overrides the declaration of another method, a compile-time error occurs if they have different return types.

---

### CHALLENGE 20.3

At Oozinoz, the method MachineSimulator.clone() returns Object, even though the method always returns an instance of MachineSimulator. Will this method be more effective if you change it to return MachineSimulator?

*The answer appears on page 411.*

A signature specifies which method is invoked when a client makes a call. So how is *signature* different from *operation*? After all, both terms refer to the specification of a service. The terms differ mainly in the context in which they are typically used. The term *operation* applies when discussing the idea that methods in different classes may have the same interface. The term *signature* applies when discussing the rules that govern how Java matches a method call to a method in the receiving object.

In Java, a method declaration includes a *header* and a *body*. A method's body is the series of instructions that can be called into action by invoking the method's signature. A method's *header* includes the method's return type and signature and may include modifiers and a `throws` clause. The form of a method header is:

```
modifiers type signature throws-clause
```

Each of the four aspects of a method's header contains subtleties and challenges.

Method modifiers include visibility modifiers: `abstract`, `static`, `final`, `synchronized`, and `native`. Several earlier chapters have discussed visibility and the `abstract` modifier. The remaining modifiers are all important, of course, but only `static` appears frequently when implementing the patterns this book describes.

A static method is invoked without reference to a particular object. This can lead to surprising results. Consider the classes `Firework` and `Rocket` in Figure 20.2. Each class defines a static `flies()` method. Most fireworks don't fly, so `Firework` defines this to return `false`, whereas `Rocket` defines it to return `true`.

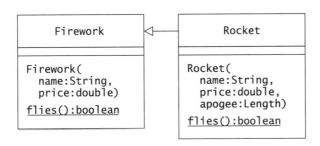

**FIGURE 20.2:** The classes `Firework` and `Rocket` each have a static method with the same signature and same return value.

---

**CHALLENGE 20.4**

What does the following program print out?

```
package com.oozinoz.applications;
import com.oozinoz.units.*;
import com.oozinoz.fireworks.*;
public class ShowStatic implements UnitConstants
{
    public static void main(String[] args)
    {
        Length apogee = (Length) METER.times(75);
        Firework r = new Rocket("Byebaby", 13.95, apogee);
        System.out.println(r.flies());
    }
}
```

*The solution appears on page 411.*

---

In addition to modifiers, return type, and signature, a method header may include a throws *clause*. This clause limits some of the exceptions that may occur during the method's execution.

## Exceptions in Methods

A method header may declare that the method throws exceptions. An *exception* in Java is an instance of any subclass of Throwable, including the Exception class and the Error class. Note that the word exception refers to an instance of Throwable but not necessarily to an instance of Exception. Figure 20.3 shows part of the Throwable hierarchy.

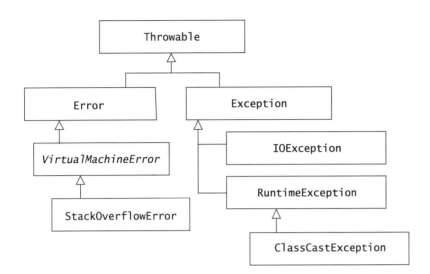

**FIGURE 20.3:** Of the classes shown, only `Throwable`, `Exception`, and `IOException` must be handled.

Exceptions are normally *checked*, meaning they must be declared by a method that might throw them. The `Error` class and its subclasses and the `RuntimeException` class and its subclasses are *unchecked*, meaning that they need not be declared. *The Java™ Language Specification* (Gosling et al. 2000) says:

> `Error` and its subclasses are exempted from compile-time checking because they can occur at many points in the program and recovery from them is difficult or impossible. (p. 221)

and

> `RuntimeException` and its subclasses are exempted from compile-time checking because, in the judgment of the designers of the Java programming language, having to declare such exceptions would not aid significantly in establishing the correctness of programs. (p. 222)

The existence of unchecked exceptions means that methods may throw exceptions that you don't have to declare. For example, you can perform casts without handling `ClassCastException` in either a try/ catch statement or in the signature of the method.

---

**CHALLENGE 20.5**

The designers of the Java programming language created a distinction between checked and unchecked exceptions. Explain why you think this was a good idea or a bad idea.

*A solution appears on page 412.*

## Summary

Although it is common to intermingle the meanings of *operation, method, signature,* and *algorithm,* preserving distinctions among these terms helps to describe important concepts. An operation is, like a signature, a specification of a service. The word *operation* applies when talking about the idea that many methods may have the same interface. The word *signature* applies when discussing method lookup rules. A method definition includes its signature—its name and parameter list—along with modifiers, return type, a throws clause, and the method's body. A method *has* a signature and *implements* an operation.

An *algorithm* is a procedure that accepts inputs and produces outputs. Methods accept inputs, produce outputs, and contain a procedural method body, so it is common to refer to a method as an algorithm. However, an algorithm's procedure may involve many operations and methods, or it may exist as part of another method. The word *algorithm* best applies when you are discussing a procedure that produces a result.

Many design patterns involve distributing an operation across several classes. You can also say that these patterns rely on *polymorphism,* the principle that method selection depends on the class of the object that receives a method call. The decision of which method executes depends on many rules and various aspects of method headers. In particular, it is important to understand that the static modifier means that the decision of which method to execute depends on the receiver's declared type, not the class of the object.

Methods execute until they return, unless they produce an exception. The potential for some exceptions is so commonplace that methods need not declare them. Other, *checked* exceptions must appear in a method's throws clause. The decision of whether an exception should be checked or unchecked is a matter of judgment.

## ■ BEYOND ORDINARY OPERATIONS

Different classes can implement an operation in different ways. In other words, Java supports polymorphism. The power of this seemingly simple idea appears in several design patterns.

| If you intend to | Apply the pattern |
|---|---|
| • Implement an algorithm in a method, deferring the definition of some steps of the algorithm so that subclasses can redefine them | TEMPLATE METHOD (Chapter 21) |
| • Distribute an operation so that each class represents a different state | STATE (Chapter 22) |
| • Encapsulate an operation, making implementations interchangeable | STRATEGY (Chapter 23) |
| • Encapsulate a method call in an object | COMMAND (Chapter 24) |
| • Distribute an operation so that each implementation applies to a different type of composition | INTERPRETER (Chapter 25) |

Operation-oriented patterns address contexts in which you need more than one method, usually with the same signature, to participate in a design. For example, the TEMPLATE METHOD pattern allows subclasses to implement methods that adjust the effect of a procedure defined in a superclass.

# 21

# TEMPLATE METHOD

IN A SENSE, almost every method is a template. Ordinary methods have bodies that define a sequence of instructions. It is also quite ordinary for a method to invoke methods on the current object and on other objects. Ordinary methods are, in this sense, "templates" that merely outline a series of instructions for the computer to follow. The TEMPLATE METHOD pattern, however, involves a more specific type of template.

When you write a method, you may want to define the outline of an algorithm, understanding that there may be differences in how you want to implement certain steps. In this case, you can define the method but leave some steps as abstract methods, as stubbed-out methods, or as methods defined in a separate interface. This produces a more rigid "template" that specifically defines which steps of an algorithm other classes can or must supply. The intent of TEMPLATE METHOD is to implement an algorithm in a method, deferring the definition of some steps of the algorithm so that other classes can redefine them.

## A Classic Example of TEMPLATE METHOD: Sorting

An ancient example of TEMPLATE METHOD that is not only pre-Java but also prehistoric occurs in *sorting*.[1] Sorting has various algorithms, but in most settings, you can establish a single algorithm and use it to sort various collections of objects. Any algorithm that you use for sorting will rely

---

1. Some developers think of sorting as an example of STRATEGY. Challenge 23.6 on page 247 will ask you to compare STRATEGY and TEMPLATE METHOD.

**FIGURE 21.1:** The `sort()` method can sort any list, using a method that you supply to perform the comparison step of the algorithm.

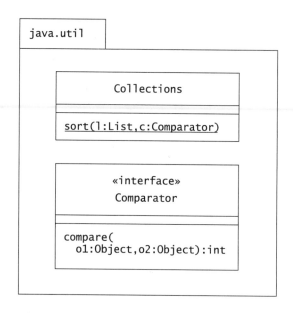

on the primitive step of comparing two items, or attributes. If you can compare, say, the sharpness of two arrowheads, your sorting algorithm will let you sort the arrowheads in a collection.

In recent times, sorting probably reigns as the most frequently reimplemented algorithm, with implementations outnumbering the number of existing computer programmers. But unless you are sorting a huge collection, you need not write your own sorting algorithm. The `Collections` class in `java.util`, shown in Figure 21.1, provides a sorting algorithm as a TEMPLATE METHOD, deferring the comparison step to you.

The static `sort()` method accepts a list and an instance of `Comparator`. The `Comparator` interface requires its implementer to supply the comparison step of the sorting algorithm. The `compare()` method must return a number less than, equal to, or greater than 0. These values correspond to the idea that, in a sense that you define, object o1 is less than, equal to, or greater than object o2. For example, you might implement `compare()` to compare the sharpness of two rocks or the apogee of two rockets.

The following class sorts a collection of rockets by their apogees:

```
package com.oozinoz.applications;
import java.util.*;
```

```java
import com.oozinoz.units.*;
import com.oozinoz.fireworks.*;
public class ShowComparator implements UnitConstants
{
    public static void main(String[] args)
    {
        Rocket r1 = new Rocket(
            "Mach-it", 22.95, (Length) METER.times(1000));
        Rocket r2 = new Rocket(
            "Pocket", 2.95, (Length) METER.times(12));
        Rocket r3 = new Rocket(
            "Sock-it", 9.95, (Length) METER.times(100));
        Rocket r4 = new Rocket(
            "Sprocket", 3.95, (Length) METER.times(50));

        List rockets =
            Arrays.asList(new Rocket[] { r1, r2, r3, r4 });

        Comparator c = new Comparator()
            {
                public int compare(Object o1, Object o2)
                {
                    /* ? */
                }
            };

        Collections.sort(rockets, c);
        Iterator i = rockets.iterator();
        while (i.hasNext())
        {
            System.out.println(i.next());
        }
    }
}
```

The program printout depends on how Rocket implements toString()
but shows the rockets sorted by apogee:

```
Pocket $2.95 (12.0 meters)
Sprocket $3.95 (50.0 meters)
Sock-it $9.95 (100.0 meters)
Mach-it $22.95 (1000.0 meters)
```

---

**CHALLENGE 21.1**

The `Rocket` class supplies a `getApogee()` method that returns the height a rocket can reach. This height is of type `Length`, a measure whose magnitude you can fetch with a call to `getMagnitude()`. Fill in the `compare()` method in the `ShowComparator` program to sort a collection of rockets by apogee.

*A solution appears on page 412.*

---

The `sort()` method and the `Comparator` interface let you supply a domain-specific step to an ancient algorithm. It can also happen that the entire algorithm is domain specific.

## Completing an Algorithm

As in the ADAPTER pattern, a thoughtful developer may foresee that you have a role in completing his or her design. In ADAPTER, you supply an object that responds to the needs of the other developer's code. In TEMPLATE METHOD, you supply a step of an algorithm.

Consider the Aster star press that Figure 21.2 shows. A star press from Aster Corporation accepts empty metal molds and presses fireworks stars into them. The machine has **hoppers**, not shown in the diagram, that dispense the chemicals that the machine mixes into a paste and presses into the molds. When the machine shuts down, it stops working on the mold in the processing area, and *ushers* any molds on its input conveyor through the processing area to the output, without processing the molds. Then the machine discharges its current batch of paste and flushes its processing area with water. The machine orchestrates all of this activity by using an on-board computer and the `AsterStarPress` class shown in Figure 21.3.

The Aster star press is smart and independent, and it is also aware that it may be running in a smart factory with which it must communicate.

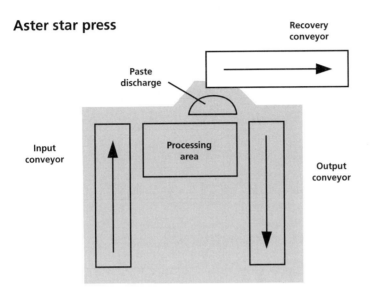

**FIGURE 21.2:** An Aster star press comes with input and output conveyors that move star press molds. Oozinoz adds a recovery conveyor that saves discarded star press paste.

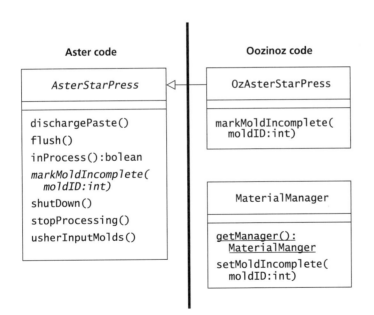

**FIGURE 21.3:** Star presses from Aster Corporation come with an abstract class that you must subclass to work at Oozinoz.

For example, the `shutDown()` method informs the factory if the mold it was processing is left incomplete:

```
public void shutDown()
{
    if (inProcess())
    {
        stopProcessing();
        markMoldIncomplete(currentMoldID);
    }
    usherInputMolds();
    dischargePaste();
    flush();
}
```

The `markMoldIncomplete()` method and the `AsterStarPress` class are abstract. At Oozinoz, you create a subclass that implements the required method and download this code to the star press computer. You can implement `markMoldIncomplete()` by passing the information about the incomplete mold to the `MaterialManager` singleton that tracks material status.

---

## CHALLENGE 21.2

Write the code for the `markMoldIncomplete()` method of `OzAsterStarPress`.

```
package com.oozinoz.aster.client;
import com.oozinoz.aster.*;
public class OzAsterStarPress extends AsterStarPress
{
    public MaterialManager getManager()
    {
        return MaterialManager.getManager();
    }
    public void markMoldIncomplete(int id)
    {
        /* ? */
    }
}
```

*A solution appears on page 413.*

The Aster star press developers are well aware of how fireworks factories work and have done a good job of communicating with the factory at the right processing points. Nonetheless, you may need to establish communication at a point that the Aster developers have not foreseen.

## TEMPLATE METHOD Hooks

A **hook** is a method call that a developer places in his or her code to give other developers a chance to insert code at a specific spot in a procedure. When you are adapting another developer's code and you need control at a point where you don't currently have it, you can request a hook. An obliging developer can add a method call at the point that you need it. The developer will also usually supply a stubbed-out version of the hook method so that other clients need not necessarily override the hook method.

Consider the Aster star press that discharges its chemical paste and flushes itself with water when shutting down. The press has to discharge this paste to keep it from drying and clogging the machine. At Oozinoz, you recover this paste so that you can dice it for use as tiny stars in Roman candles. (A **Roman candle** is a stationary tube that contains a mixture of explosive charges, sparks, and stars.) After the star press discharges the paste, you arrange for a robot to move the paste to a separate conveyor, as Figure 21.2 shows. It is critical that you remove the paste before the machine flushes its processing area with water, which would ruin the paste mixture.

The problem is that you want to gain control between the two statements:

```
dischargePaste();
flush();
```

You might override `dischargePaste()` with a method that adds a call to collect the paste:

```
public void dischargePaste()
{
    super.dischargePaste();
    getFactory().collectPaste(this);
}
```

This method uses a `Factory` singleton to collect discarded paste from a star press. This is dangerous code, though, because paste collection is a surprising side effect. Developers at Aster will certainly be unaware that you're defining `dischargePaste()` in this way. If they modify their code to discharge paste at a time that you don't want to collect it, an error will occur.

Developers usually strive to solve problems by writing code. But here the challenge is to solve a problem by communicating with other developers.

---

**CHALLENGE 21.3**

Write a note to the developers at Aster, asking for a change that will let you safely collect discarded star paste before the machine flushes its processing area.

*A solution appears on page 414.*

---

The step that a subclass supplies in TEMPLATE METHOD may be required to complete the algorithm, or it may be an optional step that hooks in a subclass's code, often at another developer's request. Although the intent of the pattern is to let a separate class define part of an algorithm, you can also apply TEMPLATE METHOD when you refactor an algorithm that appears in multiple methods.

### Refactoring to TEMPLATE METHOD

When you apply TEMPLATE METHOD, classes in a hierarchy share the outline of an algorithm that you or someone else codes in an abstract superclass. The opportunity for TEMPLATE METHOD may also crop up when you implement similar algorithms in more than one method. Consider the `Machine` and `MachinePlanner` parallel hierarchy that you worked with in Chapter 16, FACTORY METHOD. As Figure 21.4 shows, the `Machine` class provides a `createPlanner()` method as a FACTORY METHOD that returns an appropriate subclass of `MachinePlanner`.

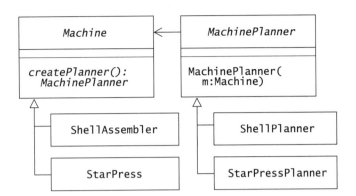

**FIGURE 21.4:** A
Machine object can
create an appropriate
MachinePlanner
instance for itself.

Suppose that you notice that subclasses of Machine include similar techniques for lazy-initializing a planner. The ShellAssembler class has a ShellPlanner attribute that it calls planner and that ShellAssembler initializes in its getPlanner() method:

```
public MachinePlanner getPlanner()
{
    if (planner == null)
    {
        planner = new ShellPlanner(this);
    }
    return planner;
}
```

The StarPress class also has a planner attribute but declares it to be of type StarPressPlanner. The getPlanner() method of StarPress also lazy-initializes the planner attribute:

```
public MachinePlanner getPlanner()
{
    if (planner == null)
    {
        planner = new StarPressPlanner(this);
    }
    return planner;
}
```

The other subclasses of Machine have similar approaches to creating a planner only when it is first needed.

**CHALLENGE 21.4**

Suppose that you provide the Machine class with a planner attribute of type MachinePlanner and delete the existing getPlanner() methods in the subclasses. Write the code for getPlanner() in the Machine class.

*A solution appears on page 414.*

You can often refactor your code into an instance of TEMPLATE METHOD. You do so by abstracting the outline of the similar methods, moving the outline method up to a superclass, and letting subclasses supply just the step where they differ in their implementation of the algorithm.

## Summary

Ordinary methods are usually templates in that you can't tell exactly what code will execute just by looking at a single method. The TEMPLATE METHOD pattern, however, does not merely note that ordinary methods are templates. Rather, the intent of TEMPLATE METHOD is to define an algorithm in a method, leaving some steps abstract, stubbed out, or defined in an interface so that other classes can fill them in.

TEMPLATE METHOD often functions as a contract between developers. One developer supplies the outline of an algorithm, and another developer supplies a certain step of the algorithm. This may be a step that lets the algorithm complete, or it may be a step that the algorithm developer includes to hook in your code at specific points in the procedure.

The intent of TEMPLATE METHOD does not imply that you will always write the template method in advance of defining subclasses. You may discover similar methods in an existing hierarchy. In this case, you may be able to distill the outline of an algorithm and move it up to a superclass, applying TEMPLATE METHOD to simplify and to organize your code.

# 22

# STATE

THE **STATE** of an object is a combination of the current values of its attributes. When you call a set- method, you typically change an object's state, and an object can change its own state as its methods execute.

In some cases, an object's state can be a prominent aspect of its behavior, such as when modeling transactions and machines. Logic that depends on the object's state may spread through many of the class's methods. To counter this spread, you can move state-specific behavior into a group of classes, with each class representing a different state. This lets you avoid having deep or complex if statements, relying instead on polymorphism to execute the right implementation of an operation. The intent of the STATE pattern is to distribute state-specific logic across classes that represent an object's state.

## Modeling States

When you model an object whose state is important, you may find that you have a variable that tracks how the object should behave, depending on its state. This variable may appear in complex, cascading if statements that focus on how to react to the events that an object can experience. One problem with this approach to modeling state is that if statements can become complex. Another problem is that when you adjust how you model the state, you often have to adjust if statements in several methods. The STATE pattern offers a cleaner, simpler approach, using a distributed operation.

**FIGURE 22.1:** A carousel door provides one-touch control with a single button that changes the door's state.

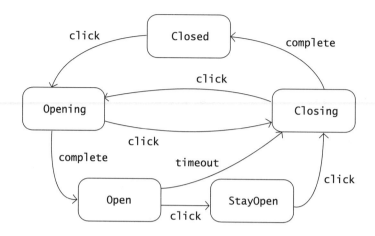

Consider the Oozinoz software that models the state of a carousel door. A **carousel** is a large, smart rack that accepts material through a doorway and stores the material according to a bar code ID on the material. The door operates with a single button. If the door is closed, clicking the button makes the door start opening. If you click again before the door opens fully, the door will begin closing. If you let the door open all the way, it will automatically begin closing after a 2-second timeout. You can prevent this by clicking again when the door is open. Figure 22.1 shows the states and transitions of the carousel's door.

The diagram in Figure 22.1 is a UML *state machine*. Such diagrams can be much more informative than a corresponding textual description.

---

**CHALLENGE 22.1**

Suppose that you open the door and place a material bin in the doorway. Is there a way to make the door begin closing without waiting for it to time out?

*A solution appears on page 415.*

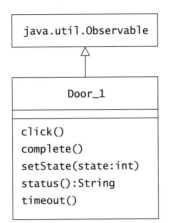

**FIGURE 22.2:** The
Door_1 class models a
carousel door, relying on
state change events sent
by the carousel machine.

You can supply a Door_1 object that the carousel software will update
with state changes in the carousel. (The underscore in the class name is a
hint that we will soon refactor this class.) Figure 22.2 shows the Door_1
class.

The Door_1 class subclasses Observable so that clients, such as a GUI,
can observe a door. The class definition declares its superclass and establishes the states that a door can enter:

```
package com.oozinoz.carousel;
public class Door_1 extends Observable
{
    public static final int CLOSED   = -1;
    public static final int OPENING  = -2;
    public static final int OPEN     = -3;
    public static final int CLOSING  = -4;
    public static final int STAYOPEN = -5;

    private int state = CLOSED;
    //...
}
```

Not surprisingly, a textual description of the state of a door depends on
the door's state:

```
public String status()
{
    switch (state)
    {
```

```
                case OPENING :
                    return "Opening";
                case OPEN :
                    return "Open";
                case CLOSING :
                    return "Closing";
                case STAYOPEN :
                    return "StayOpen";
                default :
                    return "Closed";
            }
    }
```

When a user clicks the carousel's one-touch button, the carousel generates a call to a Door object's click() method. The Door_1 code for a state transition mimics the information in Figure 22.1:

```
public void click()
{
    if (state == CLOSED)
    {
        setState(OPENING);
    }
    else if (state == OPENING || state == STAYOPEN)
    {
        setState(CLOSING);
    }
    else if (state == OPEN)
    {
        setState(STAYOPEN);
    }
    else if (state == CLOSING)
    {
        setState(OPENING);
    }
}
```

The setState() method of the Door_1 class notifies observers of the door's change:

```
private void setState(int state)
{
    this.state = state;
    setChanged();
    notifyObservers();
}
```

**CHALLENGE 22.2**

Write the code for the complete() and timeout() methods of the Door_1 class.

*Solutions appear on page 415.*

## Refactoring to STATE

The code for Door_1 is somewhat complex because the use of the state variable is spread throughout the class. In addition, you might find it difficult to compare the state transition methods, particularly click(), with the state machine in Figure 22.1. The STATE pattern can help you to simplify this code. To apply STATE in this example, make each state of the door a separate class, as Figure 22.3 shows.

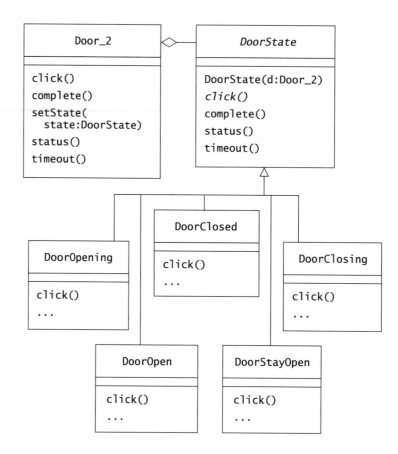

The refactoring that Figure 22.3 shows uses the Door_2 class to contain the context of the state machine. A **context** is an object that contains information that is environmental and relevant to a group of other objects. In particular, STATE uses a context object to record which instance of DoorState is the current state.

The DoorState class constructor requires a Door_2 object. Subclasses of DoorState use this object to communicate changes in state back to the door. By giving these classes an attribute that ties them to a specific Door object, this design requires that a DoorState object be referenced by a single Door object. In turn, this requires the Door class to define its states as local variables:

```
package com.oozinoz.carousel;
public class Door_2 extends Observable
{
    public final DoorState CLOSED   = new DoorClosed(this);
    public final DoorState OPENING  = new DoorOpening(this);
    public final DoorState OPEN     = new DoorOpen(this);
    public final DoorState CLOSING  = new DoorClosing(this);
    public final DoorState STAYOPEN = new DoorStayOpen(this);
    //
    private DoorState state = CLOSED;
    // ...
}
```

The abstract DoorState class requires subclasses to implement click().
This is consistent with the state machine, in which every state has a
click() transition. The DoorState class stubs out other transitions, so
that subclasses can override or ignore irrelevant messages:

```
public abstract class DoorState
{
    protected Door_2 door;

    public DoorState(Door_2 door)
    {
        this.door = door;
    }

    public abstract void click();

    public void complete()
    {
    }

    public String status()
    {
        String s = getClass().getName();
        return s.substring(s.lastIndexOf('.') + 1);
    }

    public void timeout()
    {
    }
}
```

Note that the status() method works for all the states and is much simpler than its predecessor before refactoring.

**CHALLENGE 22.3**

The new status() method returns a slightly different description of a door's state. What's
the difference?

*Solutions appear on page 415.*

The new design doesn't change the role of a Door object in receiving state
changes from the carousel. But now the Door_2 object simply passes these
changes to its current state object:

```
package com.oozinoz.carousel;
public class Door_2 extends Observable
    {
    // ... (DoorState variables)

    public void click()
    {
        state.click();
    }

    public void complete()
    {
        state.complete();
    }

    protected void setState(DoorState state)
    {
        this.state = state;
        setChanged();
        notifyObservers();
    }

    public String status()
    {
        return state.status();
    }
```

```
    public void timeout()
    {
        state.timeout();
    }
}
```

The click(), complete(), status(), and timeout() methods show the pure polymorphism of this approach. Each of these methods is still a kind of switch. In each case, the operation is fixed, but the class of the receiver—the class of state—varies. The rule of polymorphism is that the method that executes depends on the operation signature and the class of the receiver. What happens when you call click()? The answer depends on the door's state. The code still effectively performs a switch, but by relying on polymorphism, the code is simpler than before.

The setState() method in the Door_2 class is now used by subclasses of DoorState. These subclasses closely resemble their counterparts in the state machine in Figure 22.1. For example, the code for DoorOpen handles calls to click() and timeout(), the two transitions from the Open state in the state machine:

```
package com.oozinoz.carousel;
public class DoorOpen extends DoorState
{
    public DoorOpen(Door_2 door)
    {
        super(door);
    }

    public void click()
    {
        door.setState(door.STAYOPEN);
    }

    public void timeout()
    {
        door.setState(door.CLOSING);
    }
}
```

**CHALLENGE 22.4**

Write the code for DoorClosing.java.

*Solutions appear on page 415.*

The new design leads to much simpler code, but you might feel a bit dissatisfied that the "constants" that the Door class uses are in fact local variables.

### Making States Constant

Suppose that you decide to move the state constants to a DoorConstants interface. For this approach to work, you have to eliminate the Door instance variable from the DoorState class. You can drop this variable by changing the click(), complete(), and timeout() transition methods in the DoorState class to require a Door object as an input parameter. In this design, a Door object that receives, for example, a click() method from the carousel forwards this call as state.click(this).

**CHALLENGE 22.5**

Complete the class diagram in Figure 22.4 to show a design that moves the door states to an interface.

*A solution appears on page 416.*

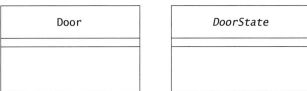

## Summary

Generally speaking, the state of an object depends on the collective value of the object's instance variables. In some cases, an object's state can be a prominent aspect of a class's behavior. This often occurs when an object is modeling a real-world entity whose state is important. In such a situation, complex logic that depends on the object's state may appear in many methods. You can simplify such code by moving state-specific behavior to a hierarchy of state objects. This lets each state class contain the behavior for one state in the domain. It also allows the state classes to correspond directly to states in a state machine.

To handle transitions between states, you can let states retain a context reference that contains a set of states. Alternatively, you can pass around, in state transition calls, the object whose state is changing. Regardless of how you manage state transitions, the STATE pattern simplifies your code by distributing an operation across a collection of classes that represent an object's various states.

# 23

# STRATEGY

A STRATEGY is a plan, or approach, for achieving an aim, given certain input conditions. A strategy is similar to an algorithm: An algorithm is a well-defined procedure that produces an output from a set of inputs. A strategy is a plan that pursues an output given a set of inputs. Usually, however, a strategy has more latitude in how to pursue its goal than an algorithm does. This latitude also means that strategies often appear in groups, or families, of alternatives. When multiple strategies are available, the logic that surrounds the strategies must select one and then execute it. Complexity in the selection and use of strategies can lead to complex and tangled code. You can clean up such code with the STRATEGY pattern.

The intent of STRATEGY is to encapsulate alternative strategies, or approaches, in separate classes, each of which implements a common operation. The strategic operation defines the inputs and output of a strategy but leaves implementation up to the individual classes. Classes that implement the various approaches implement the same operation and are thus interchangeable, presenting the same interface to clients.

## Modeling Strategies

Consider the Oozinoz advertising policy that suggests a firework to purchase when the customer is visiting the Oozinoz Web site or calling into the call center. Oozinoz uses two commercial off-the-shelf recommendation engines to help choose the right firework to offer a customer. The

`Customer` class chooses and applies one of these engines to decide on which firework to recommend to a customer.

One of the recommendation engines, the `Re18` engine, suggests a purchase based on the customer's similarity to other customers. For this recommendation to work, the customer must have registered and given information about likes and dislikes about fireworks and other entertainments.

If the customer has not registered, Oozinoz uses `LikeMyStuff`, another vendor's engine, that suggests a purchase based on the customer's recent purchases. If data is insufficient for either engine to function, the advertising software picks a firework at random. However, a special promotion can override all these considerations to promote a specific firework that Oozinoz wants to sell. Figure 23.1 shows the classes that collaborate to suggest a firework to a customer.

The `LikeMyStuff` and `Re18` engines both accept a `Customer` object and suggest something to advertise to the customer. Both engines are configured to work for fireworks, although `LikeMyStuff` requires a database and `Re18` works entirely from an object model. The code for `getRecommended()` in class `Customer` mirrors Oozinoz's advertising policies:

**FIGURE 23.1:** The `Customer` class relies on other classes for its recommendations, including two off-the-shelf recommendation engines.

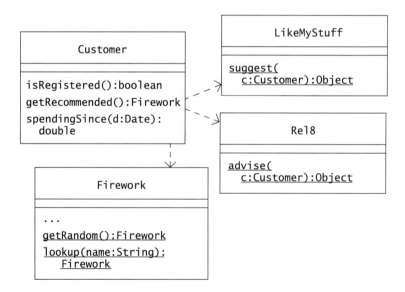

```java
public Firework getRecommended()
{
    // see if we're promoting a particular firework
    try
    {
        Properties p = new Properties();
        p.load(
            ClassLoader.getSystemResourceAsStream(
                "config/strategy.dat"));
        String promotedFireworkName =
            p.getProperty("promote");


        if (promotedFireworkName != null)
        {
            Firework f = Firework.lookup(
                promotedFireworkName);
            if (f != null)
            {
                return f;
            }
        }
    }
    catch (Exception e)
    {
    }

    // if registered, compare to other customers
    if (isRegistered())
    {
        return (Firework) Rel8.advise(this);
    }

    // check spending over the last year
    Calendar cal = Calendar.getInstance();
    cal.add(Calendar.YEAR, -1);
    if (spendingSince(cal.getTime()) > 1000)
    {
        return (Firework) LikeMyStuff.suggest(this);
    }

    // oh well!
    return Firework.getRandom();
}
```

This code expects that if a promotion is on, it will be named in a strategy.dat file in a config directory that lies in the running program's class path. Barring this, the code will use the Re18 engine if the customer is registered or the LikeMyStuff engine if the customer has a known purchase record. If the customer is not registered and not a big purchaser, the code selects and recommends a firework at random. The code works, and you might feel that this is not the worst code you've ever seen. But we can make it better.

## Refactoring to STRATEGY

The getRecommended() method presents several problems. First, it's long—long enough that comments have to explain its various parts. Short methods are easy to understand, seldom need explanation, and are usually preferable to long methods. In addition, the getRecommended() method chooses a strategy and then executes it; these are two different and separable functions. You can clean up this code by applying STRATEGY. To do so, you need to

- Create an interface that defines the strategic operation
- Implement the interface with classes that represent each strategy
- Refactor the code to select and to use an instance of the right strategic class

Suppose that you create an Advisor interface and begin your refactoring by introducing a GroupAdvisor class and an ItemAdvisor class. These classes can implement a common recommend() operation by applying the off-the-shelf recommendation engines, as Figure 23.2 shows.

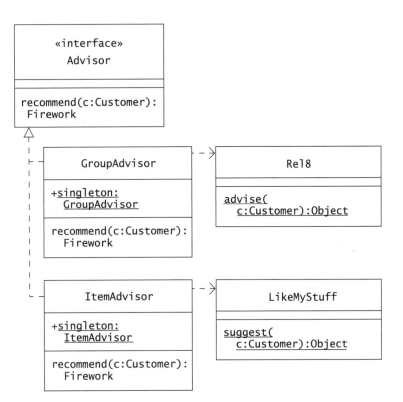

**FIGURE 23.2:** Implementations of the `Advisor` interface provide the strategic `recommend()` operation, relying on off-the-shelf engines.

To provide a strategy for a client, you can pass it a particular implementation of the `Advisor` interface. Interfaces can define only instance methods, so `GroupAdvisor` and `ItemAdvisor` must be instantiated to support the `Advisor` interface. However, only one such object is ever necessary, and so these classes define publicly accessible singletons.

The advisor classes translate calls to `recommend()` into the interfaces that the underlying engines require. For example, the `GroupAdvisor` class translates calls to `recommend()` into the `advise()` interface that the `Re18` engine requires:

```
public Firework recommend(Customer c)
{
    return (Firework) Re18.advise(c);
}
```

## CHALLENGE 23.1

In addition to SINGLETON and STRATEGY, what pattern appears in the GroupAdvisor and ItemAdvisor classes?

*A solution appears on page 418.*

## CHALLENGE 23.2

Fill in the class diagram in Figure 23.3, which shows the recommendation logic refactored into a collection of strategy classes.

*A solution appears on page 418.*

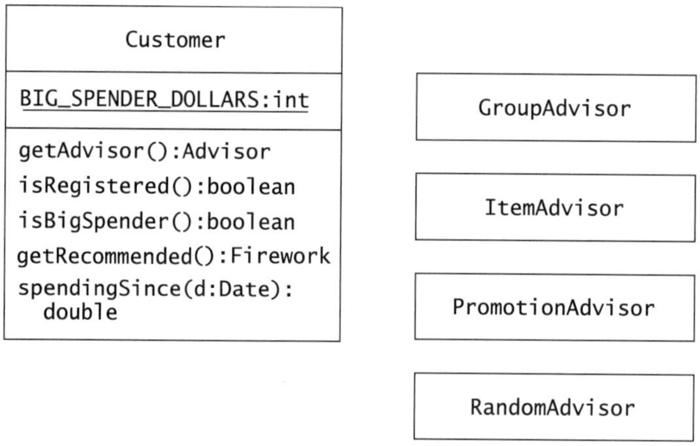

**FIGURE 23.3:** Complete this diagram to show a refactoring of the recommendation software, with strategies appearing as implementations of a common interface.

```
         Customer
─────────────────────────
BIG_SPENDER_DOLLARS:int
─────────────────────────
getAdvisor():Advisor
isRegistered():boolean
isBigSpender():boolean
getRecommended():Firework
spendingSince(d:Date):
   double
```

```
GroupAdvisor
```

```
ItemAdvisor
```

```
PromotionAdvisor
```

```
RandomAdvisor
```

Each implementation of the Advisor interface should supply a singleton that offers the recommend() operation. You might correspondingly give each class a single, private constructor to prevent other classes from instantiating it.

The constructor for PromotionAdvisor should investigate whether a promotion is on. You might then supply this class with a hasItem() method that indicates whether there is a promoted item.

```java
package com.oozinoz.recommend;
import java.io.*;
import java.util.*;
import com.oozinoz.fireworks.*;
public class PromotionAdvisor implements Advisor
{
    public static final PromotionAdvisor singleton =
        new PromotionAdvisor();
    private Firework promoted;

    private PromotionAdvisor()
    {
        try
        {
            Properties p = new Properties();
            p.load(
                ClassLoader.getSystemResourceAsStream(
                    "config/strategy.dat"));
            String promotedFireworkName =
                p.getProperty("promote");
            if (promotedFireworkName != null)
            {
                promoted = Firework.lookup(
                    promotedFireworkName);
            }
        }
        catch (Exception e)
        {
        }
    }

    public boolean hasItem() {
        return promoted != null;
    }

    public Firework recommend(Customer c) {
        return promoted;
    }
}
```

The RandomAdvisor class is simple:

```
package com.oozinoz.recommend;
import com.oozinoz.fireworks.*;
public class RandomAdvisor implements Advisor
{
    public static final RandomAdvisor singleton =
        new RandomAdvisor();

    private RandomAdvisor()
    {
    }

    public Firework recommend(Customer c)
    {
        return Firework.getRandom();
    }
}
```

---

**CHALLENGE 23.3**

Write the code for ItemAdvisor.java.

*A solution appears on page 418.*

---

The refactoring of Customer separates the *selection* of a strategy (or "advisor") from the *use* of the strategy. An advisor attribute of a Customer object holds the context, or current choice, of the strategy to apply. The refactored Customer class lazy-initializes this attribute with logic that reflects Oozinoz's advertising policies:

```
private Advisor getAdvisor()
{
    if (advisor == null)
    {
```

```
        if (PromotionAdvisor.singleton.hasItem())
        {
            advisor = PromotionAdvisor.singleton;
        }
        else if (isRegistered())
        {
            advisor = GroupAdvisor.singleton;
        }
        else if (isBigSpender())
        {
            advisor = ItemAdvisor.singleton;
        }
        else
        {
            advisor = RandomAdvisor.singleton;
        }
    }
    return advisor;
}

private boolean isBigSpender()
{
    Calendar cal = Calendar.getInstance();
    cal.add(Calendar.YEAR, -1);
    return
        spendingSince(cal.getTime()) > BIG_SPENDER_DOLLARS;
}
```

## CHALLENGE 23.4

Write the code for Customer.getRecommended().

*A solution appears on page 419.*

**CHALLENGE 23.5**

In the new design, four singletons implement the `Advisor` interface in four ways, encapsulating four strategies. Is the presence of multiple similar singletons reminiscent of a design pattern?

*A solution appears on page 419.*

## Comparing STRATEGY and STATE

The refactored code consists almost entirely of simple methods in simple classes. This is an advantage in its own right and makes adding new strategies easy. The refactoring relies primarily on the idea of distributing an operation across a related group of classes. In this regard, STRATEGY is identical to STATE. In fact, many developers wonder whether these are really different patterns.

On the one hand, in the real world, strategies (such as recommending a firework) and states (such as a carousel door with a one-touch control button) are clearly different ideas. This real difference leads to different problems in modeling states and strategies. For example, transitions are important when modeling states but usually irrelevant when choosing a strategy. Another difference is that STRATEGY might allow a client to select or to provide a strategy, an idea that rarely applies to STATE. On the other hand, the differences in modeling states and strategies may seem subtle. Certainly, the reliance on polymorphism makes STATE and STRATEGY appear almost identical structurally. Either way, if you decide that these are or are not two separate patterns, you will be in good company.

## Comparing STRATEGY and TEMPLATE METHOD

Chapter 21, TEMPLATE METHOD, described sorting as an example of the TEMPLATE METHOD pattern. You can use the `sort()` algorithm from the `Collections` class to sort any list of objects, so long as you supply a step to compare two objects. But you might argue that when you supply a comparison step to a sorting algorithm, you are changing the strategy. For instance, if you are selling rockets, presenting them sorted by price is a different marketing strategy from presenting them sorted by thrust.

---

**CHALLENGE 23.6**

Provide an argument as to whether the `Collections.sort()` method provides an example of TEMPLATE METHOD or an example of STRATEGY.

*A solution appears on page 419.*

---

## Summary

Strategies that occur in the real world may not naturally lie down as separate methods in a collection of classes. Logic that models alternative strategies may appear in a single class, often in a single method. Such methods may be too complicated and may mix strategy-selection logic with strategy execution.

To simplify such code, create a group of classes, one for each strategy. Define an operation and distribute it across these classes. This lets each class encapsulate one strategy, creating simpler code. You also need to arrange for the client that uses a strategy to be able to select one. This selection code may be complex even after refactoring, but you should be able to reduce this code so that it is nearly equivalent to pseudocode that describes strategy selection in the problem domain.

Typically, a client will hold a selected strategy in a context variable. This makes the execution of a strategy a simple matter of forwarding the strategic operation call to the context, using polymorphism to execute the right strategy. By encapsulating alternative strategies in separate classes that each implement a common operation, the STRATEGY pattern lets you create clean, simple code that models a family of approaches to solving a problem.

## 24

# COMMAND

POLYMORPHISM LETS YOU encapsulate a request, or a command as an object: Establish the signature of a method to call, and vary the effect of calling the method by varying the implementation. The COMMAND pattern establishes a method signature, most often `execute()` or `perform()`, and lets you define various implementations of this interface. This lets you encapsulate a request as an object, so that you can parameterize clients with different requests, queue, time, or log requests, and require companion operations, such as `undo()`.

## A Classic Example: Menu Commands

Menus provide a classic example of the need for the COMMAND pattern. When you add a menu to an application, you have to configure the menu with words that describe actions that the user can choose, such as Save and Load. You also have to configure the menu so that it can take action, calling a method in response to a user's click. However, the developers who wrote the code for the `JMenuItem` class had no way of knowing what action you will want when an item is selected.

How can you arrange for a class to call a method of yours when the user clicks? The answer is to use polymorphism: Make the name of the operation fixed, and let the implementation vary. For `JMenuItem`, the operation is `actionPerformed()`. When the user makes a choice, a `JMenuItem` object calls the `actionPerformed()` method of any object that has registered as a listener.

**CHALLENGE 24.1**

The mechanics of Java menus make it easy to apply the COMMAND pattern, but they do not *require* that you organize your code as commands. In fact, it is common to develop an application in which a single object listens to all the events in a GUI. What pattern does that follow?

*A solution appears on page 420.*

When you develop a Swing application, you may want to register a single listener for all of an application's GUI events, especially if the GUI components interact. For menus, however, this may not be the best pattern to follow. If you use a single object as a listener, that object has to sort out which GUI object generated an event. If you have many menu items that take independent actions, it may be better to apply COMMAND.

The method that a menu item calls when a user selects it is `actionPerformed()`, but you might think of it as `execute()`. When you create a `JMenuItem` object, you can supply it with a command to execute when the user selects the item. Your task is to create an object that implements `actionPerformed()` with a method that takes an action that corresponds to the user's command. Rather than define a new class to implement this one little behavior, it is often better to use an anonymous class to outfit menu items with action commands.

Consider the `Visualization2` class from the `com.oozinoz.visualization` package. This class provides a menu that lets the user save and restore visualizations of a simulated Oozinoz factory. The application has a menu bar that includes, at present, just a file menu:

```
protected JMenuBar menuBar()
{
    if (menuBar == null)
    {
        menuBar = new JMenuBar();
```

```
        Menu fileMenu = new Menu("File");
        menuBar.add(fileMenu());
    }
    return menuBar;
}
```

The file menu creates Save and Load menu items and registers listeners that wait for the user to choose them. The listeners are instances of anonymous classes that implement the actionPerformed() method by calling the save() and load() methods of the Visualization2 class:

```
protected JMenu fileMenu()
{
    if (fileMenu == null)
    {
        fileMenu = new JMenu("File");
        Font f = SwingFacade.getStandardFont();
        fileMenu.setFont(f);

        JMenuItem save = new JMenuItem("Save");
        save.setFont(f);
        fileMenu.add(save);
        save.addActionListener
            (
                new ActionListener()
                {
                    // challenge!
                }
            );


        JMenuItem load = new JMenuItem("Load");
        load.setFont(f);
        fileMenu.add(load);
        load.addActionListener
            (
                new ActionListener()
                {
                    // challenge!
                }
            );
    }
    return fileMenu;
}
```

When you outfit a menu with commands, you are plugging your commands into a context provided by another developer. In other cases of COMMAND, you will take the role of the context developer, providing the context in which commands will execute. For example, you might want to provide a timing service that records how long methods take to execute.

## Using COMMAND to Supply a Service

Suppose that you want to let developers time how long a method takes to execute. Figure 24.1 shows a `Command` interface and a `time()` utility that times the execution of a command.

**FIGURE 24.1:** The `time()` method returns the number of milliseconds that a command takes to execute.

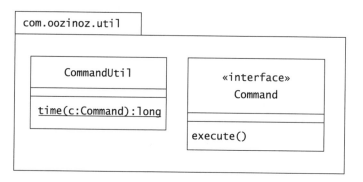

The code for `time()` captures the system time before and after executing the command and returns the difference:

```
public static long time(Command c)
{
    long t1 = System.currentTimeMillis();
```

```
        c.execute();
        long t2 = System.currentTimeMillis();
        return t2 - t1;
    }
```

Suppose that you decide to test the time() method with an automated testing tool. One reasonable test is that a command that sleeps for, say, 2,000 milliseconds should take about 2,000 milliseconds to execute:

```
package com.oozinoz.util;
import junit.framework.*;
public class TestCommand extends TestCase
{
    public TestCommand(String name)
    {
        super(name);
    }

    public static void main(String[] args)
    {
        new junit.awtui.TestRunner().start(
            new String[] { "com.oozinoz.util.TestCommand" });
    }

    public void testSleep()
    {
        Command doze = new Command()
            {
                public void execute()
                {
                    try
                    {
                        Thread.sleep(2000);
                    }
                    catch (InterruptedException ignore)
                    {
                    }
                }
            };
        long t = /* ? */
        assertEquals(2000, t, 50);
    }
}
```

The assertEquals() method checks that the expected value, 2,000, is within 50 milliseconds of the actual value.

---

**CHALLENGE 24.3**

Complete the assignment statement that times the execution of the doze command.

*A solution appears on page 421.*

---

## COMMAND in Relation to Other Patterns

The COMMAND pattern has interesting relationships to many other patterns. For example, COMMAND provides an alternative to TEMPLATE METHOD. Recall the Aster star press code that let you override the method that marks a mold as incomplete if it is in process when you shut down the press. The AsterStarPress class is abstract, requiring you to subclass it with a class that has a markMoldIncomplete() method. The shutdown() method of AsterStarPress relies on this method to ensure that your domain object knows that the mold is incomplete:

```
public void shutDown()
{
    if (inProcess())
    {
        stopProcessing();
        markMoldIncomplete(currentMoldID);
    }
    usherInputMolds();
    dischargePaste();
    flush();
}
```

You might find it inconvenient to subclass AsterStarPress with a class that you have to move to the star press's on-board computer. Suppose that you ask the developers at Aster to provide the hook in a different way, using the COMMAND pattern. Figure 24.2 shows a Hook interface that the AsterStarPress class can use, letting you parameterize the star press code at runtime.

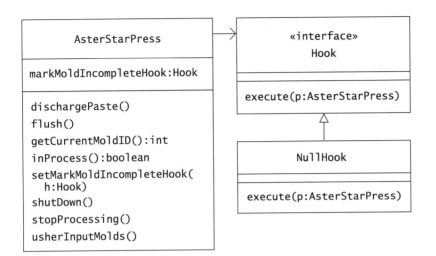

**FIGURE 24.2:** A class can provide a hook—a way to insert custom code—by calling a supplied object's execute() command at a specific point in a procedure.

The AsterStarPress class initially sets its hook to be a NullHook object. The execute() method of NullHook does nothing. You can supply your own implementation of Hook for the shutDown() method to call. The shutDown() method now relies on this hook, executing it and passing it the AsterStarPress object at the right moment:

```
public void shutDown()
{
    if (inProcess())
    {
        stopProcessing();
        markMoldIncompleteHook.execute(this);
    }
    usherInputMolds();
    dischargePaste();
    flush();
}
```

Using the previous version of the AsterStarPress class, you created a subclass that handled the effects of a shutdown, leaving a mold incomplete:

```
public class OzAsterStarPress extends AsterStarPress
{
    public MaterialManager getManager()
    {
        return MaterialManager.getManager();
```

```
        }
        public void markMoldIncomplete(int id)
        {
            getManager().setMoldIncomplete(id);
        }
    }
```

You no longer need the OzAsterStarPress class, but you do need to set the command hook in the AsterStarPress class.

---

**CHALLENGE 24.4**

Write an expression that creates an object that you can pass to setShutdownHook() and that will notify the Oozinoz material manager of the mold's state.

*A solution appears on page 422.*

---

The execute() command of Hook accepts an instance of AsterStarPress as an argument. The idea here is that the developer of a hook—namely you—will need some information about that state of the press when your hook is called. If the mark-mold-incomplete hook were the only hook for star press processing, it would make more sense to use the ID of the mold machine as the parameter of the execute() command. The chosen design, however, anticipates that other hooks will come along. Passing the complete AsterStarPress object is a hedge that makes it likely that future hooks can be added without changing the Hook interface.

The COMMAND pattern affords an alternative design to a TEMPLATE METHOD for hooks and is similar in intent, or structure, to several other patterns. The COMMAND pattern is similar to ADAPTER, in that a class such as JMenuItem or JTable arranges to call a client's code at the right moment. COMMAND is also similar to INTERPRETER; Challenge 25.3 on page 268 will ask you to compare them. Finally, COMMAND is similar to a pattern in which a client knows when an action is required but doesn't know exactly which operation to call.

---

**CHALLENGE 24.5**

Which pattern addresses the situation in which a client knows *when* to create an object but doesn't know which class to instantiate?

*A solution appears on page 422.*

---

The COMMAND pattern often names its standard operation execute() or perform(). But nothing limits the operation to this name; nor is there a limitation that this pattern may use only a single operation. In particular, instances of COMMAND often include an undo() operation to reverse the effects of an execute(). In some cases, you may be able to implement undo(), relying only on information in a command object. More often, you will need to restore a complete system to the state it was in before a command executed.

---

**CHALLENGE 24.6**

Which pattern provides for the storage and restoration of an object's state?

*A solution appears on page 422.*

---

## Summary

The COMMAND pattern lets you encapsulate a request in an object so that you can modify at runtime the method that a client will call. A classic example of the usefulness of COMMAND comes with menus. Menus know *when* to execute an action but don't know which method to call. COMMAND lets you parameterize a menu with the method calls that correspond to menu labels.

When you use a Java menu you can supply commands into a context that other developers have created. In other cases, you may take the role of the context provider, developing an environment in which to execute commands. Your environment may allow for parameterization of a service, as Java menus do. You may also provide hooks, or add extra value, such as timing an operation.

COMMAND fixes the signature of an operation and lets classes vary, applying this trick of polymorphism to encapsulate an operation in an object. Perhaps because this idea is so fundamental, COMMAND has interesting relationships to many other patterns. COMMAND can be an alternative to MEDIATOR or TEMPLATE METHOD and often interacts with other patterns.

# 25

# INTERPRETER

THE INTERPRETER PATTERN, like the STATE and STRATEGY patterns, distributes an operation across a collection of classes. In such patterns, the effect of calling the operation depends on the class of the object that receives the call. In both STATE and STRATEGY, the receiver of an operation call is a single object. INTERPRETER takes the same idea and applies it to a composition—in particular, a **rich composite**, or one with various ways of forming groups.

The INTERPRETER pattern is similar to the COMPOSITE pattern, which defines a common interface for individual items and groups of items. COMPOSITE does not require various, interesting ways of forming groups, although it allows this. For example, the `ProcessComponent` hierarchy in Chapter 5, COMPOSITE, allows sequences and alternations of process flows. In INTERPRETER, the idea that there are various types of composition is essential.

The way a class composes other components defines how an INTERPRETER class will implement, or interpret, a distributed operation. Each composite class in an instance of INTERPRETER models a rule for how composition may occur. The intent of the INTERPRETER pattern is to let you compose executable objects according to a set of composition rules that you define. An **interpreter** object conducts the execution, or evaluation of a collection of rules, letting you build expression evaluators and command languages.

## An INTERPRETER Example

The robots that Oozinoz uses to move material along a processing line come with an interpreter that controls the robot and that has limited control of machines on the line. The interpreter comes as a hierarchy of classes that encapsulate robot commands. At the head of the hierarchy is an abstract Command class. Distributed across the hierarchy is an execute() operation. The interpreter performs the same role as an API (application programming interface) but lets you create new machine programs at runtime. Figure 25.1 shows the commands that the robot interpreter supports.

The interpreter hierarchy includes commands that let you start up, shut down, and unload machines. (These commands require a bit of customization to work with our machinery.) The interpreter hierarchy also provides a command that carries material from one machine to another and provides sequence, for, and if commands that are compositions of other commands.

**FIGURE 25.1:** An interpreter hierarchy provides for runtime programming of a factory robot.

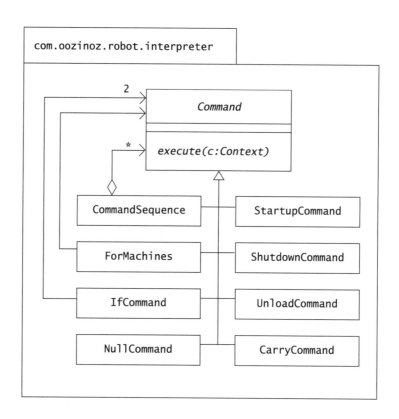

The ForMachines class uses another command as the body of a for loop. This command can be either a single command or a sequence embodied in a CommandSequence object. The IfCommand class constructor takes a condition term, not shown, and two commands, one of which it executes, depending on the condition. The NullCommand class implements execute() to do nothing. You can use this, for example, to nullify the else part of an if command.

Each class in the Command hierarchy is an interpreter. Polymorphism lets each class interpret the execute() operation differently, in a way that matches the name of the class. You might also say that each *instance* of a class in the hierarchy is an interpreter. The CommandSequence, ForMachines, and IfCommand classes let you compose new, arbitrarily complex interpreters that can interpret the execute() command as a complete program.

The Command interpreter design uses a Term hierarchy to contain references to machines, letting you create commands either for specific machines or by using variables. For example, the CarryCommand class has a constructor that requires two Term objects, as Figure 25.2 shows.

The Term class defines an abstract eval() method that returns a machine and that subclasses must implement. This provides flexibility to

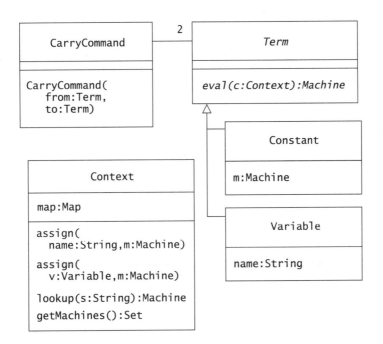

**FIGURE 25.2:** Command classes, such as Carry-Command, use Term objects as parameters. A Context object holds a mapping from machine and variable names to Machine objects.

such classes as CarryCommand. If you want to create a CarryCommand object that carries material between two specific machines, you can use Constant objects to represent those machines. Alternatively, you can create a CarryCommand object that will carry material between two variables, perhaps fromMachine and toMachine. You can assign those variables in any context, such as within a for loop, reusing the CarryCommand object.

The com.oozinoz.robot.interpreter package includes, for demonstration purposes, a MachineLine class. This class offers a static create-Context() method that returns a context with a mapping of machines in a particular line. The contents of this initial context are:

```
"Mixer1201"          -> Mixer1201
"StarPress1401"      -> StarPress1401
"ShellAssembler1301" -> ShellAssembler1301
"Fuser1101"          -> Fuser1101
"UnloadBuffer1501"   -> UnloadBuffer1501
```

This context maps machine names to instances of Machine. You can program a CarryCommand object, for example, to carry material from two machines to the buffer:

```
package com.oozinoz.robot.interpreter;
import java.util.*;
import com.oozinoz.machine.*;
public class ShowCarry
{
    public static void main(String[] args)
    {
        Context c = MachineLine.createContext();
        Variable x = new Variable("x");
        Machine ub = c.lookup("UnloadBuffer1501");
        CarryCommand comm =
            new CarryCommand(x, new Constant(ub));

        c.assign(x, c.lookup("Mixer1201"));
        comm.execute(c);
        c.assign(x, c.lookup("StarPress1401"));
        comm.execute(c);
    }
}
```

The `CarryCommand` object directs the robot to move material. A log of the machine line's response to the command executions is:

```
Robot will carry from Mixer1201 to UnloadBuffer1501
Mixer1201 unloading
Robot will carry from StarPress1401 to UnloadBuffer1501
StarPress1401 unloading
```

Note that the `CarryCommand` object is reusable. To obtain this kind of flexibility, other `Command` classes also define themselves using `Term` objects, as Figure 25.3 shows.

The interpreter classes let you compose programs that control the machine line. Each class interprets the `execute()` command in a way that

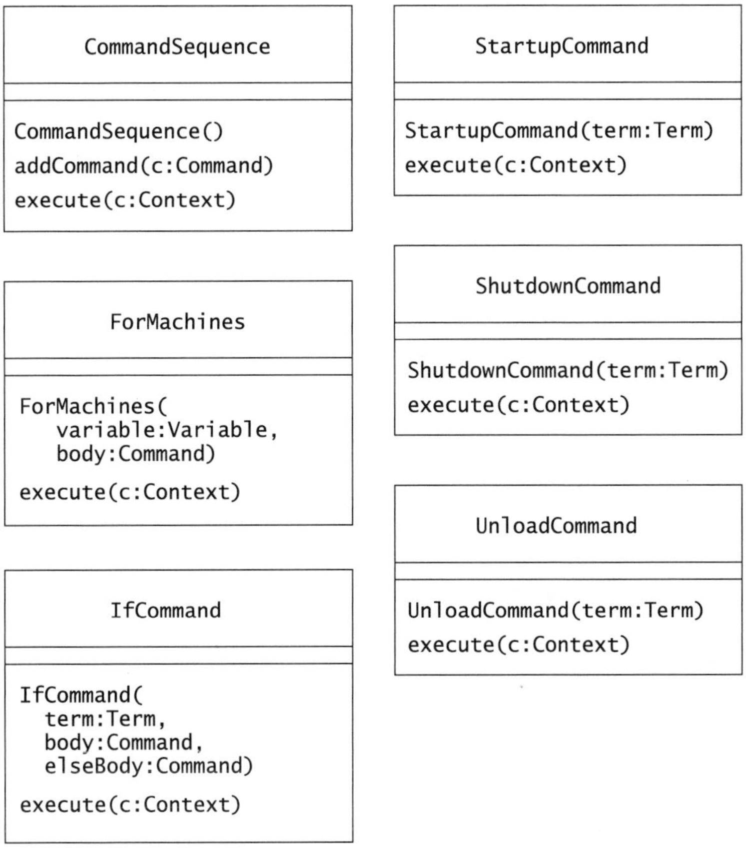

```
CommandSequence

CommandSequence()
addCommand(c:Command)
execute(c:Context)
```

```
ForMachines

ForMachines(
    variable:Variable,
    body:Command)
execute(c:Context)
```

```
IfCommand

IfCommand(
  term:Term,
  body:Command,
  elseBody:Command)
execute(c:Context)
```

```
StartupCommand

StartupCommand(term:Term)
execute(c:Context)
```

```
ShutdownCommand

ShutdownCommand(term:Term)
execute(c:Context)
```

```
UnloadCommand

UnloadCommand(term:Term)
execute(c:Context)
```

**FIGURE 25.3:** Command classes generally define themselves using terms that may be variables, specific machines, or Boolean expressions.

is consistent with the class's name. For example, the execute() method
for StartupCommand is:

```
public void execute(Context c)
{
    Machine m = term.eval(c);
    m.startup();
}
```

For the ForMachines class, execute() is:

```
public void execute(Context c)
{
    Iterator i = c.machines.iterator();
    while (i.hasNext())
    {
        Machine m = (Machine) i.next();
        c.assign(variable, m);
        body.execute(c);
    }
}
```

This code iterates over the machines in the provided context, assigning
a variable to each machine and executing the loop's body. The idea here
is for clients to create a body that depends on the variable, as in a normal
for loop. Consider a short Java program that shuts down all the
machines in the MachineLine context:

```
package com.oozinoz.robot.interpreter;
import com.oozinoz.machine.*;
public class ShowForCommand
{
    public static void main(String[] args)
    {
        Context c = MachineLine.createContext();
        Variable m = new Variable("m");
        ForMachines fm =
            new ForMachines(m, new ShutdownCommand(m));
        fm.execute(c);
    }
}
```

The body of the for command shuts down machine "m". The for command assigns this variable to each machine in the provided context and
executes the body. The program produces a log of the command execution:

```
Mixer1201 shutting down
Fuser1101 shutting down
StarPress1401 shutting down
ShellAssembler1301 shutting down
UnloadBuffer1501 shutting down
```

Implementors of the `Term` interface must implement `eval()` so that it returns an object of type `Machine`. However, the `Term` hierarchy includes two classes that are effectively Boolean operators that return `null` to mean false and return a `Machine` object to mean true. Figure 25.4 shows the Boolean subclasses of `Term`.

The `Equals` class and the `HasMoreMaterial` class return `null` to indicate false. You can create, for example, an `Equals` term that compares a variable to the constant value of the unload buffer:

```
Constant ub = new Constant(c.lookup("UnloadBuffer1501"));
Term t = new Equals(m, ub);
```

You can use an instance of `Equals` as the conditional term in an `IfCommand` object. An `IfCommand` object has a term, a body command, and an `elseBody` command. When it executes, an `IfCommand` object executes its

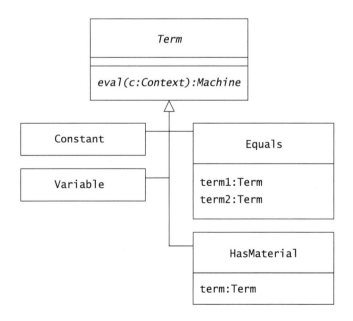

**FIGURE 25.4:** The `Term` hierarchy includes classes that are effectively Booleans.

main body command unless its term evaluates to `null`, in which case it executes its `elseBody` command:

```
package com.oozinoz.robot.interpreter;
import com.oozinoz.machine.*;
public class IfCommand extends Command
{
    protected Term term;
    protected Command body;
    protected Command elseBody;


    public IfCommand(
        Term term, Command body, Command elseBody)
    {
        this.term = term;
        this.body = body;
        this.elseBody = elseBody;
    }
    public void execute(Context c)
    {
        if (term.eval(c) != null)
        {
            body.execute(c);
        }
        else
        {
            elseBody.execute(c);
        }
    }
}
```

## CHALLENGE 25.1

Write a program that creates and uses an interpreter to shut down all the machines that `MachineLine` controls, except for the unload buffer.

*A solution appears on page 423.*

Now suppose that you want to unload all the material from a machine. The HasMaterial class takes another term—usually a machine—as a constructor argument. A HasMaterial term returns null if its term has no material and otherwise returns the term's value:

```
package com.oozinoz.robot.interpreter;
import com.oozinoz.machine.*;
public class HasMaterial extends Term
{
    protected Term term;
    public HasMaterial(Term term)
    {
        this.term = term;
    }
    public Machine eval(Context c)
    {
        Machine m = term.eval(c);
        return m.hasMaterial() ? m : null;
    }
}
```

To unload a machine and to keep unloading it until it's empty, you need a WhileCommand class. Suppose that you call up the machine line company and ask for this class. While you wait for a patch or the next release, you can also temporarily create the class yourself. The code for WhileCommand should be similar to the code in IfCommand.java.

---

**CHALLENGE 25.2**

Write the code for WhileCommand.java.

*A solution appears on page 423.*

---

You might put your `WhileCommand` class into use with an interpreter that unloads a star press:

```
package com.oozinoz.robot.interpreter;
import com.oozinoz.machine.*;
public class ShowWhile
{
    public static void main(String[] args)
    {
        Context c = MachineLine.createContext();
        Constant sp =
            new Constant(c.lookup("StarPress1401"));
        Constant ub =
            new Constant(c.lookup("UnloadBuffer1501"));
        WhileCommand wc =
            new WhileCommand(
                new HasMaterial(sp),
                new CarryCommand(sp, ub));
        wc.execute(c);
    }
}
```

The wc object is an interpreter that interprets `execute()` to mean unload all the bins from star press 1401.

The machine command interpreter hierarchy lets you create arbitrary programs at runtime by composing new interpreter objects. In this regard, INTERPRETER is similar to COMMAND.

---

**CHALLENGE 25.3**

What is the difference, if any, between the COMMAND and INTERPRETER patterns?

*A solution appears on page 424.*

---

## Interpreters, Languages, and Parsers

The INTERPRETER pattern addresses how interpreters work but does not specify how you should compose new interpreters at runtime. In this chapter, you have built new interpreters "manually," by writing lines of Java code. But by far the most common way to create a new interpreter is with a parser. A parser can read textual commands from a file or from a user prompt and can use the text to create an interpreter. Powerful! Another reason to learn about building parsers is that if you want to understand the INTERPRETER chapter in *Design Patterns* (Gamma et al. 1995), you really need to understand the interrelation of interpreters, parsers, and computer languages.

A **parser** is an object that can recognize text and decompose its structure according to a set of rules into a form suitable for further processing. For example, you can write a parser that will create a machine command interpreter object that corresponds to a textual program, such as:

```
while StarPress1401 hasMoreMaterial
{
    carry from StarPress1401 to UnloadBuffer1501;
}
```

When you write a parser, the set of strings it recognizes is a **language**. When you create a new little computer language, you will most often create a **context-free language**, a pattern of text that follows a **grammar**—a collection of rules that determine how you can compose an element of the language. A parser decomposes a string according to the rules of composition.

In a somewhat abstract sense, a language need not be a set of strings. *Design Patterns* uses the word *language* to mean the set of possibilities that can occur by applying the set of rules that an interpreter hierarchy models. For example, the machine command interpreter hierarchy establishes a language: the set of all possible objects that you might compose from the hierarchy. An IfCommand object, for example, is an element, or *sentence*, of this language.

Using this terminology, you might state the intent of INTERPRETER as: Define a class hierarchy that represents a grammar—a set of composition rules—and define an operation throughout this hierarchy to interpret, or bring meaning to, instances of the set of possible compositions. This explanation is similar to the *Design Patterns* statement of the intent of INTERPRETER: "Given a language, define a representation for its grammar along with an interpreter that uses the representation to interpret sentences in the language" (p. 243).

If you think of the possible compositions of the machine command hierarchy as a language, the job of a parser is to translate a textual language into an equivalent interpreter language. Many tools perform this translation. You can search the Web for "parser generator" tools to find the latest freeware parsers. You can also use the code that comes with *Building Parsers with Java™* (Metsker 2001). That book's intent is to make it easier for you to create new little computer languages.

You don't have to develop your own parsers to understand INTERPRETER. You should, however, understand why an interpreter often needs a parser.

---

### CHALLENGE 25.4

Close this book and write a sentence that describes the association of interpreters, languages, and parsers.

*A solution appears on page 424.*

---

### Summary

Interpreters let you compose new commands, using the classes in a hierarchy that you create. Each class in the hierarchy defines a way of composing commands—a grammar rule. This composition rule determines how the class implements, or interprets, an operation that you distribute throughout the hierarchy.

The operation in an interpreter is often named `execute()` or `evaluate()`. The operation name is necessarily vague, becoming meaningful only when combined with the name of the class that implements it. Like STATE, STRATEGY, and COMMAND, the INTERPRETER pattern fixes the name of an operation and uses various classes to implement the operation. INTERPRETER applies this idea to let you compose executable objects according to a set of composition rules that you define.

# PART V

## EXTENSION PATTERNS

# 26

# INTRODUCING EXTENSIONS

Aʀ *EXTENSION* is the addition of a class, an interface, or a method to an existing code base. The most common way to extend code is to write a new class, although you can also extend a class through delegation. In particular, when you'd like to subclass from two parents, you can subclass from one parent and use delegation to "inherit" the behavior of the other class.

Object-oriented development in Java does not begin from scratch. Rather, it's fair to say that object-oriented software development *is* extension. To develop in Java, learn what is available in an existing code base, including a company's code and the Java class libraries. After seeing where your changes fit in, add the code you need for your application. In Java, application development is extension, and extension begins where reuse leaves off.

## Reuse as an Alternative to Extension

When you shop around before you code, you have less code to maintain, you benefit from the wisdom of developers who have gone before you, and you can ensure that your own code dovetails with the class you are extending. Every class that you create will inherit from the Object class, and this is a natural place to start shopping for existing code. Figure 26.1 shows the Object class.

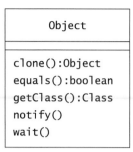

| Object |
| --- |
| clone():Object<br>equals():boolean<br>getClass():Class<br>notify()<br>wait() |

Earlier examples in this book have reused most of the behavior available in `Object`, including the `clone()`, `equals()`, and `getClass()` methods. As a Java developer, you should be able to reuse the `wait()` and `notify()` methods that `Object` provides.

Suppose that the Oozinoz robot can stack bins of material but only to a height of, say, three bins. If you command the robot to stack a fourth bin, it will wait until a human removes a bin. Figure 26.2 shows a Swing application—the `ShowWaitAndNotify` class in `com.oozinoz.applications`—that models this situation.

With the application in the state that Figure 26.2 shows, a fourth, unseen bin awaits stacking. Clicking Unload will remove a bin, letting the thread complete that is waiting to load a bin. This will leave three bins in the stack and will reenable the Load button. Clicking Unload four more

**FIGURE 26.2:** The user of this application has pressed Load a fourth time, launching a thread that will wait until the user clicks Unload.

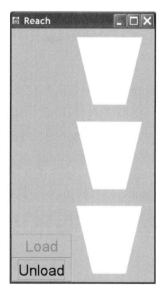

times will clear the stack and then put the Unload button in a wait state, awaiting a bin that it will immediately clear.

At the heart of an application is a BinStack class that uses wait() and notify() to suspend threads that load or unload more bins than the stack can handle. Figure 26.3 shows the application classes.

This application depends on the monitors that Java supplies to every object. The wait() method relinquishes a thread's possession of an object's monitor and makes the thread wait to get it back. The notify() method

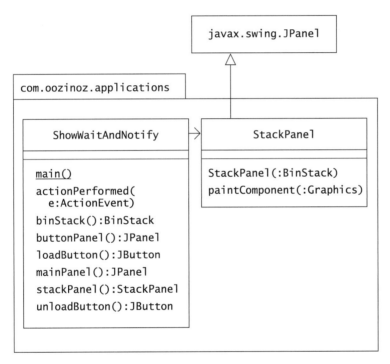

**FIGURE 26.3:** These classes collaborate to produce the bin-stacking application.

wakes up a thread that will obtain the monitor when it becomes available. Either of these methods can execute only in a thread that has the monitor. One way to obtain an object's monitor is to execute a synchronized instance method of that object. This is the technique that the BinStack class uses:

```java
package com.oozinoz.machine;
import java.util.*;
public class BinStack
{
    public static final int STACK_LIMIT = 3;
    private Stack stack = new Stack();

    synchronized public Bin pop()
    {
        while (stack.size() == 0)
        {
            try
            {
                wait();
                Thread.sleep(500);
            }
            catch (InterruptedException ignore)
            {
            }
        }
        if (stack.size() == STACK_LIMIT)
        {
            notify();
        }
        return (Bin) stack.pop();
    }

    synchronized public void push(Bin b)
    {
        /* ? */
    }

    public int size()
    {
        return stack.size();
    }
}
```

If the stack is empty, the pop() method causes the thread that called it to wait. This thread will wait until the push() method—which you are about to write—awakens it. When the pop() method wakes up after waiting, it waits another half second. This lets a newly stacked bin briefly appear in the GUI before this method snatches it away. The pop() method checks the size of the stack in a while loop in case other threads might pop the stack, although this won't occur in the ShowWaitAndNotify application.

When the stack is nonempty, the pop() method checks to see whether the stack is full. If the stack is full, another thread may be waiting to push another bin, so the pop() method calls notify(). This will cause any thread waiting on the BinStack object's monitor to wake up when pop() completes. The pop() method concludes by popping the top Bin object.

---

**CHALLENGE 26.1**

Write the code for the push() method of the BinStack class.

*A solution appears on page 424.*

---

You may have noticed that the pop() method of BinStack calls notify() before it pops an object from the stack. If a waiting thread were to wake up and start accessing the stack before this method pops an object, the stack would overflow.

---

**CHALLENGE 26.2**

There is, in fact, no danger in the BinStack code that a thread waiting to push an object will start executing before the pop() method completes its pop. Why is that?

*A solution appears on page 426.*

The Object class comments provide a surprising amount of documentation on how wait() and notify() work. Another excellent reference on these methods is *The Java™ Class Libraries, Volume 1* (Chan, Lee, and Kramer 1998). For an extensive work on many applications of Java's locking facilities, I also recommend *Concurrent Programming in Java™* (Lea 2000).

To use a BinStack object, create a thread that pushes or pops an object to the stack. The actionPerformed() method of ShowWaitAndNotify provides an example:

```java
public void actionPerformed(ActionEvent e)
{
    Object source = e.getSource();

    if (source.equals(loadButton()))
    {
        new Thread()
        {
            public void run()
            {
                loadButton().setEnabled(false);
                binStack().push(new Bin("a bin"));
                loadButton().setEnabled(true);
                stackPanel().repaint();
            }
        }
        .start();
    }

    if (source.equals(unloadButton()))
    {
        new Thread()
        {
            public void run()
            {
                unloadButton().setEnabled(false);
                binStack().pop();
                unloadButton().setEnabled(true);
```

```
                    stackPanel().repaint();
                }
            }
          .start();
        }
    }
```

You might want to refactor this code, applying OBSERVER, so that the StackPanel object will repaint itself when the stack changes.

Shopping around and discovering such tools as Java's support for locking may occasionally make you feel overwhelmed. There is so much to learn! Avid learning is good, but it has the downside that you are coding today with much less knowledge than you'll have in a year. A good balance is to spend an hour a day learning and to spend the rest of your work time applying what you know. Although you are learning all the time, you have to write code today, creating your own extensions to an existing software base.

## Extending by Subclassing

When you create a new class, you should ensure that it is a logical and consistent extension of the class you extend, as Chapter 7, Introducing Responsibility, explores. A Java compiler will enforce certain aspects of consistency.

---

**CHALLENGE 26.3**

What four aspects of the model in Figure 26.4 will a Java compiler take exception to?

*A solution appears on page 426.*

---

**FIGURE 26.4:** What's wrong with this picture?

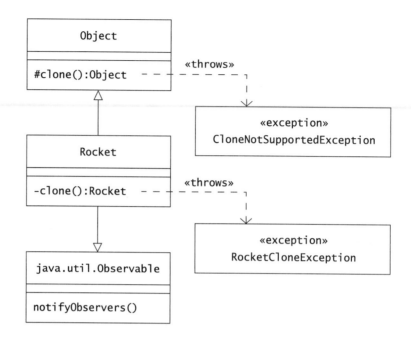

A Java compiler helps to ensure the consistency of your classes, but many potential extension problems will elude a compiler. In particular, class names have a meaning in English that only human-level intelligence can appreciate. For example, an overt error is to make `Customer` a subclass of `Sparkler`. (A **sparkler** is a wire coated with a combustible paste saturated with iron filings that do, in fact, sparkle.)

Other errors are subtler and, as such, subject to judgment as to whether they are in fact errors.

---

### CHALLENGE 26.4

List three aspects of the Figure 26.5 model that are problems or at least questionable.

*A solution appears on page 426.*

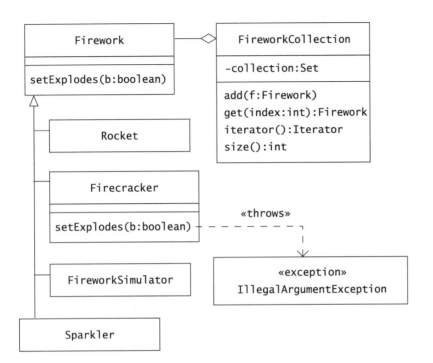

## The Liskov Substitution Principle

New classes should be logical, consistent extensions of their superclasses, but what does it mean to be *logical* and *consistent*? A Java compiler will ensure a certain level of consistency, but many principles of consistency will elude a compiler. One principle you should consider in your designs is the *Liskov Substitution Principle* (LSP). This principle, documented in Liskov (1987), can be paraphrased: An instance of a class should function as an instance of its superclass.

Basic LSP compliance is built into OO languages, such as Java. For example, it is legal to refer to a Rocket object as a Firework, as Rocket is a subclass of Firework:

```
Firework f = new Rocket();
```

Some aspects of LSP compliance require human-level intelligence, or at least more intelligence than today's compilers possess. For example, does code that sets a collection of fireworks to be nonexploding violate LSP?

```
public void defuse(FireworkList list)
{
    for (int i = 0; i < list.size(); i++)
    {
        Firework f = list.get(i);
        f.setExplodes(false);
    }
}
```

The Firework class provides the setExplodes() method so that you can specify whether certain types of fireworks explode. In particular, rockets may or may not explode. The setExplodes() method is useful for rockets, but some subclasses of Firework cannot entirely support this operation. It is a modeling error, for example, to indicate that a Firework instance explodes if that instance is in fact an instance of Sparkler. The model violates LSP because subclasses do not support a superclass method. However, violations of LSP are not necessarily bad. In this example, a modeling error occurs only when setExplodes() is called with an argument that doesn't make sense for a particular type of firework.

Violations of LSP can occur outside of domain-specific code and can occur in the Java class libraries. Consider a program that converts an array to a list, prints it, and adds an element to the list:

```
package com.oozinoz.applications;
import java.util.*;
public class ShowAsList
{
    public static void main(String[] args)
    {
        String[] names =
            new String[] {
                "Mixer", "Star Press", "Shell Assembler" };
        System.out.println(names);
        List L = Arrays.asList(names);
        System.out.println(L);
        L.add("Fuser");
    }
}
```

This program prints two lines of text and then crashes:

```
[Ljava.lang.String;@7259da
[Mixer, Star Press, Shell Assembler]
Exception in thread
    "main"java.lang.UnsupportedOperationException
          at java.util.AbstractList.add(Unknown Source)
...
```

The first line is an array's representation of itself. The second line is a list's self-representation. The remaining output reflects an unhandled exception that occurs because the add() method throws an Unsupported-OperationException. The implementation of List that asList() returns does not support adding values to the list. You can work around this limitation by defining the list as follows:

```
List L = new ArrayList(Arrays.asList(names));
```

---

**CHALLENGE 26.5**

Does Arrays.asList() violate LSP? Can you justify why this method returns an implementation of List that does not support the full List interface?

*A solution appears on page 427.*

---

## Extending by Delegating

Extension through delegation occurs when a class has methods that forward calls to identical operations supplied by another object. This technique makes available the behavior of the forwarded-to class on the class you are extending, but this is usually not the best way to achieve extension. If you want to inherit the exact methods of an existing class, the most straightforward approach is to subclass it. However, this is not always possible. The class whose behavior you need may be declared final—as String is, for example—or your class may already be subclassing something else. In these cases, you can extend your class through delegation.

---

**CHALLENGE 26.6**

Suppose that you want to make a class in an existing hierarchy observable, so that interested clients can register for notification of changes. Name an existing class from which you can "inherit" these features, and describe how the delegation works.

*A solution appears on page 427.*

---

Extending a `final` class using delegation is usually questionable, or just a plain bad idea. Suppose that a colleague asks for your thoughts about extending the `String` class with an `OoString` class that adds a few new behaviors. Specifically, he wants Oozinoz strings to provide `setTitle-Case()` and `setRandomCase()` methods. (**Title case** means that characters after whitespace are in uppercase. **Random case** means that characters in the string are uppercase or lowercase at random.) Figure 26.6 shows the proposed `OoString` class, which adds functions that change the case of text, such as ad copy for a Web site:

**FIGURE 26.6:** In this questionable design, the `OoString` class extends the `String` class, delegating certain operations to an underlying `String` instance.

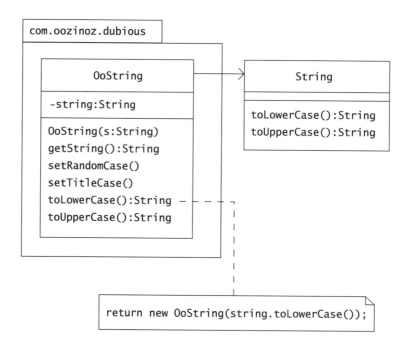

```
package com.oozinoz.dubious;
public class ShowOoString
{
    public static void main(String args[])
    {
        OoString os =
            new OoString(
                "Launch our newest rocket "
                    + "from any international waters!");
        os.setRandomCase();
        os.setTitleCase();
        System.out.println(os);
    }
}
```

This code prints out something like:

```
LaUnch OUr NeWEsT ROcKEt FrOm ANY InternatIOnal WATers!
```

---

**CHALLENGE 26.7**

Which of the following objections are valid?

A. You can achieve the desired case effects by introducing similar operations in a utility class.

B. One reason `String` is `final` is to preserve immutability, and the `OoString` class undermines this.

C. Classes such as `StringReader` cannot effectively be extended to work with `OoString` objects instead of the `String` objects they expect.

D. To "extend" `String`, the `OoString` class should provide all the operations that the `String` class provides.

E. Strings are built into the compiler in a special way that `OoString` cannot emulate.

*A solution appears on page 428.*

## Summary

A major change that has accompanied the advent of object-oriented programming is that programming is now a matter of extending an existing code base. Talented Java developers spend more time reading than writing, to understand how their code will fit with and benefit from the voluminous class libraries. One class that you should be especially sure to understand is `Object`, the superclass from which all your classes will derive.

The subclasses you create should be logical and consistent extensions of their superclasses. The Java compiler will enforce some aspects of consistency; in many areas, however, consistency is a matter of judgment. The Liskov Substitution Principle suggests that subtypes should uphold the behavior of supertypes. A good policy is to violate this principle only when you have a compelling justification.

In addition to subclassing, you can extend through delegation. This is more fragile than subclassing but may be necessary if your class needs to provide the behavior of multiple superclasses.

A healthy view is that development is a matter of extending the Java code base with just the changes you need for your application. Aggressive reuse of the Java class libraries will you help you reduce the chances for introducing defects and will let you benefit from the hard work of many developers who have preceded you. With a good understanding of the existing code base, you can develop rich applications as minimal extensions of existing code.

## ■ BEYOND ORDINARY EXTENSION

The ordinary way to extend a software system is to find a suitable superclass—usually `Object`—and to subclass it. You can also "inherit" behavior from more than one class by copying some of the operations of a second class and delegating calls to an instance of that class. Both of these extension techniques, however, require that you know at compile time what behaviors you want to add. If you need to add behavior to an object without changing its class, you may be able to apply the TEMPLATE METHOD (Chapter 21), COMMAND (Chapter 24), DECORATOR (Chapter 27), or VISITOR (Chapter 29) design patterns.

Ordinary extension also adds behavior to individual instances of a class. You may need to add behaviors that apply to a *collection* of instances of your class. The ITERATOR pattern addresses one such case.

| If you intend to | Apply the pattern |
|---|---|
| • Allow a client to hook in an operation at a step in an algorithm | TEMPLATE METHOD (Chapter 21) |
| • Let a client outfit your code with an operation to execute in response to an event | COMMAND (Chapter 24) |
| • Attach additional responsibilities to an object dynamically | DECORATOR (Chapter 27) |
| • Provide a way to access a collection of instances of a class that you create | ITERATOR (Chapter 28) |
| • Allow for the addition of new operations to a class without changing the class | VISITOR (Chapter 29) |

Extension-oriented patterns address contexts in which you need to add behavior specific to a collection of objects or to add new behaviors to an object without altering the object's class. For example, when you need to be able to add new behavior to an object dynamically, you can apply the DECORATOR pattern.

# 27

# DECORATOR

ORDINARILY, AN OBJECT inherits behaviors from its superclasses. As earlier chapters have shown, you can apply the STATE and the STRATEGY patterns to alter the behavior of an object dynamically. Like STATE and STRATEGY, the DECORATOR pattern relies on polymorphism, but DECORATOR combines polymorphism with delegation to let you *extend* an object's behavior. The intent of DECORATOR is to let you compose an object's behavior dynamically.

## A Classic Example of DECORATOR: Streams

The Java class libraries provide a classic example of the DECORATOR pattern in the overall design of Java input and output streams. A **stream** is a serial collection of bytes or characters, such as those that appear in a document. In Java, each stream object usually contains another stream object to which it forwards its operations. This structure is typical of DECORATOR.

The DECORATOR pattern arranges for each decorator object to contain another decorator object. In this regard, a decorator is like a slim composite whose elements each have a single child. Unlike the COMPOSITE pattern, whose purpose is to compose aggregate objects, the purpose of DECORATOR is to compose *behavior*.

Structurally, DECORATOR arranges classes in a hierarchy and distributes operations across this hierarchy. Each class in the hierarchy typically has a constructor that requires another instance of a class in the hierarchy. For example, Figure 27.1 shows a portion of the OutputStream hierarchy from the Java class libraries.

**FIGURE 27.1:** Java
input/output (I/O)
streams provide a
classic example of
DECORATOR.

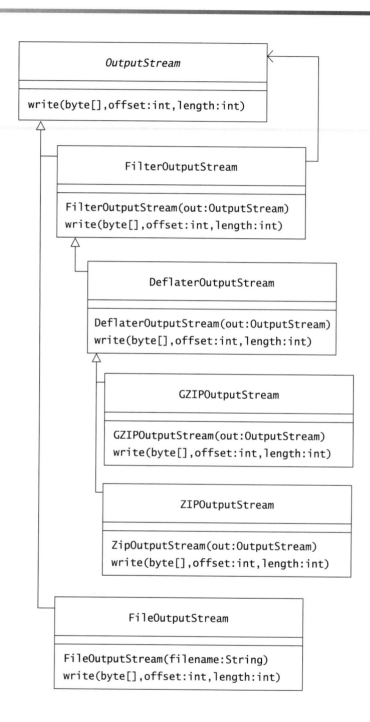

DECORATOR classes typically implement their operations by relying on the decorator object they receive in their constructors. For example, the GZIPOutputStream class implements its write() operations by compressing the bytes it receives and then writing them to the OutputStream object that its constructor requires. In other words, the GZIPOutputStream class adds the behavior of compression to the OutputStream object it receives. This is typical of the intent of Decorator.

Requiring an OutputStream object in each OutputStream constructor is a recursive idea. Like Composite, the Decorator pattern requires some classes in a hierarchy to act as leaf nodes. For example, you can instantiate the FileOutputStream class without already having an OutputStream object.

Most of Java's stream classes are part of the java.io package, but the DeflaterOutputStream, GZIPOutputStream, and ZipOutputStream classes that Figure 27.1 shows are part of the package java.util.zip. The ZipOutputStream class lets you create a compressed file with multiple entries, whereas the GZIPOutputStream class compresses a single input file. Which of these classes you choose depends on how you want to "decorate" the output. For example, you can wrap a GZIPOutputStream object around a FileOutputStream object to create a zipped version of an existing file:

```
package com.oozinoz.applications;
import java.io.*;
import java.util.zip.*;
public class ShowGzip
{
    public static void main(String args[])
    throws IOException
    {
        String fileName = "demo.doc";
        java.net.URL url =
            ClassLoader.getSystemResource(fileName);
        InputStream in = url.openStream();

        GZIPOutputStream out =
            new GZIPOutputStream(
                new FileOutputStream(
                    url.getFile() + ".gz"));

        byte[] data = new byte[100];
        while (true)
        {
            int n = in.read(data);
            if (n == -1)
            {
```

```
                    break;
                }
                out.write(data, 0, n);
            }
            out.close();
            in.close();
        }
    }
```

This program uses the `ClassLoader` class to find the URL (uniform resource locator) of the `demo.doc` file. If you set the class path for the `ShowGzip` class to include the parent directory of a `demo.doc` file, the `getSystemResource()` method will find it. The `ShowGzip` class's `main()` method tacks a `.gz` extension onto the output file and places it into the same directory as the input. The program creates a compressed `demo.doc.gz` file that any zip utility can decompress.

The `OutputStream` class has many more subclasses, and you can create your own. The `FilterOutputStream` class is designed specifically to simplify the creation of new output streams. This class provides stub implementations of the `OutputStream` class methods that forward their operations to the underlying stream. You can subclass `FilterOutputStream` and override just the methods that you need. In this regard, `FilterOutputStream` is similar to its counterpart, `FilterWriter`.

In addition to its support for *byte* streams, Java includes a somewhat parallel collection of classes that manage streams of *characters*. Like the byte stream hierarchies, Java provides `Reader` and `Writer` hierarchies for managing character streams. These hierarchies include `Filter` subclasses that, like their byte-oriented counterparts, are designed for subclassing. The `FilterWriter` class, as shown in Figure 27.2, has three versions of `write()` methods.

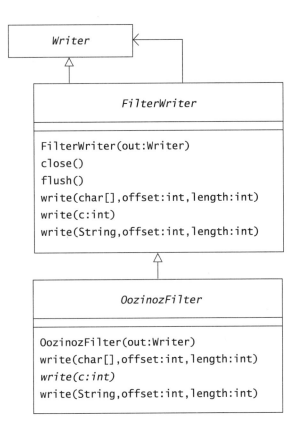

**FIGURE 27.2:** Oozinoz developers use the `OozinozFilter` class as the superclass for classes that decorate output character streams.

The `OozinozFilter` class directs its two concrete `write()` methods to call its abstract `write()`, so that subclasses have only one method to override:

```
package com.oozinoz.io;
import java.io.*;
public abstract class OozinozFilter extends FilterWriter
{
    protected OozinozFilter(Writer out)
    {
        super(out);
    }

    public void write(char cbuf[], int off, int len)
    throws IOException
```

```
    {
        for (int i = 0; i < len; i++)
        {
            write(cbuf[i]);
        }
    }

    public abstract void write(int c) throws IOException;

    public void write(String s, int off, int len)
    throws IOException
    {
        write(s.toCharArray(), off, len);
    }
}
```

Oozinoz has a variety of output character stream decorators that manipulate text for display in the company's Web site. Figure 27.3 shows the Oozinoz decorators.

For example, the `WrapFilter` class compresses whitespace and wraps text at a specified line length. (The contents of `WrapFilter.java` and all the filter classes are available at oozinoz.com.) The following program line-wraps text in an input file and puts it in title case:

**FIGURE 27.3:** The Oozinoz filters can decorate a `Writer` object with behaviors that manipulate ad copy text for a Web site.

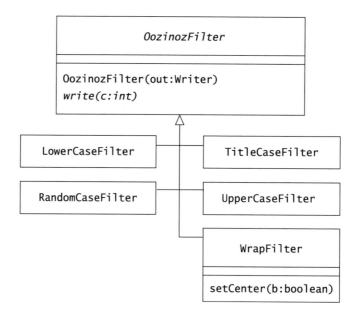

```java
package com.oozinoz.applications;
import java.io.*;
import com.oozinoz.io.*;
public class ShowFilters
{
    public static void main(String args[])
    throws IOException
    {
        BufferedReader in =
            new BufferedReader(new FileReader(args[0]));

        Writer out = new FileWriter(args[1]);
        out = new WrapFilter(new BufferedWriter(out), 40);
        out = new TitleCaseFilter(out);


        while (true)
        {
            String s = in.readLine();
            if (s == null)
            {
                break;
            }
            out.write(s + "\n");
        }
        out.close();
        in.close();
    }
}
```

The BufferedReader class provides the ability to read one line at a time from a file. The ShowFilters program creates a FileWriter object and decorates it with behaviors to wrap the text at 40 characters and to title-case the text. Suppose that a file named demo.txt contains:

```
The "SPACESHOT" shell       hovers
          at 100 meters for 2 to 3
minutes,       erupting star bursts  every 10 seconds that
generate            abundant reading-level light for a
typical    stadium.
```

Running this file through the ShowFilters program cleans up the text:

```
> java -classpath \oozinoz\classes com.oozinoz.applica-
tions.ShowFilters demo.txt demo-out.txt
```

```
>type demo-out.txt

The "Spaceshot" Shell Hovers At 100
Meters For 2 To 3 Minutes, Erupting Star
Bursts Every 10 Seconds That Generate
Abundant Reading-level Light For A
Typical Stadium.
```

## CHALLENGE 27.1

If you want to direct output to System.out instead of to a file, you can create a Writer object that directs its output to System.out:

```
Writer out = new PrintWriter(System.out);
```

Write a snippet of code to define a Writer object that wraps text at 15 characters, centers the text, sets the text to random casing, and directs the output to System.out.

*A solution appears on page 429.*

The code for most of the filter classes is simple. For example:

```
import java.io.*;
public class LowerCaseFilter extends OozinozFilter
{
    protected LowerCaseFilter(Writer out)
    {
        super(out);
    }
    public void write(int c) throws IOException
    {
        out.write(Character.toLowerCase((char) c));
    }
}
```

The code for the `TitleCaseFilter` class is a bit more complex, as it has to keep track of whether the stream is in whitespace:

```java
import java.io.*;
public class TitleCaseFilter extends OozinozFilter
{
    boolean inWhite = true;
    protected TitleCaseFilter(Writer out)
    {
        super(out);
    }

    public void write(int c) throws IOException
    {
        out.write(
            inWhite
                ? Character.toUpperCase((char) c)
                : Character.toLowerCase((char) c));
        inWhite = Character.isWhitespace((char) c) ||
                c == '"';
    }
}
```

---

**CHALLENGE 27.2**

Write the code for RandomCaseFilter.java.

*A solution appears on page 430.*

---

Input and output streams provide a classic example of how the DECORATOR pattern lets you assemble the behavior of an object at runtime. Another important application of DECORATOR occurs when you need to create mathematical functions at runtime.

## Function Decorators

You can combine DECORATOR with the idea of treating functions as objects to allow for runtime composition of new functions. In Chapter 4, FACADE, you refactored an application that shows the flight path of a nonexploding aerial shell. The original code calculated the path in the paintComponent() method of a JPanel subclass:

```java
public void paintComponent(Graphics g)
{
    super.paintComponent(g); // paint the background
    int nPoint = 101;
    double w = getWidth();
    double h = getHeight();
    int[] x = new int[nPoint];
    int[] y = new int[nPoint];

    for (int i = 0; i < nPoint; i++)
    {
        // t goes 0 to 1
        double t = ((double) i) / (nPoint - 1);
        // x goes 0 to w
        x[i] = (int) (t * w);
        // y is h at t = 0 and t = 1, and y is 0 at t = .5
        y[i] = (int) (4 * h * (t - .5) * (t - .5));
    }
    g.drawPolyline(x, y, nPoint);
}
```

This method hard-codes the function it plots. Suppose that you want to be able to create functions for x and y at runtime. A first step is to apply polymorphism: Make the name of the method fixed, and provide classes with varying implementations of this method. Figure 27.4 shows a FunPanel class that accepts functions to plot.

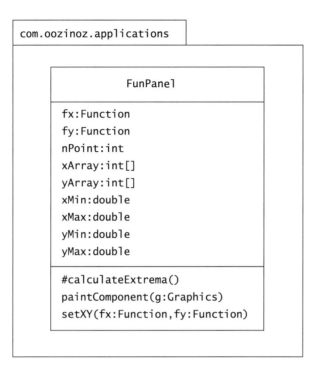

**FIGURE 27.4:** The Fun-Panel class accepts x and y functions to plot.

The setXY() method in the FunPanel class accepts x and y functions and calculates the minimum and maximum values of these curves:

```
public void setXY(Function fx, Function fy)
{
    this.fx = fx;
    this.fy = fy;
    calculateExtrema();
    repaint();
}
```

The functions that the setXY() method accepts are parametric functions of time. Any code that works with the curve of a function will evaluate the function as time varies from 0 to 1. We shall see that this approach will let us plot parabolas, circles, and other types of curves for which y is not strictly a function of x. The idea that time varies from 0 to

1 appears several places in the function-plotting code, such as the calculation of the extreme values of the functions:

```
protected void calculateExtrema()
{
    for (int i = 0; i < nPoint; i++)
    {
        double t = ((double) i) / (nPoint - 1);
        double dx = fx.f(t);
        double dy = fy.f(t);
        if (i == 0 || dx > xMax)
        {
            xMax = dx;
        }
        if (i == 0 || dx < xMin)
        {
            xMin = dx;
        }

        if (i == 0 || dy > yMax)
        {
            yMax = dy;
        }
        if (i == 0 || dy < yMin)
        {
            yMin = dy;
        }
    }
}
```

The `paintComponent()` method also lets time vary from 0 to 1 and scales the curves to fill the panel:

```
public void paintComponent(Graphics g)
{
    super.paintComponent(g);
    double h = (double) (getHeight() - 1);
    double w = (double) (getWidth() - 1);

    for (int i = 0; i < nPoint; i++)
    {
        double t = ((double) i) / (nPoint - 1);
        xArray[i] = (int)
            (w * (fx.f(t) - xMin) / (xMax - xMin));
        yArray[i] = (int)
```

```
                (h - h * (fy.f(t) - yMin) / (yMax - yMin));
    }
    g.setColor(Color.black);
    g.drawPolyline(xArray, yArray, nPoint);
}
```

The FunPanel class lets you supply various implementations of the f()
method in separate classes. If you were to implement the f() method
directly, you would wind up with classes like FlightPathX and Flight-
PathY, which provide x and y functions. Rather than creating new classes
for each new function, DECORATOR lets you assemble a function from an
existing hierarchy. Figure 27.5 shows a hierarchy of function classes that
implement a common operation f(). These classes appear in the com.ooz-
inoz.function package.

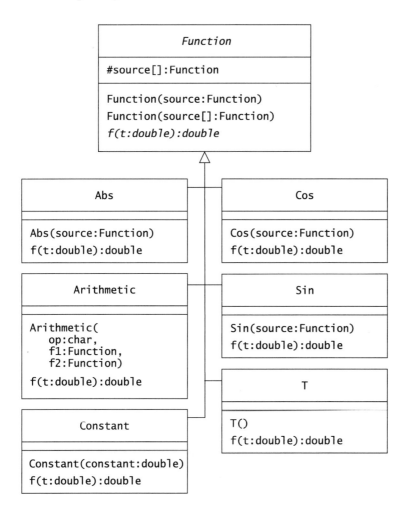

**FIGURE 27.5:** Each
subclass of Function
implements f(t) in a
way that corresponds
to the class name.

You can use classes from the Function hierarchy to compose, for example, the flight path of a dud:

```
package com.oozinoz.applications;
import com.oozinoz.function.*;
public class ShowFunFlight
{
    public static void main(String args[])
    {
        FunPanel p = new FunPanel();
        p.setPreferredSize(
            new java.awt.Dimension(200, 200));
        Function x = new T();

        //     y = 1 - 4 * (t - .5)**2;
        Function ft =
            new Arithmetic('-', new T(), new Constant(.5));
        Function y =
            new Arithmetic(
                '-',
                new Constant(1),
                new Arithmetic(
                    '*',
                    new Constant(4),
                    new Arithmetic('*', ft, ft)));
        p.setXY(x, y);
        com.oozinoz.ui.SwingFacade.launch(
            p, " Flight Path");
    }
}
```

Figure 27.6 shows the results of this code, as well as the following code, which plots a circle without requiring a new class:

```
package com.oozinoz.applications;
import com.oozinoz.function.*;
public class ShowFunZone
{
    public static void main(String args[])
    {
        FunPanel p = new FunPanel();
        p.setPreferredSize(
            new java.awt.Dimension(200, 200));
```

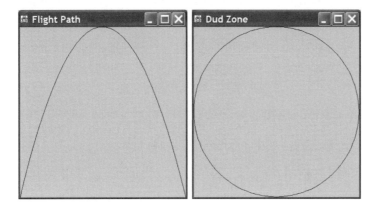

```
        Function theta =
            new Arithmetic(
                '*',
                new Constant(2 * Math.PI),
                new T());
        Function x = new Cos(theta);
        Function y = new Sin(theta);
        p.setXY(x, y);
        com.oozinoz.ui.SwingFacade.launch(p, " Dud Zone");
    }
}
```

Most of the classes in the Function hierarchy work by wrapping their namesake function around another function that they receive in a constructor. The Function class holds an array of "sources," the source functions that each instance of a subclass will wrap:

```
package com.oozinoz.function;
public abstract class Function
{
    protected Function[] source;
    public Function(Function[] source)
    {
        this.source = source;
    }
    public Function(Function f)
    {
        this(new Function[] {f});
    }
    public abstract double f(double t);
}
```

Most `Function` subclasses wrap a single function. Consider the code for `Abs.java`:

```
package com.oozinoz.function;
public class Abs extends Function
{
    public Abs(Function f)
    {
        super(f);
    }
    public double f(double t)
    {
        return Math.abs(source[0].f(t));
    }
}
```

The constructor for the `Abs` class collaborates with its superclass to store a source function in `source[0]`.

The `f()` method of class `Abs` shows DECORATOR at work. This method applies an absolute-value function *to the value of another function* at the given time. In other words, the `Abs.f()` method decorates its source function with an absolute-value function. This simple idea lets us compose an infinite number of functions from a small hierarchy of classes. The code for the `Cos` and `Sin` classes is almost identical to the code for the `Abs` class.

The `T` class provides a trivial identity function:

```
package com.oozinoz.function;
public class T extends Function
{
    public T()
    {
        super(new Function[0]);
    }
    public double f(double t)
    {
        return t;
    }
}
```

The `T` class lets you model functions that vary linearly with time. For example, in the `ShowFunZone` class, the arc of a circle varies from 0 to 2 times pi as time varies from 0 to 1:

```
Function theta = new Arithmetic(
                    '*',
                    new Constant(2 * Math.PI),
                    new T());
```

The Constant class represents a value that does not change over time:

```
package com.oozinoz.function;
public class Constant extends Function
{
    private double constant;
    public Constant(double constant)
    {
        super(new Function[0]);
        this.constant = constant;
    }
    public double f(double t)
    {
        return constant;
    }
}
```

The Arithmetic class requires an operator and two Function arguments:

```
package com.oozinoz.function;
public class Arithmetic extends Function
{
    protected char operator;

    public Arithmetic(
        char operator,
        Function f1,
        Function f2)
    {
        super(new Function[] { f1, f2 });
        this.operator = operator;
    }
    public double f(double t)
    {
        switch (operator)
        {
            case '+' :
                return source[0].f(t) + source[1].f(t);
```

```
                                  case '-' :
                                      return source[0].f(t) - source[1].f(t);
                                  case '*' :
                                      return source[0].f(t) * source[1].f(t);
                                  case '/' :
                                      return source[0].f(t) / source[1].f(t);
                                  default :
                                      return 0;
                          }
                      }
                  }
```

---

## CHALLENGE 27.3

Write the code for an Exp class that wraps Math.exp() around its source function.

*A solution appears on page 431.*

---

Suppose that the brightness of a star is a sine wave that decreases exponentially:

$$brightness = e^{-5t} \cdot \sin(\pi t)$$

As before, a plot of brightness versus time requires no new classes:

```
package com.oozinoz.applications;
import com.oozinoz.function.*;
public class ShowBrightness
{
    public static void main(String args[])
    {
        FunPanel p = new FunPanel();
        p.setPreferredSize(
            new java.awt.Dimension(200, 200));

        // ??
        Function brightness =
        // ??
```

```
        p.setXY(new T(), brightness);
        com.oozinoz.ui.SwingFacade.launch(
            p, " Brightness");
    }
}
```

This code produces the plot in Figure 27.7.

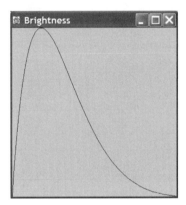

**FIGURE 27.7:** A star's brightness peaks quickly and then tails off.

---

**CHALLENGE 27.4**

Write the code to define a brightness object that represents the brightness function.

*A solution appears on page 431.*

---

You can add other functions to the Function hierarchy as needed. For example, you might add Random, Sqrt, and Tan classes. You can also create new hierarchies that work on different types, such as strings, or that have a different notion of how to define the f() operation. For example, you might define f() as a two- or three-dimensional function of time. Regardless of the hierarchy you create, if you apply DECORATOR and you wrap functions around each other, you will develop a rich set of functions that you can compose at runtime.

## Decorating without DECORATOR

Having seen some good examples of DECORATOR, it is important to note that similar designs allow for "decorating" an object without applying the DECORATOR pattern. Two areas that can be mistaken for DECORATOR are the use of Swing borders and listeners.

A GUI framework developer might apply DECORATOR in establishing how GUI components get borders. To do so, you can create a hierarchy of components that expect another component in their constructor and distribute a paint() method across this hierarchy. Border classes in this hierarchy would paint their border and then forward the paint() call to the component they wrap. Swing, however, does not work this way.

Swing anticipates that any component might need a border, and so the JComponent class includes a setBorder() method. If you want to "decorate" a component with more than one border, you can apply the CompoundBorder class. The following code gives an example with results shown in Figure 27.8.

```
package com.oozinoz.applications;
import javax.swing.*;
import javax.swing.border.*;
import java.awt.*;
import com.oozinoz.ui.*;
public class ShowBorders
{
    protected static JButton createButton(String label)
    {
        JButton b = new JButton(label);
        b.setFont(SwingFacade.getStandardFont());
        b.setFocusPainted(false);
        return b;
    }

    public static void main(String[] args)
    {
        JButton ignite = createButton("Ignite");
        JButton launch = createButton("Launch");
        launch.setBorder(
            new CompoundBorder(
                new LineBorder(Color.black, 4),
```

```
            new CompoundBorder(
                new BevelBorder(BevelBorder.RAISED),
                new EmptyBorder(10, 10, 10, 10))));

        JPanel p = new JPanel();
        p.add(ignite);
        p.add(launch);
        SwingFacade.launch(p, " Borders");
    }
}
```

**FIGURE 27.8:** Borders can make a component more appealing.

If you think of painting a border as a behavior, you might design borders by using the DECORATOR pattern. On the other hand, if you think of borders as attributes, there is no need compose behavior and no need for DECORATOR.

Another feature of Java that might be mistaken for DECORATOR is the ability to add behaviors at runtime through the use of listeners. Suppose that you introduce a rollover effect for a button by listening to the mouse, as the following code and Figure 27.9 show.

```
package com.oozinoz.applications;
import com.oozinoz.ui.*;
import java.awt.event.*;
import java.awt.*;
import javax.swing.*;
public class ShowListen
{
    protected static JButton createButton(String label)
    {
        JButton b = new JButton(label);
        b.setFont(SwingFacade.getStandardFont());
        b.setFocusPainted(false);
        return b;
    }

    public static void main(String[] args)
    {
```

```
JPanel p = new JPanel();
p.add(createButton("Normal"));
final JButton b = createButton("Nifty");


b.addMouseListener
(
    new MouseAdapter()
    {
        public void mouseEntered(MouseEvent e)
        {
            b.setBackground(Color.cyan);
            b.repaint();
        }
        public void mouseExited(MouseEvent e)
        {
            b.setBackground(Color.lightGray);
            b.repaint();
        }
    }
);

b.setBackground(Color.lightGray);
p.add(b);
SwingFacade.launch(p, " Rollover");
    }
}
```

**FIGURE 27.9:** Listeners let you add behavior, such as rollover effects, without creating new component subclasses.

---

**CHALLENGE 27.5**

The ShowListen program outfits a JButton object at runtime with a new behavior, interacting with the cursor position. But this design is not an instance of DECORATOR. Why not?

*A solution appears on page 432.*

## Summary

When you have an object type that needs a variety of behaviors that you might compose in various ways, the DECORATOR pattern offers a flexible alternative to creating a class for every possible behavioral combination. The Java class libraries provide a classic example of DECORATOR in the implementation of input and output streams. In application code, you can apply DECORATOR to set up function hierarchies. This lets you create a large family of function objects from a fixed set of function classes.

It is easy to mistake examples of "decoration" in a design as instances of DECORATOR. A design may allow runtime customization of an object's attributes and its behavior without using DECORATOR. The intent of DECORATOR is to let you compose an object's behavior from a collection of cooperating classes.

# 28

# ITERATOR

IN ORDINARY DEVELOPMENT, you add behavior by extending classes with new methods. Occasionally, though, you need to add behavior to a *collection* of instances of the classes you create. The Java class libraries provide many features for working with collections, including behaviors for sorting, shuffling, reversing, and iterating over a collection. You may find, however, that you need iteration behaviors that go beyond those built into Java. In particular, if you need to add type safety to iteration, or if you need to create a new type of collection, you will probably need to develop your own iterator code to walk through the collection. The intent of the ITERATOR pattern is to provide a way to access the elements of collection sequentially.

## Type-Safe Collections

When you pass a collection of objects to a client, you will often imply that the contents of the collection are instances of a certain type. For example, if you have a static method `getPromotionalFireworks()` that returns an instance of `List`, the implication is that the list contains instances of the `Firework` class. You can strengthen this type of contract by creating a `FireworkList` class that guarantees that its contents are instances of `Firework`. Figure 28.1 shows this class.

**FIGURE 28.1:** The
FireworkList class
provides type-specific
lists for Firework
objects. The Itr class
is an inner class for
FireworkList.

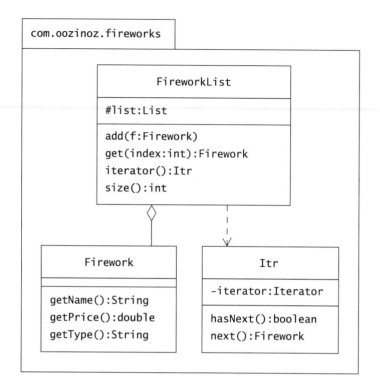

The FireworkList class stores its objects in a regular instance of Array-
List. The add() method ensures that only Firework objects enter the list.
For example, the Promo class creates and returns a list of promotional fire-
works, using a FireworkList object:

```
package com.oozinoz.fireworks;
import com.oozinoz.units.*;
public class Promo implements UnitConstants
{
    public static FireworkList getPromotionalFireworks()
    {
        FireworkList fl = new FireworkList();
        fl.add(new Sparkler("Brightful", .35));
        fl.add(new Firecracker("Frightful", .19));
        fl.add
        (
            new Rocket(
                "Heightful",
                33.95,
                (Length) METER.times(300))
```

```
        );
        return fl;
    }
}
```

The get() method in the FireworkList class relieves clients from having to cast its return value. To complete this thought, it is useful to provide an iterator that also relieves clients from casting and from getting a possible ClassCastException. The Itr class is useful only to the FireworkList class, so it is a good idea to make it an inner class:

```
package com.oozinoz.fireworks;
import java.util.*;
public class FireworkList
{
    protected List list = new ArrayList();
    public class Itr
    {
        private Iterator iterator = list.iterator();
        public boolean hasNext()
        {
            return iterator.hasNext();
        }
        public Firework next()
        {
            return (Firework) iterator.next();
        }
    }

    public void add(Firework f)
    {
        list.add(f);
    }

    public Firework get(int index)
    {
        return (Firework) list.get(index);
    }

    public FireworkList.Itr iterator()
    {
        return new Itr();
    }

    public int size()
    {
```

```
            return list.size();
        }
    }
```

Note that the `Itr` class does not implement the `Iterator` interface from the `java.util` package. The `Iterator` interface requires a `remove()` method that is not appropriate in this code. By not implementing any interface, however, the code requires clients to refer to the iterator's type with the type `Firework.Itr`.

A client can iterate over a `FireworkList` collection without having to cast its results:

```
package com.oozinoz.applications;
import com.oozinoz.fireworks.*;
public class ShowFireworkList
{
    public static void main(String[] args)
    {
        FireworkList flist =
            Promo.getPromotionalFireworks();

        ?? i = ??

        while (i.hasNext())
        {
            Firework f = i.next();
            System.out.println(
                f.getName()
                    + ", $" + f.getPrice()
                    + ", "  + f.getType());
        }
    }
}
```

Running this program prints out:

```
Brightful, $0.35, Sparkler
Frightful, $0.19, Firecracker
Heightful, $33.95, Rocket
```

---

**CHALLENGE 28.1**

Fill in the missing code in `ShowFireworkList` to instantiate the iterator.

*A solution appears on page 432.*

---

When you create a type-specific collection, you may want to inherit behavior from an existing collection, such as `ArrayList`. In this approach, you have to use different method names for `get()` and `iterator()`, as you can't change the return type of an overridden method. You will also find that using utilities, such as the `sort()` and `min()` methods of the `Collections` class, will force clients back into using casts. If you don't want to give clients this much flexibility, you can leave your type-safe class as a subclass of `Object` and add utilities as your clients need them. For example, if a client needs to know the cheapest firework in a list, you might add to `FireworkList` the following method:

```
public Firework cheapest()
{
    Comparator c = new Comparator()
        {
            public int compare(Object o1, Object o2)
            {
                Firework f1 = (Firework) o1;
                Firework f2 = (Firework) o2;
                return (int)
                    (100 * (f1.getPrice() - f2.getPrice()));
            }
        };
    return (Firework) Collections.min(list, c);
}
```

This code creates and applies a Comparator object that reflects the client's specific need to know the cheapest firework. If the client wants, say, a list of fireworks sorted by price, you can add yet another method to the FireworkList class. If you don't think that you can keep up with client demands, make your collection class a subclass of ArrayList or another class from java.util. The tradeoff is between offering flexibility versus providing type safety and applying domain-specific knowledge about what is important about your collection.

By creating type-specific collections, you can strengthen the contract between your code and your client's code, reducing the chance for defects. Iterators are a natural extension to collections, and it is usually worthwhile to accompany a type-specific collection with a type-specific iterator. Another occasion for supplying an iterator may occur when you create a new collection type, such as a composite.

## Iterating Over a Composite

In Challenge 5.3, from Chapter 5, COMPOSITE, you developed recursive behaviors that execute by traversing a composite structure. Iterators introduce a new challenge when working with composites, because you want to return control to a client as you traverse each node.

You might think that you would need a new iterator class for each domain-specific composite you model. In fact, you can design a fairly reusable composite iterator, although you have to arrange for domain classes to be able to instantiate your iterator. You may also need to handle composites that contain cycles.

As an example of a composite structure that you might want to iterate over, recall the ProcessComponent hierarchy that Chapter 5 introduced. Figure 28.2 shows the process composite hierarchy that Oozinoz uses for modeling the manufacturing work flows that produce various types of fireworks.

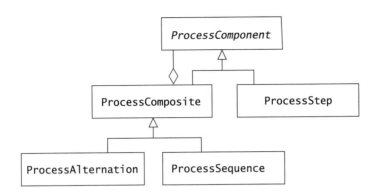

**FIGURE 28.2:** Manufacturing process flows at Oozinoz are composites.

Figure 28.3 shows the structure of the specific process flow that Oozinoz uses for making aerial shells. The code that creates the process object model creates ProcessComponent objects in static methods:

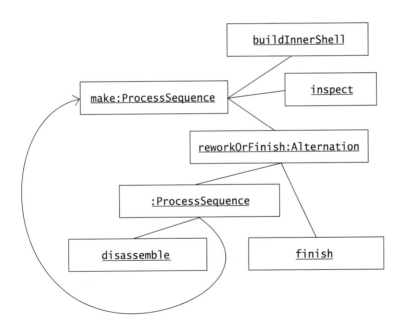

**FIGURE 28.3:** The process flow for making aerial shells is a cyclic composite. Each leaf node in this diagram is an instance of ProcessStep. The remaining nodes are instances of Process-Composite.

```java
package com.oozinoz.process;
public class ShellProcess
{
    protected static ProcessSequence make;

    public static ProcessSequence make()
    {
        if (make == null)
        {
            make = new ProcessSequence(
                "Make an aerial shell");
            make.add(buildInnerShell());
            make.add(inspect());
            make.add(reworkOrFinish());
        }
        return make;
    }

    protected static ProcessStep buildInnerShell()
    {
        return new ProcessStep("Build inner shell");
    }

    protected static ProcessStep inspect()
    {
        return new ProcessStep("Inspect");
    }

    protected static ProcessAlternation reworkOrFinish()
    {
        return new ProcessAlternation(
            "Rework inner shell, or complete shell",
            new ProcessComponent[] { rework(), finish()});
    }

    protected static ProcessSequence rework()
    {
        return new ProcessSequence(
            "Rework",
            new ProcessComponent[] { disassemble(), make()});
    }

    protected static ProcessStep disassemble()
    {
        return new ProcessStep("Disassemble");
    }
```

```
    protected static ProcessStep finish()
    {
        return new ProcessStep(
            "Finish: Attach lift, insert fusing, wrap");
    }

}
```

Suppose that you want to provide an iterator for the `ProcessComponent` hierarchy. Mechanics for iterating over a composite node will differ from those for iterating over a leaf node. These two types of iterators will presumably have some behavior or attributes in common, so you can create a hierarchy of these iterators, such as the classes that Figure 28.4 shows. The classes in Figure 28.4 provide the `hasNext()` and `next()` methods that you might expect from an iterator, as well as a `depth()` method that will tell the current depth of an iterator within a composite.

The `CompositeIterator` class needs to create new "subiterators" as it traverses over the children of a composite object. For each child, a `CompositeIterator` object must create either a new leaf node iterator or a new composite iterator, depending on the type of the child. This is an

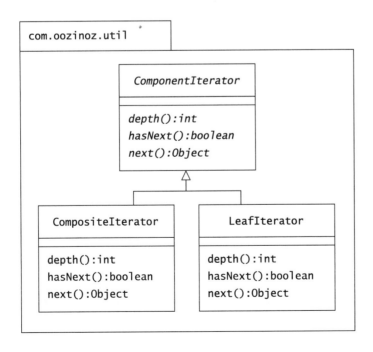

**FIGURE 28.4:** The `ComponentIterator` hierarchy anticipates different behavior for iterating over composites and leaves.

opportunity to apply polymorphism, letting the nodes decide which type of iterator to instantiate. If you have access to the collection classes that you want to iterate over, you can add an iterator() operation and let leaf and composite classes implement this operation differently. If you introduce an Iterable interface, such as Figure 28.5 shows, the CompositeIterator class can call the iterator() method for each of its children. The iterator() method produces an iterator that the composite must exhaust before getting an iterator for the next child.

The ProcessComposite class can implement iterator() to return an instance of CompositeIterator. The ProcessStep class can implement this method to return an instance of LeafIterator.

**FIGURE 28.5:** You can extend the ProcessComponent hierarchy to implement an Iterable interface, allowing CompositeIterator to build new iterators for each child of a composite node.

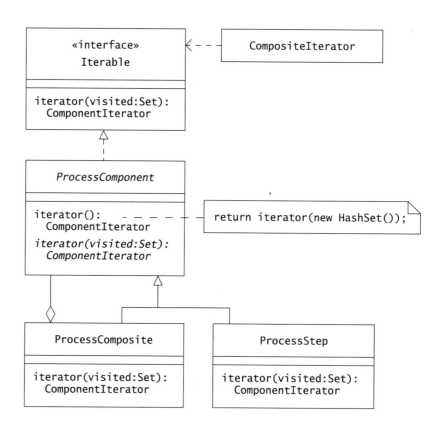

---

**CHALLENGE 28.2**

What pattern are you applying if you let classes in the ProcessComponent hierarchy implement iterator() to create instances of an appropriate iterator class?

*A solution appears on page 433.*

---

The ComponentIterator hierarchy is somewhat difficult to develop, but it is highly reusable and easy to apply. For example, a short program can print the nodes of a composite, using indentation to show each node's depth:

```
package com.oozinoz.applications;
import com.oozinoz.process.*;
import com.oozinoz.util.*;
public class ShowProcessIteration
{
    public static void main(String[] args)
    {
        ProcessComponent pc = ShellProcess.make();
        ComponentIterator i = pc.iterator();
        while (i.hasNext())
        {
            for (int j = 0; j < i.depth() * 4; j++)
            {
                System.out.print(' ');
            }
            System.out.println(i.next());
        }
    }
}
```

This program prints out:

```
Make an aerial shell
    Build inner shell
    Inspect
    Rework inner shell, or complete shell
        Rework
            Disassemble
        Finish: Attach lift, insert fusing, wrap
```

Iterating over a cyclic composite is not the best way to produce a textual description of the composite. For a composite pretty-printer, see page 346 in Chapter 29, VISITOR. The printout here demonstrates that the code completes without entering an infinite loop, a testament to the Component-Iterator hierarchy's ability to iterate over a cyclic composite. The output also shows that the iterator correctly tracks the depth of each node.

To write the code for the composite iterator, you can start at the top of the hierarchy, with the ComponentIterator class. This class defines the common operations for the hierarchy and holds a node object that represents either a leaf or an interior node. For example, when iterating over a process composite, the node object will be an instance of either ProcessStep or ProcessComposite.

```java
package com.oozinoz.util;
import java.util.*;
public abstract class ComponentIterator
{
    protected Object node;
    protected Set visited = new HashSet();


    public ComponentIterator(Object node, Set visited)
    {
        this.node = node;
        this.visited = visited;
    }
    public abstract int depth();
    public abstract boolean hasNext();
    public abstract Object next();
}
```

The `ComponentIterator` class includes a `visited` set that can keep track of whether an iterator has already traversed a node in a composite. For example, the aerial shell process flow starts with a composite `make` step that contains a rework step that contains, again, the `make` step. When you write an iterator for a composite that may contain cycles, you must ensure that you do not step into an infinite loop.

As with composites, the terminal class for a composite iterator is comparatively simple:

```
package com.oozinoz.util;
import java.util.*;
public class LeafIterator extends ComponentIterator
{
    public LeafIterator(Object node, Set visited)
    {
        super(node, visited);
    }
    public int depth()
    {
        return 0;
    }
    public boolean hasNext()
    {
        return !visited.contains(node);
    }
    public Object next()
    {
        if (visited.contains(node))
        {
            return null;
        }
        visited.add(node);
        return node;
    }
}
```

Note that the depth of an iterator is different from the depth of a node in a tree.

The depth of an iterator depends on the depth of its subiterator. Leaf iterators do not have subiterators, so their depth is always 0. The value of `depth()` for a `CompositeIterator` object is 1 plus the depth of its subiterator:

```
public int depth()
{
    if (subiterator != null)
    {
        return subiterator.depth() + 1;
    }
    return 0;
}
```

The `CompositeIterator` has to walk across the children of the component—a `ProcessComposite`, say—over which it is iterating. The `CompositeIterator` class can use a `children` variable to hold this iterator. Each child may be an arbitrarily deep composite, so the `Composite-Iterator` class needs a `subiterator` object to traverse the component that each child represents:

```
package com.oozinoz.util;
import java.util.*;
public class CompositeIterator extends ComponentIterator
{
    protected Iterator children;
    protected ComponentIterator subiterator;
    protected Object peek;


    public CompositeIterator(
        Object node, List components, Set visited)
    {
        super(node, visited);
        children = components.iterator();
    }
//...
}
```

The `CompositeIterator` uses a `peek` object to facilitate the implementation of `hasNext()`. It can be difficult to tell whether a (possibly cyclic) composite has a next node. A simple workaround is to have `hasNext()` search for the next value, and report whether or not this search was successful. The `CompositeIterator` class employs this approach:

```
public boolean hasNext()
{
    if (peek == null)
    {
        peek = next();
    }
    return peek != null;
}
public Object next() {
    if (peek != null)
    {
        Object o = peek;
        peek = null;
        return o;
    }
    if (!visited.contains(node))
    {
        visited.add(node);
        return node;
    }
    return nextDescendant();
}
```

The next() method checks whether a peek value is loaded and then checks whether it has reported the interior node of the composite that is being traversed. If not, the next() method transfers control to next-Descendant().

The nextDescendant() method exhausts the composite beneath the current child, moving onto the next child, if necessary:

```
protected Object nextDescendant()
{
    while (true)
    {
        if (subiterator != null)
        {
            if (subiterator.hasNext())
            {
                return subiterator.next();
            }
        }
        if (!children.hasNext())
        {
```

```
                return null;
            }
            Iterable i = (Iterable) children.next();
            if (!visited.contains(i))
            {
                subiterator = i.iterator(visited);
            }
        }
    }
}
```

There is a fair amount of judgment in how you design a composite iterator. A critical decision in the design just described is that we can expect to be able to add `iterator()` methods to the domain classes. You will have to use a different approach if you can't touch the classes over which you want to iterate. In addition, you may find that you want to introduce other behaviors to your composite iterators.

Suppose that you decide to add a `setShowInterior()` method to the `ComponentIterator` class. This lets you iterate over just the leaves of a composite:

```java
package com.oozinoz.applications;
import com.oozinoz.util.*;
import com.oozinoz.process.*;
public class ShowLeavesOnly
{
    public static void main(String[] args)
    {
        ProcessComponent pc = ShellProcess.make();
        ComponentIterator i = pc.iterator();
        i.setShowInterior(false);
        while (i.hasNext())
        {
            System.out.println(i.next());
        }
    }
}
```

This program prints:

```
Build inner shell
Inspect
Disassemble
Finish: Attach lift, insert fusing, wrap.
```

> **CHALLENGE 28.3**
>
> To support the setShowInterior() method, suppose that you add a showInterior Boolean attribute to the ComponentIterator class. What changes would you have to make in the CompositeIterator class so that next() will return only leaf nodes if showInterior is false?
>
> *A solution appears on page 433.*

## Thread-Safe Iterators

When it returns the next value in a collection to a client, an iterator also returns control of the program. This opens the possibility that a client will take an action that will change the collection over which you are iterating. Consider a program that can update a list in one thread while another thread is iterating over the list:

```
package com.oozinoz.applications;
import java.util.*;
public class ShowConcurrentFor implements Runnable
{
    private List list;

    protected static List upMachineNames()
    {
        return new ArrayList
            (
                Arrays.asList
                (
                    new String[]
                    {
                        "Mixer1201",
                        "ShellAssembler1301",
                        "StarPress1401",
                        "UnloadBuffer1501"
                    }
                )
            );
    }
```

```
protected void go()
{
    list = Collections.synchronizedList(
        upMachineNames());
    for (int i = 0; i < list.size(); i++)
    {
        if (i == 1)
        { // simulate wake-up
            new Thread(this).start();
        }
        System.out.println(list.get(i));
    }
}

public void run()
{
    list.add(0, "Fuser1101");
}

public static void main(String[] args)
{
    new ShowConcurrentFor().go();
}
```
}

This program uses the synchronizedList() method of the Collections utility class to improve the thread safety of the code. The resulting list guarantees that methods that access the list will execute entirely before another thread can access the list. This helps to prevent a method in one thread from altering a collection while a method in another thread is traversing the collection. To simulate a thread waking up at an inopportune time, the program launches a new thread in the middle of a for loop.

Suppose that the first time you run this program, it prints:

```
Mixer1201
ShellAssembler1301
StarPress1401
StarPress1401
UnloadBuffer1501
```

---

**CHALLENGE 28.4**

Explain the output of the ShowConcurrentFor program.

*A solution appears on page 434.*

---

The program's behavior stems partially from the fact that it uses a for loop instead of using an iterator and a while loop. The iterators that classes in the java.util package supply provide **fail-fast** recognition of concurrent modification to a collection. If you modify the list between calls to an iterator's next() method, the iterator will throw a Concurrent-ModificationException.

Suppose that you modify the program to use an iterator instead of a for loop.

```
package com.oozinoz.applications;
import java.util.*;
public class ShowConcurrentIterator implements Runnable
{
    private List list;

    public static List upMachineNames()
    {
        // ... as before
    }

    protected void go()
    {
        list = Collections.synchronizedList(
            upMachineNames());
        Iterator i = list.iterator();
        int j = 0;
        while (i.hasNext())
        {
```

```
                        j++;
                        if (j == 1)
                        { // simulate wake-up
                            new Thread(this).start();
                        }
                        System.out.println(i.next());
                    }
                }

                public void run()
                {
                    list.add(0, "Fuser1101");
                }

                public static void main(String[] args)
                {
                    new ShowConcurrentIterator().go();
                }

            }
```

With this code in place, the program crashes:

```
> java com.oozinoz.applications.ShowConcurrentIterator
Mixer1201
ShellAssembler1301
StarPress1401
UnloadBuffer1501
Exception in thread "main"
    java.util.ConcurrentModificationException
    ...
```

The program crashes because the iterator object detects that the list has
changed during the iteration. You don't need to create a new thread to
show this behavior. However, a multithreaded application is much more
likely to accidentally modify a list while an iterator is traversing it. In a
large application, you may have little control over, or even knowledge of,
the number of threads running in the application and their various roles.
In such an application, you have to avoid presenting a corrupt representation of a collection, but you can't afford to crash your application as a
preventive measure.

Two main approaches provide safe iteration over a collection in a multithreaded application. Both approaches involve the use of an object—sometimes called a **mutex**—that is shared by threads that vie for control of the object's monitor.

In one approach, your design can require that all threads gain control of the mutex monitor before accessing the collection:

```java
package com.oozinoz.applications;
import java.util.*;
public class ShowConcurrentMutex implements Runnable
{
    private List list;
    private Object mutex = new Object();
    protected static List upMachineNames()
    {
        //... as before
    }

    protected void go()
    {
        list = upMachineNames();
        synchronized (mutex) {
            Iterator i = list.iterator();
            int j = 0;
            while (i.hasNext())
            {
                j++;
                if (j == 1)
                {
                    new Thread(this).start();
                }
                System.out.println(i.next());
            }
        }
    }

    public void run()
    {
        synchronized (mutex)
        {
```

```
                    list.add(0, "Fuser1101");
            }
        }

        public static void main(String[] args)
        {
            new ShowConcurrentMutex().go();
        }
    }
```

This program will print the original list, because the run() logic must wait for the mutex monitor:

```
Mixer1201
ShellAssembler1301
StarPress1401
UnloadBuffer1501
```

This output is correct, but you will usually not want other threads to block while one thread iterates over a collection. It may be more effective to clone the collection in a synchronized operation and then work on the clone. The interfaces List and Set are not cloneable, but the implementing classes ArrayList and HashSet are.

Cloning a collection and iterating over the clone may cause problems. The clone() methods for ArrayList and HashSet produce a **shallow copy**: They merely create a new collection that refers to the same objects as the original. Relying on a clone will fail if other threads can change the underlying objects in a way that interferes with your method. But in some cases, this risk is small. For example, if you want to display a list of machine names, it may be unlikely or inconsequential whether the names change while your method iterates over a clone of the list. The advantage of cloning the list before traversing it is speed. Cloning a collection is often much faster than waiting for another method to finish operating on the collection's contents.

---

**CHALLENGE 28.5**

What changes would you make to the `ShowConcurrentMutex` program to let the primary thread iterate over a clone of the collection, allowing the second thread to work without waiting for access to the collection?

*A solution appears on page 435.*

---

## Summary

The intent of the ITERATOR pattern is to let a client access the elements of a collection sequentially. The collection classes in the Java class libraries offer rich support for operating on collections, including support for iteration. These iterators usually require a client to cast the returned objects to the appropriate type. You can strengthen your contract with clients by creating type-specific collections with type-specific iterators.

If you create a new type of collection, you will often want to create an iterator to go with it. Domain-specific composites are a common example of a new collection type. You can design a fairly generic iterator for composites that you may be able to apply against a variety of composite hierarchies.

When you instantiate an iterator, you should consider whether the collection can change while you are iterating over it. There is usually not much chance of this in a single-threaded application. In a multithreaded application, you first have to ensure that access to a collection is synchronized. The Java class libraries provide good support for this, but that support does not guarantee safe iteration. To safely iterate in a multithreaded application, you can synchronize on the monitor of a mutex object. You can either block out all access while iterating or block access briefly while you make a clone of the collection. With a proper design, you can provide thread safety and type safety to the clients of your iterator code.

# 29

# VISITOR

THE ORDINARY WAY to extend a class hierarchy's behavior is to add methods that provide the behavior you need. It may happen, though, that the behavior you need is not consistent with the thrust of the existing object model. In other cases, the developer of a hierarchy may have little information about the behaviors that later developers will need.

If the developers who control the hierarchy code can't or won't change quickly enough to meet your needs, it may be impossible to extend the hierarchy's behavior without modifying the hierarchy's classes. But VISITOR lets a hierarchy developer build in support for the prospect that another developer may want to extend the behavior of the hierarchy. The intent of VISITOR is to let you define a new operation for a hierarchy without changing the hierarchy classes.

## Supporting VISITOR

Chapter 5, COMPOSITE, introduced the MachineComponent hierarchy and suggested several possible behaviors for this composite structure. Suppose that the developers at Oozinoz have built some of these behaviors into the hierarchy and have also applied VISITOR to allow for later extensions. Figure 29.1 shows the current state of the hierarchy.

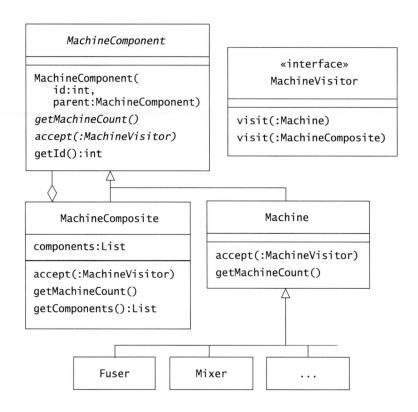

The figure doesn't explain how VISITOR works; the next section does
that. The figure simply shows some of the groundwork that lets you apply
VISITOR.

One aspect of allowing for later extensions is that the hierarchy classes
make their attributes accessible. In particular, the `getId()` method of the
`MachineComponent` class and the `getComponents()` method of the `Machine-
Composite` class make it possible for visitors to access these critical attri-
butes of hierarchy objects. The mechanics of providing support for VISITOR
also include adding an `accept()` operation to the hierarchy and adding a
visitor interface that developers can implement to create new extensions.

The `accept()` method in the `MachineComponent` class is abstract. Both
subclasses implement this method with exactly the same code:

```
public void accept(MachineVisitor v)
{
    v.visit(this);
}
```

You might think that because this method is identical in the Machine and MachineComposite class, you could move the method up to the abstract MachineComponent class. However, a compiler will see a difference in these two "identical" methods.

---

**CHALLENGE 29.1**

What difference will a Java compiler see between the accept() methods in the Machine and MachineComposite classes?

*A solution appears on page 436.*

---

The MachineVisitor interface requires implementers to define methods for visiting machines and machine composites:

```
package com.oozinoz.machine;
public interface MachineVisitor
{
    void visit(Machine m);
    void visit(MachineComposite mc);
}
```

The accept() methods in the MachineComponent, together with the visitor interface, invite developers to provide new operations to the hierarchy.

## Extending with VISITOR

Suppose that you accept an assignment to help bring up a new Oozinoz factory in Dublin, Ireland. The developers in Dublin have created an object model of the new factory's machine composition and have made this model accessible as the static dublin() method of the OozinozFactory class. To display this composite, the developers created a MachineTreeModel class to adapt the model's information to a JTree object's needs. (The code for the MachineTreeModel class is in the com.oozinoz.dublin package.) Displaying the new factory's machines requires building an instance of `MachineTreeModel` from the factory composite and wrapping this model in Swing components:

```
package com.oozinoz.applications;
import javax.swing.*;
import javax.swing.tree.*;
import com.oozinoz.ui.SwingFacade;
import com.oozinoz.dublin.MachineTreeModel;
import com.oozinoz.machine.OozinozFactory;
public class ShowMachineTreeModel
{
    public static void main(String[] args)
    {
        MachineTreeModel mtm =
            new MachineTreeModel(OozinozFactory.dublin());
        JTree tree = new JTree(mtm);
        tree.setFont(SwingFacade.getStandardFont());
        SwingFacade.launch(
            new JScrollPane(tree), " A New Oozinoz Factory");
    }
}
```

This code produces the tree browser that Figure 29.2 shows.

**FIGURE 29.2:** This GUI application presents the composition of machines at the new factory in Dublin.

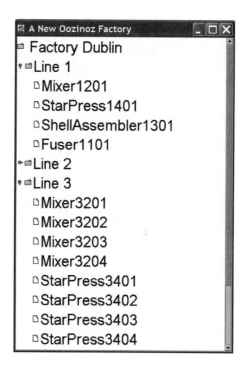

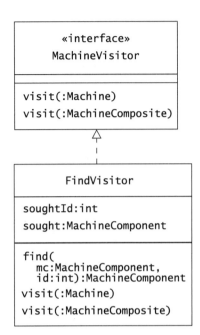

There are many possible behaviors for the machine composite that you might desire. For example, suppose that you need to find a particular machine within the factory model. To add this ability without modifying the MachineComponent hierarchy, you can create a FindVisitor class, such as Figure 29.3 shows.

The visit() methods do not return an object, so the FindVisitor class records the status of a search in its sought instance variable:

```
package com.oozinoz.dublin;
import com.oozinoz.machine.*;
import java.util.*;
public class FindVisitor implements MachineVisitor
{
    private MachineComponent sought;
    private int soughtId;

    public MachineComponent find(
        MachineComponent mc, int id)
    {
        sought = null;
        soughtId = id;
        mc.accept(this);
```

```
            return sought;
        }
        public void visit(Machine m)
        {
            if (sought == null && m.getId() == soughtId)
            {
                sought = m;
            }
        }

        public void visit(MachineComposite mc)
        {
            if (sought == null && mc.getId() == soughtId)
            {
                sought = mc;
                return;
            }
            Iterator i = mc.getComponents().iterator();
            while (sought == null && i.hasNext())
            {
                ((MachineComponent) i.next()).accept(this);
            }
        }
    }
}
```

The visit() methods frequently check the sought variable so that the tree traversal will end as soon as the desired component is found.

---

**CHALLENGE 29.2**

Write a program that finds and prints out the StarPress3404 object within the instance of MachineComponent that OozinozFactory.dublin() returns.

*A solution appears on page 437.*

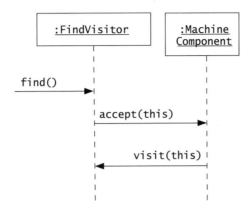

**FIGURE 29.4:** A FindVisitor object calls a MachineComponent object's accept() method to determine which visit() method to execute.

Note that the find() method does not worry about whether the machine component it receives as an argument is an instance of Machine or of MachineComposite. The find() method simply calls accept(), which in turn calls visit(). Figure 29.4 shows this sequence of method calls.

The short trip from the FindVisitor object to the MachineComponent object and back again picks up the type of the MachineComponent object, ensuring that the right visit() method of the FindVisitor class executes. This technique is called **double dispatch**. The FindVisitor object dispatches a call to the MachineComponent object. The MachineComponent object dispatches back to the visitor, calling visit() and sending itself as an argument. This call will execute either the FindVisitor class's visit(:Machine) method or its visit(:MachineComposite) method, depending on the type of the machine component.

The double dispatching in VISITOR lets you create visitor classes with methods that are specific to the various types in the visited hierarchy. As another example, consider a visitor that finds all the machines—the leaf nodes—in a machine component.

```
import com.oozinoz.machine.*;
import java.util.*;
public class RakeVisitor implements MachineVisitor
```

```
        {
            private Set leaves;
            public Set getLeaves(MachineComponent mc)
            {
                leaves = new HashSet();
                mc.accept(this);
                return leaves;
            }
            public void visit(Machine m)
            {
                ??
            }
            public void visit(MachineComposite mc)
            {
                ??
            }
        }
```

## CHALLENGE 29.3

Complete the code of the RakeVisitor class to collect the leaves of a machine component.

*A solution appears on page 437.*

A short program can find the leaves of a machine component and print them out:

```
package com.oozinoz.applications;
import com.oozinoz.machine.*;
import java.io.*;
import com.oozinoz.io.WrapFilter;
import com.oozinoz.dublin.RakeVisitor;
public class ShowRake
```

```
    {
        public static void main(String[] args)
        throws IOException
        {
            MachineComponent f = OozinozFactory.dublin();
            Writer out = new PrintWriter(System.out);
            out = new WrapFilter(new BufferedWriter(out), 60);
            out.write(
                new RakeVisitor().getLeaves(f).toString());
            out.close();
        }
    }
```

This program uses a wrap filter to produce the output:

```
[Mixer1201, StarPress3401, Mixer2202, StarPress3404,
StarPress1401, Mixer3202, StarPress2402, Fuser1101,
ShellAssembler3302, Mixer3204, Mixer2201, Fuser2101,
StarPress3403, Fuser3102, Mixer3201, StarPress3402,
StarPress2401, ShellAssembler3301, ShellAssembler1301,
Mixer3203, ShellAssembler2301, Fuser3101]
```

The FindVisitor and RakeVisitor classes each add a new behavior to the MachineComponent hierarchy, and these classes appear to work correctly. However, a danger in writing visitors is that they require an understanding of the hierarchy that you are extending. A change in the hierarchy may break your visitor, and you may misunderstand the mechanics of the hierarchy initially. In particular, you may have to handle cycles if the composite you are visiting does not prevent them.

## VISITOR Cycles

The ProcessComponent hierarchy that Oozinoz uses to model process flows is another composite structure that can benefit from building in support for VISITOR. Unlike machine composites, it is natural for process flows to contain cycles, and visitors must take care not to cause infinite loops while traversing process composites. Figure 29.5 shows the ProcessComponent hierarchy.

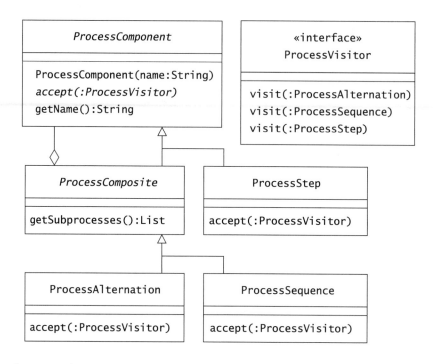

**FIGURE 29.5:** Like the MachineComponent hierarchy, the Process-Component hierarchy can build in support for VISITOR.

Suppose that you want to print out a process component in a "pretty," or indented, format. In Chapter 28, ITERATOR, you used an iterator to print out a process flow's steps. This printout looked like:

```
Make an aerial shell
    Build inner shell
    Inspect
    Rework inner shell, or complete shell
        Rework
            Disassemble
        Finish: Attach lift, insert fusing, wrap
```

You may recall that the step after "Disassemble" is "Make an aerial shell." The printout doesn't show this step, because the iterator sees that the step has already appeared once. However, it would be more informative to show the step name and to indicate that the process enters a cycle at this point. It would also be helpful to indicate which composites are alternations as opposed to sequences.

To create a pretty-printer for processes, you can create a visitor class that initializes a StringBuffer object and that adds to this buffer as the visitor visits the nodes in a process component. To indicate that a composite step is an alternation, the visitor can prepend a question mark (?)

to an alternation step's name. To indicate that a step has occurred before, the visitor can attach an ellipsis (...) to the end of the step's name.

A process component visitor has to watch for cycles, but this is easily achieved by using a Set object to keep track of the nodes the visitor has already seen:

```java
package com.oozinoz.dublin;
import java.util.*;
import com.oozinoz.process.*;
public class PrettyVisitor implements ProcessVisitor
{
    public static int INDENT_DEPTH = 4;
    private StringBuffer buf;
    private int depth;
    private Set visited;

    public StringBuffer getPretty(ProcessComponent pc)
    {
        buf = new StringBuffer();
        visited = new HashSet();
        depth = 0;
        pc.accept(this);
        return buf;
    }
    public void visit(ProcessAlternation a)
    {
        printComposite("?" + a.getName(), a);
    }

    public void visit(ProcessSequence s)
    {
        printComposite(s.getName(), s);
    }

    public void visit(ProcessStep s) {
        printTag(s.getName());
    }

    protected void printComposite(
        String tag, ProcessComposite c)
    {
        if (visited.contains(c))
        {
            printTag(tag + "...");
```

```
        }
        else
        {
            visited.add(c);
            printTag(tag);
            acceptChildren(c);
        }
    }

    protected void acceptChildren(ProcessComposite c)
    {
        Iterator i = c.getSubprocesses().iterator();
        depth++;
        while (i.hasNext())
        {
            ((ProcessComponent) i.next()).accept(this);
        }
        depth--;
    }

    protected void printTag(String tag)
    {
        for (int i = 0; i < depth * INDENT_DEPTH; i++)
        {
            buf.append(" ");
        }
        buf.append(tag);
        buf.append("\n");
    }

}
```

A short program can now pretty-print a process flow:

```
package com.oozinoz.applications;
import com.oozinoz.process.*;
import com.oozinoz.dublin.*;
public class ShowPretty
{
    public static void main(String[] args)
    {
        ProcessComponent p = ShellProcess.make();
        PrettyVisitor v = new PrettyVisitor();
        System.out.println(v.getPretty(p));
    }
}
```

Running this program prints out:

```
Make an aerial shell
    Build inner shell
    Inspect
    ?Rework inner shell, or complete shell
        Rework
            Disassemble
            Make an aerial shell...
        Finish: Attach lift, insert fusing, wrap
```

The developers of the ProcessComponent hierarchy are well aware of the need to avoid infinite loops while traversing process flows. As the PrettyVisitor class shows, the developers of the visitor also have to be aware of the potential for cycles in process components. It would help prevent errors if the ProcessComponent developers could provide some support of cycle management as part of their support of VISITOR.

---

**CHALLENGE 29.4**

How can the ProcessComponent developers include support of cycle management in the hierarchy's support for VISITOR?

*A solution appears on page 438.*

---

## VISITOR **Controversy**

VISITOR is a controversial pattern. Some developers consistently avoid applying it; others defend its use and suggest ways to strengthen it, although these suggestions usually add complexity. The fact is that many design problems tend to accompany the VISITOR pattern.

The fragility of VISITOR shows up in the examples in this chapter. For instance, in the MachineComponent hierarchy, the hierarchy developers decided to differentiate between Machine nodes and MachineComposite nodes but not to differentiate among Machine subclasses. If you need to distinguish among types of machines in your visitor, you will have to resort to using `instanceof` or another technique to tell which type of machine a `visit()` method has received. You might argue that the hierarchy developers should have included all machine types as well as a catch-all `visit(:Machine)` method in the visitor interface. But new machine types come along all the time, so this does not appear to be any sturdier.

Another example of fragility showed up in the `ProcessComponent` hierarchy. The developers of the hierarchy are aware of the danger of cycles that lurks within process flow models. How can the developers convey their concerns to a visitor developer? This may expose the fundamental problem with VISITOR: Extending a hierarchy's behavior usually requires some expert knowledge of the hierarchy's design. If you lack that expertise, you may step in a trap, such as not avoiding cycles in a process flow. If you do have expert knowledge of the hierarchy's mechanics, you may build in dangerous dependencies that will break if the hierarchy changes. For example, note that the `FindVisitor` class depends on the notion that a machine's ID number uniquely identifies the machine. If this principle changes so that identity depends on, say, the containing factory plus the machine's ID, the `FindVisitor` class may break with a composite that contains two factories. The division of expertise and code control can make VISITOR a dangerous pattern to apply.

The classic case in which VISITOR seems to work well without creating downstream problems is language development. When you develop a language parser, you may arrange for the parser to create an **abstract syntax tree**, a structure that organizes the input text according to the language's grammar. You may want to develop a variety of behaviors to accompany these trees, and the VISITOR pattern is an effective approach for allowing this. Note, though, that in this classic case, the visited hierarchy usually has little or no behavior. Thus, all the responsibility for behavior design lies with visitors, avoiding the split of responsibility that this chapter's examples must endure.

Like any pattern, VISITOR is never necessary; if it were, it would automatically appear everywhere it was needed. For VISITOR, though, alternatives often provide a sturdier design.

---

**CHALLENGE 29.5**

List two alternatives to building VISITOR into the Oozinoz machine and process hierarchies.

*A solution appears on page 438.*

---

## Summary

The VISITOR pattern lets you define a new operation for a hierarchy without changing the hierarchy classes. The mechanics for VISITOR include defining an interface for visitors and adding `accept()` methods in the hierarchy that a visitor will call. The `accept()` methods dispatch their calls back to the visitor in a double-dispatching scheme. This scheme arranges for the execution of a `visit()` method that applies to the specific type of object from the hierarchy.

A visitor developer must be aware of some, if not all, of the subtleties in the design of the visited hierarchy. In particular, visitors need to beware of cycles that may occur in the visited object model. This type of difficulty leads some developers to eschew VISITOR, regularly applying alternatives instead. Using VISITOR should probably be a team decision that depends on your methodology and the specifics of your application.

# PART VI

## APPENDIXES

# APPENDIX A: **DIRECTIONS**

I<small>F YOU HAVE READ</small> the book up to this point, allow me to say, "Congratulations!" If you have worked through all the challenges, I salute you! I feel confident that if you have read this book and worked the challenges, you have learned a lot about patterns. Now where can you go from here?

## Get the Most from This Book

If you have *not* worked through the challenges in this book, you are not alone! We are all busy, and it is quite tempting to think about a challenge momentarily and to then glance at the solution. That is certainly an ordinary experience, but you have the potential to become an extraordinary developer. Go back and rework the challenges, turning to the solutions only when you think you've got a correct answer or when you're completely stumped. Work through the challenges *now*; don't kid yourself that you'll somehow have more time later. By exercising your patterns knowledge on these challenges, you'll build the confidence you need to start applying patterns in your work.

In addition to working the challenges in this book, I suggest that you download the code from www.oozinoz.com and ensure that you can repeat the results of this book's examples on your own system. Knowing that you can get the code to run will give you more confidence than simply working examples on paper. You may also want to set up new challenges for yourself. Perhaps you will want to combine decorator filters in a new way or implement the `TableModel` interface with a class that shows data from a familiar domain.

As you build fluency with design patterns, you should start to see that you understand classic examples of design patterns. You will also begin to find ways to incorporate design patterns in your own code.

## Understand the Classics

Design patterns often make a design stronger. This is not a new idea, so it is no surprise that many design patterns are built into the Java class libraries. If you can spot the design pattern in a body of code you can grasp the design yourself and communicate it to others who understand design patterns. For example, if a developer understands the DECORATOR pattern, it is meaningful to explain that Java streams are decorators.

Here is a test of your understanding of some of the classic examples of design patterns that appear in Java.

- How do Swing listeners use the OBSERVER pattern?
- Why do menus often use the COMMAND pattern? How can you use the COMMAND pattern with Swing menus?
- Why are drivers a good example of the BRIDGE pattern? Is each particular driver an instance of the ADAPTER pattern?
- What does it mean to say that Java streams use the DECORATOR pattern?
- Why is the PROXY pattern fundamental to the design of RMI?
- If sorting provides a good example of the TEMPLATE METHOD pattern, which step of the algorithm is left unspecified?

A good goal is to be able to answer these questions without referring to this book. It is also good exercise to write down your answers and to share your answers with a colleague.

## Weave Patterns into Your Code

A primary purpose for learning design patterns is to become a better developer. Think about how to use patterns in the code base you work with most often. Here, you have two choices: Apply design patterns as you add new code, or apply design patterns through refactoring. If part of your code is complex and difficult to maintain, you may be able to improve it by refactoring the code and using a design pattern. Before diving into such a project, make sure that you have a customer for the result. Also, before you change the code, be sure to create an automated test suite for the code that you are refactoring.

Now, suppose that you understand the patterns you have studied and are determined to use them carefully and appropriately. How do you find an opportunity? Some opportunities arise fairly frequently. If you're looking for a chance to apply design patterns, consider the following.

- Does your code base have any complex code that deals with the state of a system or the state of the application user? If so, you may be able to improve the code by applying the STATE pattern.
- Does your code combine the selection of a strategy with the execution of that strategy? If it does, you may be able to make the code better by using the STRATEGY pattern.
- Does your customer or analyst supply you with flowcharts that translate into code that is difficult to comprehend? If so, you can apply the INTERPRETER pattern, letting each node of the flowchart become an instance of a class in the interpreter hierarchy. You can thus provide a direct translation from the flowchart to the code.
- Does your code contain a weak composite that doesn't allow children to be composites themselves? You may be able to strengthen such code with the COMPOSITE pattern.
- Have you encountered relational-integrity errors in your object model? You may be able to prevent them by applying the MEDIATOR pattern to centralize the modeling of object relations.
- Does your code have places where clients are using information from a service to decide which class to instantiate? You may be able to improve and to simplify such code by applying the FACTORY METHOD pattern.

By learning design patterns, you have developed a rich vocabulary of design ideas. If you are on the lookout for opportunities, it probably won't be long before you find a design that you can improve by applying a pattern.

## Keep Learning

Somehow, you had the opportunity, drive, and ambition to acquire and to read this book. All I can say is, keep it up! I think the best advice for developers is to decide how many hours a week you want to spend on your career. Take five hours off the top and pay yourself first. Spend that time away from the office, reading books and magazines or writing software related to any topic that interests you. Make this practice as regular as your office hours. Treat this aspect of your career seriously, and you'll become a much better developer, and you'll probably find that you enjoy your job more.

Now, suppose that you have given yourself plenty of time and simply need to set your direction. Before learning more about patterns, you may want to make sure that you understand the basics. If you haven't read *The Java™ Programming Language* (Arnold and Gosling 1998) or *The Unified Modeling Language User Guide* (Booch, Rumbaugh, and Jacobson 1999), let me highly recommend them. If you want to learn more about patterns, you have a lot of choices. For a walkthrough of realistic examples of applying design patterns, I recommend *Pattern Hatching* (Vlissides 1998). If you want to add to your patterns vocabulary, my experience is that most shops would benefit from having a local expert on concurrency patterns. To learn about this important and often neglected aspect of development, I recommend reading *Concurrent Programming in Java™* (Lea 2000).

Of the many directions that you can go, the most important practice is to keep going. Make learning a part of your career, and pursue the topics that interest you most. Think of how strong you can become as a developer, and become that strong. Keep up the good work!

## Introducing Interfaces  (Chapter 2)

**SOLUTION 2.1** *(from page 14)*

An abstract class with no nonabstract methods is similar to an interface in terms of its utility. However, note the following.

- A class can implement any number of interfaces but can subclass at most one abstract class.

- An abstract class can have nonabstract methods, which are usually instances of the TEMPLATE METHOD pattern. All the methods of an interface are abstract, whether or not this declaration is explicit.

- An abstract class can declare instance variables that its subclasses inherit. An interface cannot declare instance variables, although it can establish static final fields.

- An abstract class can define constructors; an interface cannot.

- An abstract class's visibility can be public, protected, private, or none (package); an interface's visibility must be public or none (package).

- An abstract class can have methods whose visibility is protected, private, or none (package); every method in an interface must be public.

- An abstract class inherits from Object, including such methods as clone() and equals().

**SOLUTION 2.2** *(from page 15)*

A. *True.* Interface methods are always abstract, whether or not they declare it.

B. *True.* Interface methods are also always public, whether or not they declare it.

C. *False!* An interface's visibility may be limited to the package in which the interface resides. The `RocketSim` interface does not declare itself to be `public`, so it is package protected. Classes outside `com.oozinoz.sim` cannot access or implement this interface.

D. *True.* For example, the `List` and the `Set` interfaces both extend the `Collection` interface in `java.util`.

E. *False.* An interface with no methods is a *marker* interface. Sometimes, a method high in a class hierarchy, such as `Object.clone()`, is not appropriate for every subclass. You can create a marker interface that requires subclasses to opt in or to opt out of participation in such a method. The `clone()` method on `Object` requires subclasses to opt in, declaring that they implement the `Cloneable` marker interface.

F. *False.* An interface cannot declare instance fields, although it can create constants by declaring fields that are `static` and `final`.

G. *False.* It might be a good idea, but there is no way for a Java interface to require implementing classes to provide any particular constructors.

**SOLUTION 2.3** *(from page 15)*

An interface does not define a contract between the caller and the implementing class when the interface is used to *register* for notification. In this case, the implementing class may need to take an action in response to a method call, but it is generally not performing a service for the caller.

For example, a class that implements the `MouseMotionListener` interface from `java.awt.event` must implement the methods:

```
public void mouseDragged(MouseEvent e)
public void mouseMoved(MouseEvent e)
```

The presence of these methods does not imply that the methods will take an action when a client calls them. In fact, it would not be uncommon to react to the mouseDragged() method but to ignore to calls to the mouseMoved() method.

**SOLUTION 2.4** *(from page 16)*

A class that implements WindowListener must implement all the methods the interface declares, even if the class will ignore these methods when called. The WindowAdapter class ignores *all* the methods in Window-Listener. This lets a subclass implement only the methods that it wants to react to, as Figure B.1 shows. The anonymous class in Figure B.1 can react to only the windowClosing() event, without having to implement dummy methods for the other methods specified in the WindowListener interface.

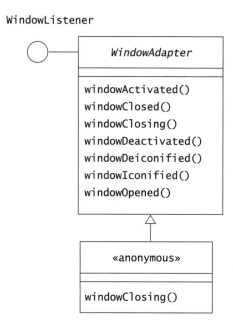

WindowListener

**FIGURE B.1:** An anonymous subclass of WindowAdapter can provide a Window-Listener object that ignores all events except a window closing.

Here is a method that accepts a JFrame object and arranges for the Java virtual machine to terminate when the user closes the frame's window:

```
public static void listen(Frame f) {
    f.addWindowListener
        (
```

```
                        new WindowAdapter()
                        {
                            public void windowClosing(WindowEvent e)
                            {
                                System.exit(0);
                            }
                        }
                    );
            }
```

This code registers with the frame an instance of an anonymous Window-Adapter subclass that overrides the windowClosing() method. The value of the WindowAdapter class is that it makes it easy to create a subclass that reacts to only the relevant window events.


**SOLUTION 2.5** *(from page 19)*

The advantage of placing constants in an interface is that a class that implements the interface can use the constants as if it had inherited them from a superclass. To make the classification constants available to a class, declare that the class implements the ClassificationConstants interface. Then you can change secureOrder() to:

```
        public void secureOrder(Firework f /*, etc. */)
        {
            //...
            if (f.classification == DISPLAY)
            {
                // issue warning
            }
            else
            {
                // proceed
            }
        }
```

The difference is that you can now refer to the constant as DISPLAY instead of Classification.DISPLAY.

## ADAPTER (Chapter 3)

**SOLUTION 3.1** *(from page 23)*

Your solution should look something like Figure B.2.

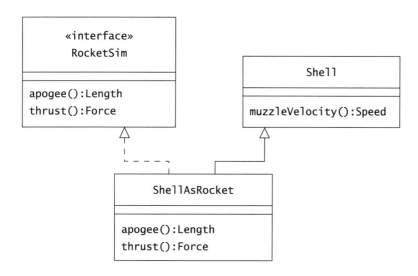

**FIGURE B.2:** This ShellAsRocket class relies on fireworks physics that can model a shell's apogee and "thrust" from its muzzle velocity.

**SOLUTION 3.2** *(from page 29)*

One set of solutions for the missing methods is:

```
package com.oozinoz.applications;
import javax.swing.table.*;
import com.oozinoz.fireworks.*;
public class RocketTable extends AbstractTableModel
{
    protected Rocket[] rockets;
    protected String[] columnNames =
        new String[] { "Name", "Price", "Apogee" };

    public RocketTable(Rocket[] rockets)
    {
        this.rockets = rockets;
    }

    public int getColumnCount()
    {
        return columnNames.length;
    }
```

```
                         public String getColumnName(int i)
                         {
                             return columnNames[i];
                         }

                         public int getRowCount()
                         {
                             return rockets.length;
                         }

                         public Object getValueAt(int row, int col)
                         {
                             switch (col)
                             {
                                 case 0 :
                                     return rockets[row].getName();
                                 case 1 :
                                     return new Double(rockets[row].getPrice());
                                 case 2 :
                                     return new Double(
                                         rockets[row].getApogee().getMagnitude());
                                 default :
                                     return null;
                             }
                         }
                     }
```

The `TableModel` interface provides a good example of the power of planning ahead for adaptation. This interface, along with its partial implementation by `AbstractTableModel`, reduces the work of showing domain objects in a standard GUI table. Your solution should show how easy it is to adapt when adaptation is supported with an interface.

**SOLUTION 3.3** *(from page 32)*

The problem with subclassing `PrintStream` and overriding only one of its many methods is that in a later version, the client code might start using methods that you don't support. The compiler won't detect a problem, because the client still needs a `PrintStream` object and you will still be supplying one.

**SOLUTION 3.4** *(from page 33)*

You should ask the client code developers to specify a Java interface, such as:

```
public interface MessageChannel
{
    void print(Object o);
}
```

The client developers also need to change the setOutput() method to accept an instance of MessageChannel instead of an instance of Print-Stream. In this scenario, you can define MessageAdapter to subclass Text-Area and implement MessageChannel. The advantage is that the client developers can't change the calls the application makes without changing the interface. If the client developers change the interface, the worst possible result is that your code won't compile. This is greatly preferable to the earlier design, in which a change on the client side would not be noticeable until runtime.

**SOLUTION 3.5** *(from page 33)*

If you have the opportunity, try to convince a colleague of your view.

- *Sample argument:* The intent of the ADAPTER pattern is to convert the interface of a class into another interface that clients expect. The MessageAdapter class achieves this, letting a TextArea object pose as a PrintStream object. Thus, MessageAdapter is a valid, if dangerous, example of ADAPTER.
- *On the other side:* The MessageAdapter class is simply delegating a call to a PrintStream object. We don't want to consider that every instance of delegation is an instance of ADAPTER. The ADAPTER pattern's intent is to translate an interface. This example has no interface, just a particular method call that we need to override.

If you can clearly articulate your own views and listen thoughtfully to opposition at the same time, you win.

**SOLUTION 3.6** *(from page 34)*

- *One argument:* When the user clicks the mouse, I need to translate, or adapt, the resulting Swing call into an appropriate action. In other words, when I need to adapt GUI events to my application's interface, I use Swing adapter classes. I am translating from one interface to another, fulfilling the intent of the ADAPTER pattern.
- *A counterargument:* The "adapter" classes in Swing are stubs. They don't translate or adapt anything. You subclass these classes, overriding the methods you need to do something. It is thus your methods and your class that form an example of ADAPTER.

## FACADE (Chapter 4)

**SOLUTION 4.1** *(from page 43)*

Your diagram should look something like Figure B.3.

**FIGURE B.3:** This diagram shows the flight path application factored into one class for calculating a flight path, one for displaying a flight path, and one that simplifies use of the Swing libraries.

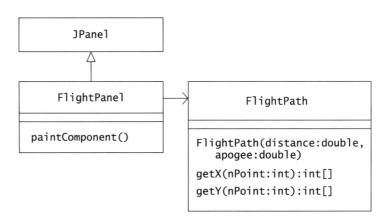

Note that all the methods of SwingFacade are static methods. Does your solution make these methods static? If not, why not?

**SOLUTION 4.2** *(from page 47)*

Some differences to note between demos and facades follow.

- A demo is usually a standalone application, whereas a facade is usually not.
- A demo usually includes sample data; a facade does not.
- A facade is usually configurable, whereas a demo is not.
- A facade is intended for reuse, whereas a demo is not.
- A facade is intended for use in production; a demo is not.

**SOLUTION 4.3** *(from page 48)*

The JOptionPane class is one of the few examples of a facade in the Java class libraries. It is production worthy, configurable, and designed for reuse. Above all else, the JOptionPane class fulfills the intent of the FACADE pattern by providing a simple interface that makes it easy to use the JDialog class. You might argue that a facade simplifies a "subsystem" and that the solitary JDialog class does not qualify as a subsystem. But it is exactly the richness of this class's features that makes a facade valuable.

Sun Microsystems bundles many demos in with the JDK. However, these classes are never part of the Java class libraries. That is, these classes do not appear in packages with a java prefix. A facade may belong on the Java class libraries, but demos do not.

The JOptionPane has dozens of static methods that effectively make it a utility. Strictly speaking, though, it does not meet the UML definition that requires a utility to possess solely static methods.

**SOLUTION 4.4** *(from page 49)*

Here are a few reasonable—but opposing—views about the paucity of facades in the Java class libraries.

- As a Java developer, you are well advised to develop a thorough knowledge of the Java class libraries. Facades necessarily limit the way you might apply any system. They would be a distraction and a potentially misleading element of the class libraries in which they might appear.

- A facade lies somewhere between the richness of a toolkit and the specificity of a particular application. To create a facade requires some notion of the types of applications the facade will support. This predictability is impossible, given the huge and diverse audience of the Java class libraries.
- The scarcity of facades in the Java class libraries is a weakness. Adding more facades would be a big help.

## COMPOSITE (Chapter 5)

**SOLUTION 5.1** *(from page 52)*

One answer is that *Design Patterns* (Gamma et al. 1995) shows Component as an abstract class, so Java developers may implement it that way without considering the use of a Java interface. Another answer is that the Component superclass often has fields and methods that its subclasses can share. For example, the Component class may have a name instance variable and a concrete toString() method that uses it.

**SOLUTION 5.2** *(from page 53)*

For the Machine class, getMachineCount() should be something like:

```
public int getMachineCount()
{
    return 1;
}
```

The class diagram shows that MachineComposite uses a List object to track its components. To count the machines in a composite, you might write:

```
public int getMachineCount()
{
    int count = 0;
    Iterator i = components.iterator();
    while (i.hasNext())
    {
        MachineComponent mc = (MachineComponent) i.next();
        count += mc.getMachineCount();
    }
    return count;
}
```

**SOLUTION 5.3** *(from page 54)*

| Method | Class | Definition |
|---|---|---|
| getMachineCount() | MachineComposite | Return the sum of the counts for each component in components. |
| | Machine | Return 1. |
| isCompletelyUp() | MachineComposite | Return if all components are "completely up." |
| | Machine | Return true if this machine is up. |
| stopAll() | MachineComposite | Tell all components to "stop all." |
| | Machine | Stop this machine. |
| getOwners() | MachineComposite | Create a set, not a list, add the owners of all components, and return the set. |
| | Machine | Return this machine's owners. |
| getMaterial() | MachineComposite | Return a collection of all the material on components. |
| | Machine | Return the material that is on this machine. |

**SOLUTION 5.4** *(from page 57)*

The program prints out the number 4.

Only three machines are in the plant factory, but machine m is counted by both plant and bay. Both of these objects contain lists of machine components that refer to machine m.

The results could be worse. If, say, an engineer adds the plant object as a component of the bay composite, a call to getMachineCount() will enter an infinite loop.

**SOLUTION 5.5** *(from page 59)*

A reasonable implementation of MachineComposite.isTree() is:

```
protected boolean isTree(Set visited)
{
    visited.add(this);
    Iterator i = components.iterator();
    while (i.hasNext())
    {
        MachineComponent c = (MachineComponent) i.next();
        if (visited.contains(c) || !c.isTree(visited))
        {
            return false;
        }
    }
    return true;
}
```

**SOLUTION 5.6** *(from page 61)*

Your solution should show the links in Figure B.4.

**FIGURE B.4:** The cycle in processing aerial shells shows up as a cycle in this object diagram.

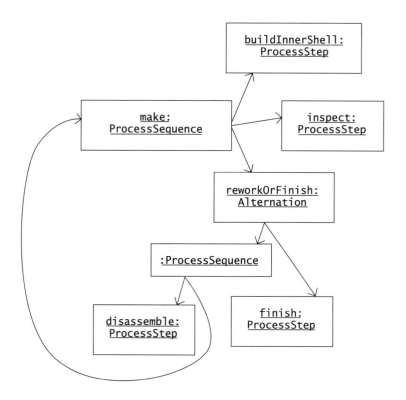

## BRIDGE (Chapter 6)

**SOLUTION 6.1** *(from page 67)*

Figure B.5 shows a completed sequence diagram that illustrates the normal steps in an application that uses a JDBC driver.

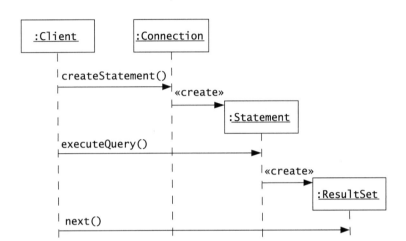

**FIGURE B.5:** A typical JDBC application creates a **Statement** object and uses it to execute one or more queries.

**SOLUTION 6.2** *(from page 69)*

You have many choices about how to illustrate the class relationships in this example. Figure B.6 shows one answer. Your figure should show the relationship between JDBCAdapter and Statement. In UML, the open arrowhead on the association between JDBCAdapter and Statement indicates that a JDBCAdapter object can use or navigate to a Statement object, but a Statement object cannot use a JDBCAdapter object.

Note that you cannot show the class that implements Statement, as the JDBC architecture isolates you from knowing how a driver writer has named this class.

**FIGURE B.6:** An `OzJDBCAdapter` object will throw a `NoQuery` exception if the adapter is asked for data before a query has made data available.

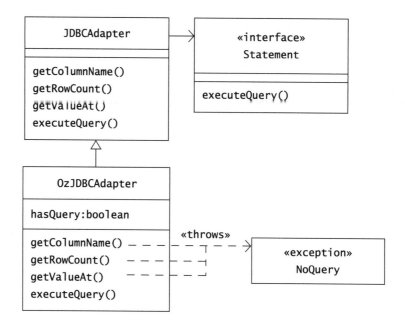

An illustration of the `OzJDBCAdapter` class should show the methods it overrides. Figure B.6 also indicates that `OzJDBCAdapter` objects use a `hasQuery` Boolean to keep track of whether they have received a query.

**SOLUTION 6.3** *(from page 72)*

Figure B.7 shows a solution.

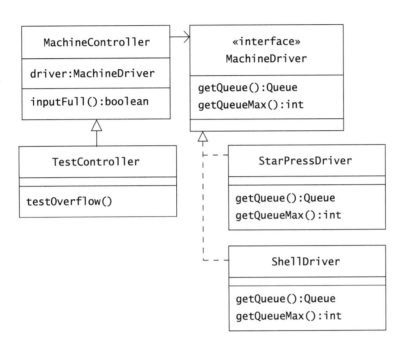

**FIGURE B.7:** The abstraction—a hierarchy of types of controllers— is separated from implementations of the abstract **driver** object that the abstraction uses.

**SOLUTION 6.4** *(from page 74)*

Figure B.8 shows one solution.

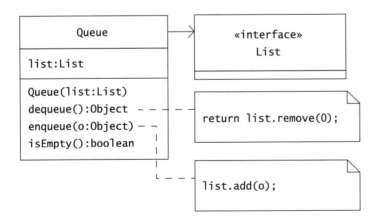

**FIGURE B.8:** The line forms at the rear: Objects enqueue at the tail of the list; dequeued objects come from the "head" of the list, at index 0.

## Introducing Responsibility (Chapter 7)

**SOLUTION 7.1** *(from page 78)*

Some problems with the given diagram follow:

- The `Rocket.thrust()` method returns a `Rocket` instead of a number or a physical quantity.
- The `LiquidRocket` class has a `getLocation()` method, although nothing in the diagram or in the problem domain suggests that we model rockets as having a location. Even if we did, there is no reason for liquid-fueled rockets to have a location, whereas other `Rocket` objects do not.
- The `isLiquid()` method may be an acceptable alternative to using the `instanceof` operator, but then we'd expect the superclass to also have an `isLiquid()` method that would return `false`.
- `CheapRockets` is plural, although class names are conventionally singular.
- We could model cheapness with attributes alone, so there is no justification for creating a class just for cheap rockets. The `CheapRockets` class also introduces a factoring that conflicts with factoring the rocket model as liquid or solid. For example, it is not clear how to model a cheap liquid rocket.
- The `CheapRockets` class implements `Runnable`, although this interface has nothing to do with cheap rocket objects from the problem domain.
- The model shows that `Firework` is a subclass of `LiquidRocket`, declaring that all fireworks are liquid rockets, which is false.
- The model shows a direct relation between reservations and types of firework, although no such relation exists in the problem domain.
- The `Reservation` class has its own copy of `city`, which it should get by delegation to a `Location` object.
- A `CheapRocket` is composed of `Runnable` objects, which is simply bizarre.

**SOLUTION 7.2** *(from page 79)*

The value of this challenge is not to get the right answer but rather to exercise your thinking about what makes up a good class. Consider whether your definition addresses the following points.

- A nuts-and-bolts description of a class is, "A class is a named collection of fields that hold data values and methods that operate on those values" (Flanagan 1999b, p. 61).
- A class establishes a collection of fields: that is, it defines the attributes of an object. The attribute types are other classes, primitive data types, such as `boolean` and `int`, or interfaces.
- A class designer should be able to justify how a class's attributes are related.
- The name of a class should reflect the meaning of the class both as a collection of attributes and with respect to the class's behavior.
- A class must support all the behaviors it defines, as well as all those in superclasses, and all methods in interfaces that the class implements. (A decision to *not* support a superclass or an interface method is occasionally justifiable.)
- A class should have a justifiable relationship to its superclass.
- The name of each of a class's methods should be a good commentary on what the method does.

**SOLUTION 7.3** *(from page 79)*

At least two earlier challenges have involved cases in which the effect of calling a method is not completely predictable from the method name.

- Challenge 2.1 on page 14 asks about methods that do not imply responsibility on the part of the implementing class to take action or to return a value. As the solution (page 359) suggests, when a class registers for notification calls, such as `mouseDragged()`, the methods do not imply an obligation to the caller.
- Chapter 6, BRIDGE, gives several examples showing that the effect of calling an abstraction's methods depends on which driver or implementation is in place.

The effects of calling a method are *purposely* unpredictable when the method is part of an abstraction and when the method exists to receive notification. In other cases, a method with unforeseeable results may simply be misnamed.

The Java class libraries contain other examples of when you might not predict a method's behavior from knowing its name. In particular, Chapter 18, PROTOTYPE, asks you to take a hard look at the behavior of `Object.clone()` in Challenge 18.3 on page 186.

### SOLUTION 7.4 *(from page 81)*

To keep another developer from burrowing into your package with subclasses that manipulate `protected` members of your classes, you might

- Offer to add the function the developer needs
- Modify your instance variables with `private` visibility and use `get-` methods within your own package
- Declare classes like `SolidRocket` to be `final`, so that they cannot be subclassed

## SINGLETON  (Chapter 8)

### SOLUTION 8.1 *(from page 84)*

To prevent other developers from instantiating your class, create a single constructor with private visibility. Note that if you create other, nonprivate constructors or create no constructors at all, other developers will likely be able to reinstantiate your class.

### SOLUTION 8.2 *(from page 85)*

As *Design Patterns* says, "You might not have enough information to instantiate every singleton at static initialization time. A singleton might require values that are computed later in the program's execution" (p. 130). When a `Factory` singleton is born, for example, it might have to establish connections with machine drivers, to set up planners, and to initialize a simulation of itself.

**SOLUTION 8.3** *(from page 87)*

Your solution should eliminate the possibility of confusion that can occur when two threads call the `recordWipMove()` method at approximately the same time:

```
public void recordWipMove()
{
    synchronized (classLock)
    {
        wipMoves++;
    }
}
```

Is it possible that a thread might activate in the middle of an increment operation? Even if you're certain that the answer is no, it's a good policy to carefully restrict access to a singleton's data in a multithreaded application.

Multithreaded applications often fail because their developers do not understand the mechanics of synchronization or do not foresee subtle problems that can occur. If you are working with a multithreaded Java application, I heartily recommend familiarizing yourself with the information in *Concurrent Programming in Java™* (Lea 2000).

**SOLUTION 8.4** *(from page 88)*

| | |
|---|---|
| `OurBiggestRocket` | This class has an inappropriate name. You should model attributes, such as "biggest," with attributes, not with class names. If a developer *must* sustain this class, perhaps it is a singleton. |
| `TopSalesAssociate` | This class has the same problem as `OurBiggestRocket`. |
| `Math` | This class is a *utility*, with all static methods and *no* instances. It is not a singleton. |
| `System` | This is a utility. |
| `PrintStream` | Although the `System.out` object is a `PrintStream` object with unique responsibilities, it is not a unique instance of `PrintStream`, which is not a singleton class. |

| PrintSpooler: | If you really have only one printer in your company, PrintSpooler might be a singleton. |
|---|---|
| PrinterManager: | At Oozinoz, you have a lot of printers, and you can look up their addresses through the PrinterManager singleton. |

## OBSERVER (Chapter 9)

**SOLUTION 9.1** *(from page 92)*

One solution is:

```
public JSlider slider()
{
    if (slider == null)
    {
        slider = new JSlider();
        sliderMax = slider.getMaximum();
        sliderMin = slider.getMinimum();
        slider.addChangeListener(this);
        slider.setValue(slider.getMinimum());
    }
    return slider;
}

public void stateChanged(ChangeEvent e)
{
    double val = slider.getValue();
    double tp = (val - sliderMin) / (sliderMax - sliderMin);
    burnPanel().setTPeak(tp);
    thrustPanel().setTPeak(tp);
    valueLabel().setText("" + tp);
}
```

**SOLUTION 9.2** *(from page 93)*

One solution is shown in Figure B.9. To allow a label to register for slider events, the design in Figure B.9 creates a subclass of JLabel that implements ChangeListener. The new design lets the components that depend on the slider register their interest and update themselves. This is arguably an improvement, but we will refactor the design again, to a model/view/control architecture.

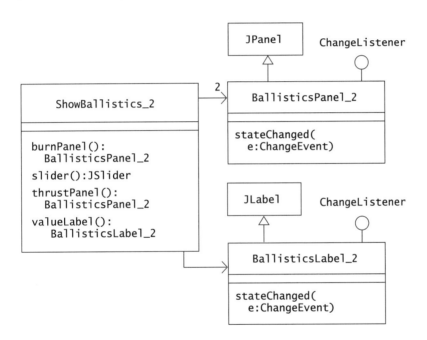

**FIGURE B.9:** In this design, components that depend on the slider implement ChangeListener so that they can register for slider events.

**SOLUTION 9.3** *(from page 96)*

One solution is:

```
package com.oozinoz.applications;
import javax.swing.*;
import java.util.*;
import com.oozinoz.ballistics.Tpeak;
public class BallisticsLabel extends JLabel
implements Observer
{
    public BallisticsLabel(Tpeak tPeak)
    {
        tPeak.addObserver(this);
    }
}
```

```
public void update(Observable o, Object arg)
{
    setText("" + ((Tpeak) o).getValue());
    repaint();
}
}
```

Note that this solution places the Tpeak class in the ballistics package and the BallisticsLabel class in the applications package.

**SOLUTION 9.4** *(from page 97)*

A solution is:

```
public JSlider slider()
{
    if (slider == null)
    {
        slider = new JSlider();
        sliderMax = slider.getMaximum();
        sliderMin = slider.getMinimum();
        slider.addChangeListener
            (
                new ChangeListener()
                {
                    public void stateChanged(ChangeEvent e) {
                        tPeak.setValue(
                            (slider.getValue() - sliderMin)
                            / (sliderMax - sliderMin));
                    }
                }
            );
        slider.setValue(slider.getMinimum());
    }
    return slider;
}
```

**SOLUTION 9.5** *(from page 98)*

Figure B.10 shows the calls that flow when a user moves the slider in the ballistics application.

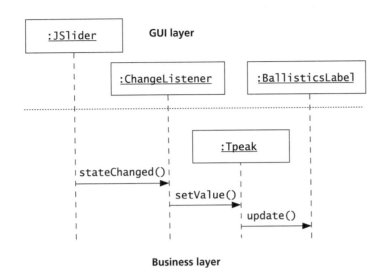

FIGURE B.10: MVC causes the path of change to loop through a business layer.

## SOLUTION 9.6 *(from page 100)*

Your diagram should look something like Figure B.11. Note that you can apply the same design with Observer and Observable. The key to the design is that the interesting class Tpeak makes itself observable by maintaining an object with good listening skills.

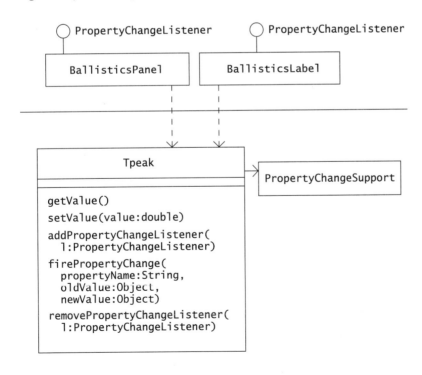

FIGURE B.11: The **Tpeak** class can add in listening behaviors by delegating listening-oriented calls to a PropertyChange-Support object.

## MEDIATOR (Chapter 10)

**SOLUTION 10.1** *(from page 106)*

Figure B.12 shows a solution. The arrowheads in the link between PlaceA-Tub and PlaceATubMediator emphasize two-way navigability between these classes. A PlaceATub object has a mediator that it registers for events:

```
public JTextField textField()
{
    if (textField == null)
    {
        textField = new JTextField();
        textField.setFont(font());
        textField.addActionListener(mediator());
        textField.addFocusListener(mediator());
    }
    return textField;
}
```

**FIGURE B.12:** The PlaceATub class handles component building, and the PlaceATubMediator class handles events.

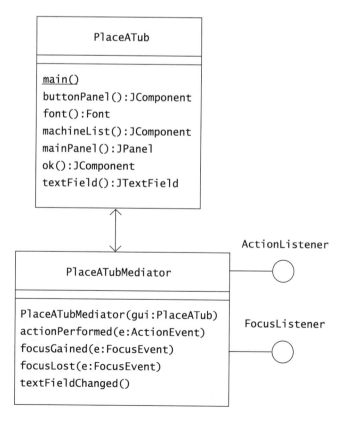

The constructor for PlaceATubMediator accepts a PlaceATub object to which
it passes back information:

```
public void focusGained(FocusEvent e)
{
    gui.textField().selectAll();
}
```

## SOLUTION 10.2 *(from page 107)*

Your solution should look something like Figure B.13. Note that although
this diagram shows only a Tub domain object, the mediator must also
update the affected machines when a user moves a tub.

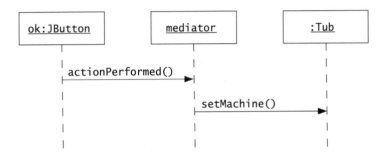

**FIGURE B.13:** When you move event handling into a mediator class, components register a mediator object for their events. When a user clicks a button, the event goes to the mediator, where domain-specific knowledge about the action to perform resides.

## SOLUTION 10.3 *(from page 111)*

Figure B.14 shows an updated object diagram. The problem that the
developer's code introduces is that StarPress-2402 still thinks that it has
tub T308. In a relational table, changing the machine attribute of a row
automatically removes the tub from the prior machine. This automated
removal does not occur when the relation is dispersed across a distributed
object model. The proper modeling of the tub/machine relation requires
special logic that you can remove to a separate mediator object.

**FIGURE B.14:** Two machines think that they contain tub T308. The object model accepts a situation that neither a relational table nor reality will allow.

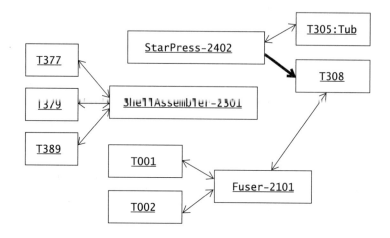

**SOLUTION 10.4** *(from page 113)*

The contents of Tub.java should look something like:

```
package com.oozinoz.chemical;
import com.oozinoz.machine.*;
public class Tub
{
    protected String id;
    protected Mediator mediator;

    public Tub(String id, Mediator mediator)
    {
        this.id = id;
    }

    public Machine getMachine()
    {
        return mediator.getMachine(this);
    }

    public void setMachine(Machine machine)
    {
        mediator.set(this, machine);
    }

    public String toString()
    {
        return id;
    }
}
```

**SOLUTION 10.5** *(from page 113)*

- The FACADE pattern may help to refactor a large application.
- The BRIDGE pattern moves abstract operations to an interface.
- The OBSERVER pattern may appear as you refactor code to support an MVC architecture.
- The FLYWEIGHT pattern extricates the immutable part of an object so that this part can be shared.
- The BUILDER pattern moves the construction logic for an object outside the class to instantiate.
- The FACTORY METHOD pattern lets you reduce the amount of responsibility in a class hierarchy by moving an aspect of behavior to a parallel hierarchy.
- The STATE and STRATEGY patterns let you move state-specific and strategy-specific behavior into separate classes.

## PROXY (Chapter 11)

**SOLUTION 11.1** *(from page 119)*

The image-display methods of `ImageIconProxy` forward their calls to the current image:

```
public int getIconHeight()
{
    return current.getIconHeight();
}

public int getIconWidth()
{
    return current.getIconWidth();
}

public synchronized void paintIcon(
    Component c, Graphics g, int x, int y)
{
    current.paintIcon(c, g, x, y);
}
```

**SOLUTION 11.2** *(from page 122)*

The load() method sets the image to Loading..., whereas the run() method, executing in a separate thread, loads the desired image:

```
public void load(JFrame callbackFrame)
{
    this.callbackFrame = callbackFrame;
    setImage(LOADING.getImage());
    callbackFrame.repaint();
    new Thread(this).start();
}

public void run()
{
    setImage(new ImageIcon(filename).getImage());
    callbackFrame.pack();
}
```

**SOLUTION 11.3** *(from page 127)*

As the class diagram shows, a RocketImpl constructor accepts a price and an apogee:

```
Rocket biggie = new RocketImpl(29.95, 820);
```

You could declare biggie to be of type RocketImpl. However, what is important about biggie is that it fulfills the Rocket interface that a client will look for.

**SOLUTION 11.4** *(from page 128)*

The completed diagram should appear as in Figure B.15. A legitimate but less informative labeling would name both receivers of getApogee() as being of type Rocket. In fact, both the server and the client programs refer to these objects as instances of the Rocket interface.

**FIGURE B.15:** A proxy forwards a client's calls so that to the client, the remote object appears as if it were local.

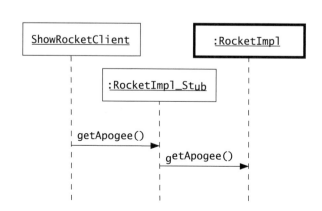

## CHAIN OF RESPONSIBILITY (Chapter 12)

**SOLUTION 12.1** *(from page 132)*

Two possible answers follow.

- Method lookup searches across a well-defined series of *classes*. The CHAIN OF RESPONSIBILITY pattern directs the search for a responsible method to occur across a series of *objects*.
- The mechanics of method lookup are part of the Java language specification, whereas CHAIN OF RESPONSIBILITY is under your control as a developer.

**SOLUTION 12.2** *(from page 134)*

Your diagram should looking similar to Figure B.16. With this design, any client of any simulated item can simply ask the item for the responsible engineer. As the next challenge shows, the code for the various implementations of getResponsible() gets simpler, too.

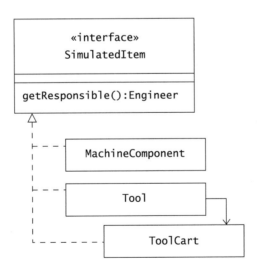

**FIGURE B.16:** Every `SimlulatedItem` object can respond to a `getResponsible()` call. Internally, a `Simulated-Item` object may forward the request to its parent.

**SOLUTION 12.3** *(from page 135)*

A.  A MachineComponent object may have an explicitly assigned responsible person. If it doesn't, it passes the request to its parent:

```
public Engineer getResponsible()
{
    if (responsible != null)
    {
        return responsible;
    }
    if (parent != null)
    {
        return parent.getResponsible();
    }
    return null;
}
```

B.  The code for Tool.getResponsibility() reflects the statement that "tools are always assigned to tool carts":

```
public Engineer getResponsible()
{
    return toolCart.getResponsible();
}
```

C.  The ToolCart code reflects the statement that "tool carts have a responsible engineer":

```
public Engineer getResponsible()
{
    return responsible;
}
```

**SOLUTION 12.4** *(from page 135)*

Your solution should look something like Figure B.17. Your constructors should allow Machine and MachineComposite objects to be instantiated with or without an assigned engineer. Whenever a MachineComponent object does not have an assigned engineer, it can get a responsible engineer from its parent.

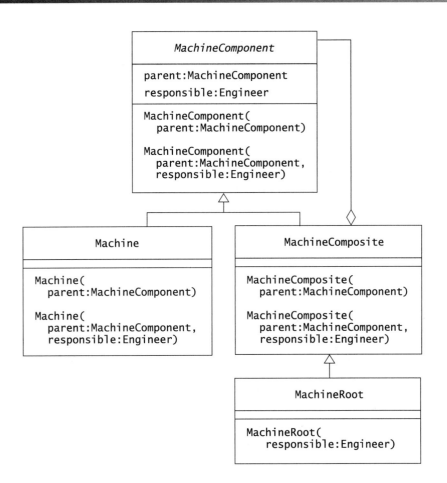

**FIGURE B.17:** The constructors in the `MachineComponent` hierarchy support the rules that a `MachineRoot` object must have a responsible engineer, and every `MachineComponent` object except a root must have a parent.

**SOLUTION 12.5** *(from page 137)*

Two examples of when CHAIN OF REPONSIBILITY might apply to objects that do not form a composite are

- A chain of on-call engineers that follows a standard rotation. If the primary on-call engineer does not answer a production support page in a specific amount of time, the notification system pages the next engineer in the chain.
- When users enter such information as the date of an event, a chain of parsers can take turns trying to decode the user's text.

## FLYWEIGHT (Chapter 13)

**SOLUTION 13.1** *(from page 140)*
The BorderFactory class in javax.swing is a good example of FLYWEIGHT. As its class comment says, "Wherever possible, this factory will hand out references to shared Border instances." When a Border object can be safely shared, BorderFactory will return the same border more than once. For example, every call to createEmptyBorder() will return the same, empty border.

**SOLUTION 13.2** *(from page 140)*

- An argument *for* the immutability of strings: In practice, strings are frequently shared between clients and thus frequently the crux of defects that emerge when one client inadvertently affects another. For example, a method that returns a customer's name as a string will typically retain its reference to the name. If the client, say, uppercases the string to use it in a hash table, the Customer object's name would change as well, if not for the immutability of strings. In Java, you can produce an uppercase version of a string, but this must be a new object, not an altered version of the initial string. The immutability of strings makes them safe to share among multiple clients.
- Against: The immutability of strings protects us from certain errors but at a heavy price. First, developers are cut off from any ability to change a string, regardless of how we might justify this need. Second, adding special rules to a language makes the language more difficult to learn and to use. Java is far, far more difficult to learn than the equally powerful Smalltalk language. Finally, no computer language can keep me from making errors. I'd be much better off if you let me learn the language quickly, so that I have time to also learn how to set up and use a testing framework.

**SOLUTION 13.3** *(from page 143)*

The name, symbol, and atomic weight of chemicals do not change, so you can refactor the Substance class as Figure B.18 shows. The refactoring moves the immutable, or *intrinsic*, aspect of a particular substance into the Chemical class. Note that the Chemical class's immutability relies on the fact that its attributes cannot change once the Chemical object is created. The class's immutability also relies on the immutability of its attributes. If Chemical contained, say, a List object, a chemical could change if its list changed.

Clients of the Chemical class can pass in the mass of a batch of a given chemical to determine its molality. The code for getMoles() in the Chemical class accepts a mass parameter:

```
public double getMoles(double grams)
{
    return grams / atomicWeight;
}
```

The Substance version of getMoles() applies the mass of the chemical batch it represents:

```
public double getMoles()
{
    return chemical.getMoles(grams);
}
```

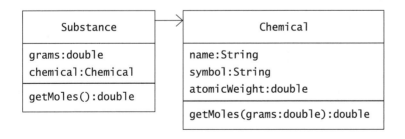

**FIGURE B.18:** This diagram shows the immutable part of the Substance class extracted into a separate class, Chemical.

**SOLUTION 13.4** *(from page 145)*

To prevent developers from instantiating the Chemical class themselves, you can place Chemical and ChemicalFactory in the same package and give the Chemical class's constructor package visibility. Note that if you make its constructor private, even ChemicalFactory won't be able to create Chemical objects.

**SOLUTION 13.5** *(from page 147)*

Controlling the instantiation of Chemical objects by applying an inner class is a more complex but more thorough approach. The resulting code will look something like this:

```java
package com.oozinoz.chemical;
import java.util.*;
public class ChemicalFactory
{
    private static Map chemicals = new HashMap();
    static
    {
        chemicals.put(
            "carbon",
            new ChemicalImpl("Carbon", "C", 12));
        //...
    }

    private static class ChemicalImpl implements Chemical
    {
        private String name;
        private String symbol;
        private double atomicWeight;
        //
        private ChemicalImpl(
            String name, String symbol, double atomicWeight)
        {
            this.name = name;
            this.symbol = symbol;
            this.atomicWeight = atomicWeight;
        }

        public double getMoles(double grams)
        {
```

```
            return grams / atomicWeight;
        }

        public String getName()
        {
            return name;
        }

        public String getSymbol()
        {
            return symbol;
        }

        public double getAtomicWeight()
        {
            return atomicWeight;
        }
    }

    public static Chemical getChemical(String name)
    {
        return (Chemical) chemicals.get(name.toLowerCase());
    }
}
```

## Introducing Construction (Chapter 14)

**SOLUTION 14.1** *(from page 151)*

Special rules regarding constructors include the following.

- You must use new to invoke a constructor.
- Constructor names must match the class name. This results in the oddity that, unlike most methods, constructor names normally begin with an uppercase letter.
- If you do not supply a constructor for a class, Java will provide a default.
- You can invoke other constructors with this() and super() so long as this invocation is the first statement in a constructor.

There are also several rules governing the order of field initialization and special rules for the instantiation of arrays.

**SOLUTION 14.2** *(from page 153)*

A constructor that allows Fountain to compile is:

```
public Fountain(String name)
{
    super(name);
}
```

This constructor allows the Fountain class to compile, as it invokes the superclass's constructor in its first statement. We have also corrected an important inconsistency in our classes. By introducing a Firework constructor that accepts a name, we established that all Firework objects must have a name. Logically, all fountains are fireworks, and all Fountain objects must have a name if all Firework objects have a name. The constructor in this solution respects the design of its superclass, accepting a name and passing it up so that the superclass can uniformly apply it.

**SOLUTION 14.3** *(from page 154)*

One way to provide default values for an object's attributes is to provide a constructor that omits the attribute. That constructor can fill in the default value, passing control to another constructor with this():

```
public Firework(String name)
{
    this(name, DISPLAY);
}

public Firework(String name, Classification classification)
{
    this.name = name;
    this.classification = classification;
}
```

You can also define default values in the declarations of the attributes for the class. For example, you could declare the classification variable with:

```
protected Classification classification = DISPLAY;
```

Establishing defaults with constructors has the advantage of placing all an object's initialization in one place—its constructors—rather than partly in its constructors and partly in its attribute declarations.

**SOLUTION 14.4** *(from page 155)*

Here are a pair of Fountain constructors that mirror the constructors in the Firework superclass:

```
public Fountain(String name)
{
    super(name);
}

public Fountain(
    String name, Classification classification)
{
    super(name, classification);
}
```

The first constructor could invoke this() with the name parameter and with a default classification. The code here has the advantage of leaving the decision of which classification is the default in one place, the superclass. On the other hand, you may have picked up on the fact that fountains are always "consumer" fireworks in the United States, and you may have built that into your solution, which is arguably an improvement on the code shown here.

## BUILDER (Chapter 15)

**SOLUTION 15.1** *(from page 159)*

The point of making the Reservation constructor protected is that it limits the ability to instantiate your class. You want to compel other developers to create Reservation objects with a builder rather than with the Reservation constructor. You could make the constructor package protected, which would ensure that only other classes within your package can construct Reservation objects. Making the constructor protected leaves open the possibility of subclassing Reservation from another package. Note that making the constructor's visibility private would break the builder classes' ability to instantiate the Reservation class.

**SOLUTION 15.2** *(from page 161)*

The `build()` method of `UnforgivingBuilder` throws an exception if any attribute is invalid and otherwise returns a valid `Reservation` object. Here is one implementation:

```
public Reservation build() throws BuilderException
{
    if (date == null)
    {
        throw new BuilderException("Valid date not found");
    }
    if (city == null)
    {
        throw new BuilderException("Valid city not found");
    }
    if (headcount < MINHEAD)
    {
        throw new BuilderException(
            "Minimum headcount is " + MINHEAD);
    }
    if (dollarsPerHead * headcount < MINTOTAL)
    {
        throw new BuilderException(
            "Minimum total cost is " + MINTOTAL);
    }
    return new Reservation(
        date,
        headcount,
        city,
        dollarsPerHead,
        hasSite);
}
```

Note that `UnforgivingBuilder` "inherits" constants, such as `MINHEAD`, from the `ReservationConstants` interface.

**SOLUTION 15.3** *(from page 162)*

Here is one solution for a builder that creates a reasonable counteroffer from an incomplete request:

```
public Reservation build() throws BuilderException
{
    boolean noHeadcount = (headcount == 0);
```

```
        boolean noDollarsPerHead = (dollarsPerHead == 0.0);
        boolean counteroffer = noHeadcount || noDollarsPerHead;


        if (noHeadcount && noDollarsPerHead)
        {
            headcount = MINHEAD;
            dollarsPerHead = MINTOTAL / headcount;
        }
        else if (noHeadcount)
        {
            headcount =
                (int) Math.ceil(MINTOTAL / dollarsPerHead);
            headcount = Math.max(headcount, MINHEAD);
        }
        else if (noDollarsPerHead)
        {
            dollarsPerHead = MINTOTAL / headcount;
        }

        check();
        return new Reservation(
            date,
            headcount,
            city,
            dollarsPerHead,
            hasSite,
            counteroffer);
    }
```

This solution factors out a check() method that verifies the validity of a
potentially modified request:

```
    protected void check() throws BuilderException
    {
        if (date == null)
        {
            throw new BuilderException("Valid date not found");
        }
        if (city == null)
        {
            throw new BuilderException("Valid city not found");
        }

        if (headcount < MINHEAD)
        {
```

```
                  throw new BuilderException(
                      "Minimum headcount is " + MINHEAD);
              }
              if (dollarsPerHead * headcount < MINTOTAL)
              {
                  throw new BuilderException(
                      "Minimum total cost is " + MINTOTAL);
              }
          }
      }
```

## FACTORY METHOD (Chapter 16)

**SOLUTION 16.1** *(from page 165)*

Many answers are possible, but toString() is probably the most commonly used method that creates a new object. For example, the following code creates a new String object:

```
          String s = new java.util.Date().toString();
```

The creation of strings often happens behind the scenes. Consider:

```
          System.out.print(new Date());
```

This method creates a String object from the Date object, ultimately by calling the toString() method of class Date. It is interesting to walk through this in debugger, to see the details of what happens within a common print() method.

Another method that creates a new object is clone(). You may discover other methods that are "factories" for creating objects without necessarily exemplifying the FACTORY METHOD pattern.

**SOLUTION 16.2** *(from page 167)*

The intent of the FACTORY METHOD pattern is to let an object provider determine which class to instantiate when creating an object. By comparison, clients of BorderFactory know exactly what object types they're getting. The pattern at play in BorderFactory is FLYWEIGHT, in that BorderFactory uses sharing to efficiently support large numbers of borders. The BorderFactory class isolates clients from managing the reuse of objects, whereas FACTORY METHOD isolates clients from knowing which class to instantiate.

### SOLUTION 16.3 *(from page 168)*

A good answer, perhaps, is that you do not need to know what class of object an iterator() method returns. What is important is that you know the interface that the iterator supports, which lets you walk through the elements of a collection. However, if you *must* know the class, you can print out its name, with a line like:

```
System.out.println(i.getClass().getName());
```

In the version of Java used in this book, this statement prints out:

```
java.util.AbstractList$Itr
```

The class Itr is an inner class of AbstractList. You should probably never see this class in your work with Java.

### SOLUTION 16.4 *(from page 170)*

Figure B.19 shows that the two credit check classes implement the CreditCheck interface. The factory class provides a method that returns a CreditCheck object. The client that calls createCreditCheck() does not know the precise class of the object it receives.

**FIGURE B.19:** Two classes implement the CreditCheck interface. The decision of which class to instantiate lies with the service provider rather than with the client that needs a credit check.

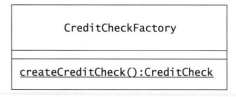

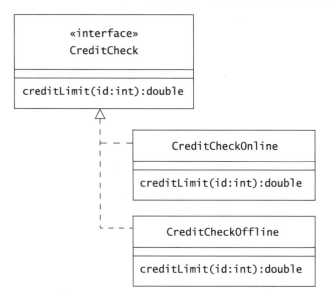

The createCreditCheck() method is a static method, so clients need not instantiate the CreditCheckFactory class in order to get a CreditCheck object. You can make this class abstract or give it a private constructor if you want to actively prevent other developers from instantiating it.

### SOLUTION 16.5 *(from page 171)*

If you take the leap of faith that the static method isAgencyUp() accurately reflects reality, the code for createCreditCheck() is simple:

```
public static CreditCheck createCreditCheck()
{
    if (isAgencyUp())
    {
        return new CreditCheckOnline();
    }
    else
    {
        return new CreditCheckOffline();
    }
}
```

**SOLUTION 16.6** *(from page 172)*

Figure B.20 shows a reasonable diagram for the Machine/MachinePlanner parallel hierarchy. This diagram indicates that subclasses of MachinePlanner must implement the method getAvailable(). The diagram also depicts MachinePlanner as an abstract class. Alternatively, you might make MachinePlanner concrete, letting it take the role of the BasicPlanner class.

The diagram also indicates that classes in the MachinePlanner hierarchy accept a Machine object in their constructors. This allows the planner to interrogate the object it is planning for, regarding such criteria as the machine's location and the amount of material it is currently processing.

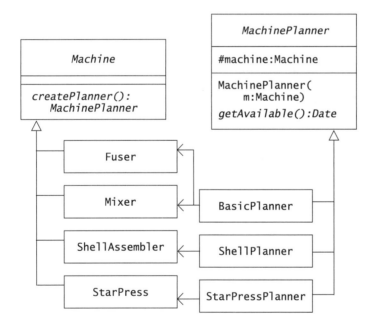

**FIGURE B.20:** Planning logic is now in a separate hierarchy. Each subclass of Machine knows which planner to instantiate in response to a createPlanner() call.

**SOLUTION 16.7** *(from page 173)*

A `createPlanner()` method for the `Fuser` class might look like:

```
public MachinePlanner createPlanner()
{
    return new BasicPlanner(this);
}
```

For `StarPress`, the `createPlanner()` method might be:

```
public MachinePlanner createPlanner()
{
    return new StarPressPlanner(this);
}
```

These methods shows the FACTORY METHOD pattern at work. When we need a planner object, we call the `createPlanner()` message of the machine we want to plan for. The specific planner that we receive depends on the machine.

## Abstract Factory  (Chapter 17)

**SOLUTION 17.1** *(from page 177)*

Figure B.21 shows a solution to providing concrete `com.oozinoz.check.canada` classes that implement the interfaces and abstract class in `com.oozinoz.check`. One subtlety is that you need only one concrete class for offline credit checking, because at Oozinoz, offline checking is the same for calls from the United States and Canada.

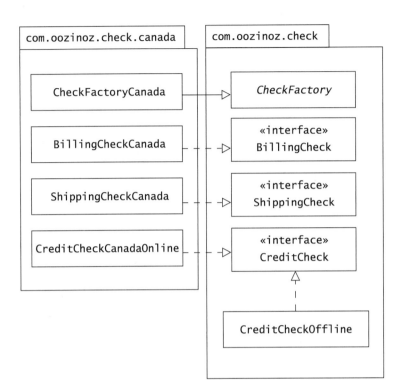

**FIGURE B.21:** The canada package provides a family of concrete classes that conduct a variety of checks for Canadian calls.

**SOLUTION 17.2** *(from page 178)*

Here is one solution:

```java
package com.oozinoz.check.canada;
import com.oozinoz.check.*;
public class CheckFactoryCanada extends CheckFactory
{
    public BillingCheck createBillingCheck()
    {
        return new BillingCheckCanada();
    }

    public CreditCheck createCreditCheck()
    {
        if (isAgencyUp())
        {
            return new CreditCheckCanadaOnline();
        }
        else
        {
            return new CreditCheckOffline();
        }
    }
```

```
            public ShippingCheck createShippingCheck()
            {
                return new ShippingCheckCanada();
            }
    }
```

Your solution should

- Have create- methods for each interface in com.oozinoz.check
- Have the proper interface for the return type of each create-method
- Return a CreditCheckOffline object if the agency is down


**SOLUTION 17.3** *(from page 179)*

A version of CheckFactory.java that makes U.S. and Canada factories readily available is:

```
package com.oozinoz.check;

import com.oozinoz.check.us.CheckFactoryUS;
import com.oozinoz.check.canada.CheckFactoryCanada;

public abstract class CheckFactory {
    public static final CheckFactory US =
        new CheckFactoryUS();

    public static final CheckFactory CANADA =
        new CheckFactoryCanada();

    public abstract BillingCheck createBillingCheck();

    public abstract CreditCheck createCreditCheck();

    public abstract ShippingCheck createShippingCheck();
}
```

A user of your software can import com.oozinoz.check.* and then refer to whichever factory he or she needs. For example, application code might contain:

```
// ...
CheckFactory f = CheckFactory.CANADA;
BillingCheck b = f.createBillingCheck();
// ...
```

**SOLUTION 17.4** *(from page 180)*

- *An example justification*: Placing country-specific classes in separate packages helps our developers at Oozinoz to organize our software and our development efforts. By placing the classes for each country in a separate package, we keep country-specific packages independent. We can be confident, for example, that U.S.-specific classes have no impact on Canada-specific classes. We can also add support for new countries easily. For example, when we start doing business with Mexico, we can create a new package that provides the check services we need in a way that makes sense in that country. This has the further advantage of letting us assign the `mexico` package to a developer who has expertise in working with services and data from Mexico.

- *An argument against*: Although this separation is nice in theory, it's overwrought in practice. I'd rather have one package with all the classes in it, at least until we expand to nine or ten countries. In my development environment, this lets me see and compare all the classes of a given type at once.

**SOLUTION 17.5** *(from page 181)*

Reasons for specifying different look-and-feel standards include the following.

- We might want to have one set of components for new users and one for power users.
- We might have different display types, such as handheld and full-screen displays. For a smaller display, our standard components should typically be smaller. Even the difference between, say, a 15-inch and a 19-inch display might warrant different standard components.
- We might want to distinguish major release versions of our application suite by including changes in look-and-feel. For example, we might change the standard background color from ivory to canary yellow when a user upgrades to version 3.0 of our application.

In the call center, it will be instantly recognizable which version of our application a user is running.

• For beta software, we might want to, say, put a red stripe around the outermost panel.

**SOLUTION 17.6**  *(from page 181)*

Figure B.22 shows a sample solution:

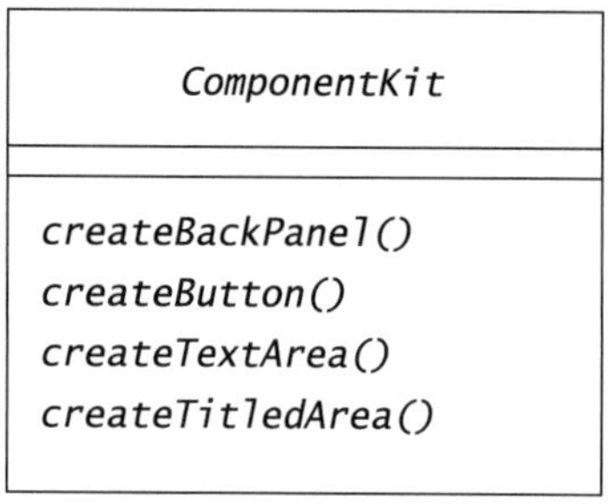

**FIGURE B.22:** The abstract `ComponentKit` class establishes the palette of components that concrete subclasses must supply.

```
┌─────────────────────────────┐
│        ComponentKit         │
├─────────────────────────────┤
│                             │
├─────────────────────────────┤
│ createBackPanel()           │
│ createButton()              │
│ createTextArea()            │
│ createTitledArea()          │
│                             │
└─────────────────────────────┘
```

The word **kit**, a synonym for an abstract factory, is often used when the factory creates user interface components. For this reason, Figure B.22 names the component factory `ComponentKit`.

## PROTOTYPE  (Chapter 18)

**SOLUTION 18.1**  *(from page 184)*

Figure B.23 shows a solution. Note that this class is concrete. You will soon establish instances of this class as complete user interface factories.

**FIGURE B.23:** A `UIKit` object is a wellspring of GUI components that have a consistent look.

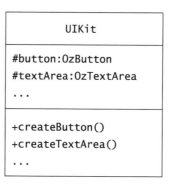

```
┌─────────────────────────────┐
│            UIKit            │
├─────────────────────────────┤
│ #button:OzButton            │
│ #textArea:OzTextArea        │
│ ...                         │
├─────────────────────────────┤
│ +createButton()             │
│ +createTextArea()           │
│ ...                         │
└─────────────────────────────┘
```

**SOLUTION 18.2** *(from page 185)*

Here is an example solution:

```
public static UIKit handheld()
{
    UIKit k = new UIKit();
    Font f = new Font("Dialog", Font.PLAIN, 8);
    k.button.setFont(f);
    k.textArea.setFont(f);
    Cursor c = new Cursor(Cursor.HAND_CURSOR);
    k.textArea.setCursor(c);
    return k;
}
```

The object k is a kit that can create components suitable for a handheld display.

**SOLUTION 18.3** *(from page 186)*

The comment for `Object.clone()` in JDK 1.2.2 says that this method "creates a new instance of the class of this object and initializes all its fields with exactly the contents of the corresponding fields of this object, as if by assignment; the contents of the fields are not themselves cloned. Thus, this method performs a 'shallow copy' of this object, not a 'deep copy' operation." To remember the precise function of `Object.clone()`, it helps to think of this method as if it were named `Object.newObject-SameFields()`.

**SOLUTION 18.4** *(from page 187)*

One solution is:

```
public Object clone()
{
    OzTextArea ta = new OzTextArea();
    ta.setFont(textArea().getFont());
    ta.setCursor(getCursor());
    return ta;
}
```

To copy an OzTextArea object, this code creates a new object and explicitly sets the instance variables that the new object must reproduce from its prototype.

**SOLUTION 18.5** *(from page 190)*

The code given in the challenge produces three objects, as Figure B.24 shows. The current version of the clone() method for MachineSimulator calls super.clone(), which class Object implements. This method creates a new object with the same fields. Primitive types, such as the int instance fields in a MachineSimulator, are copied. In addition, object references, such as the Location field in MachineSimulator, are copied. Note that the *reference* is copied, not the object. This means that Object.clone() produces the situation that Figure B.24 shows.

**FIGURE B.24:** An insufficient design for cloning can create an incomplete copy that shares some objects with its prototype.

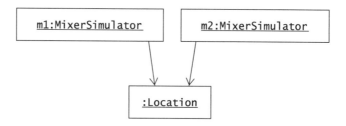

The code in the challenge changes the bay and the coordinates of the second machine's location. However, because there is only one Location object, these modifications change the location of both simulations. Thus, the println() statement displays 2 as the value of m1.location.bay.

**SOLUTION 18.6** *(from page 191)*

A reasonable solution is as follows:

```
public Object clone()
{
    try
    {
        MachineSimulator copy =
            (MachineSimulator) super.clone();
        copy.location = (Location) location.clone();
        return copy;
    }
```

```
    catch (CloneNotSupportedException e)
    {
        // this shouldn't happen, since we are Cloneable
        throw new InternalError();
    }
}
```

Note that the return type of `Object.clone()` is `Object`, so your `clone()` method must also return this type. You also have to cast the return value of the `clone()` method to be the type of the field to which you assign its results.

## MEMENTO (Chapter 19)

### SOLUTION 19.1 *(from page 193)*

Storing a memento as an object assumes that the application will still be running when the user wants to restore the original object. Reasons that will force you to save a memento to persistent storage follow.

- The ability to restore an object's state has to survive a system crash.
- You anticipate that the user will exit the system and will want to resume work later.
- You need to reconstruct an object on another computer.

### SOLUTION 19.2 *(from page 196)*

Here is an implementation of `createMemento()` for `FactorySimulator`:

```
public List createMemento()
{
    List list = new ArrayList();
    Iterator i = machines.iterator();
    while (i.hasNext())
    {
        MachineImage mi = (MachineImage) i.next();
        list.add(mi.clone());
    }
    return list;
}
```

When you write a `createMemento()` method, you should convince your-self or your colleagues that the method returns all the information nec-essary to reconstruct the receiving object. In this example, a machine simulator can reconstruct itself from a clone, and a factory simulator can reconstruct itself from a list of machine simulator clones.

### SOLUTION 19.3 *(from page 196)*

Here is a solution that performs the described behavior of the Undo button:

```
protected void undo()
{
    if (mementos.size() > 1)
    {
        mementos.pop();
        List s = (List) mementos.peek();
        factory().restore(s);
        undoButton().setEnabled(mementos.size() > 1);
        vizPanel().repaint();
    }
}
```

Note that the `factory()`, `undoButton()`, and `vizPanel()` method names match the ones given in Figure 19.2. If the other methods in the GUI application work correctly, this method should not have to check that the `mementos` stack has at least one memento. But it doesn't hurt.

### SOLUTION 19.4 *(from page 198)*

The latest memento contains the state to save, so the object to write to disk is `mementos.peek()`.

### SOLUTION 19.5 *(from page 200)*

The disadvantages of storing an object in textual format follow.

- Encapsulation flies out the window. Anyone with a text editor can manipulate the object's data.
- For this approach to work, you must be able to parse the text, either using an XML parser or writing your own parser for a pro-prietary format.

- A textual representation may be much larger than an object serialization with the same information.

On the other hand, there are many advantages to storing objects as text.

- Anyone with a text editor can verify an object's data.
- Anyone with a text editor can manipulate an object's data—an advantage in some contexts.
- It is often easier to pass text between systems than it is to set up interchange with RMI, CORBA, or other protocols.

## Introducing Operations (Chapter 20)

**SOLUTION 20.1** *(from page 206)*
CHAIN OF RESPONSIBILITY distributes an operation across a chain of objects. Each method implements the operation's service directly or forwards calls to the next object in the chain.

**SOLUTION 20.2** *(from page 207)*
The figure shows one algorithm—the procedure to determine whether an object model is a tree—two operations,which appear as two signatures in the MachineComponent class, and four methods.

**SOLUTION 20.3** *(from page 208)*
No. If you change the return value of MachineSimulator.clone(), it won't compile. The clone() signature matches the signature of Object.clone(), so the return type must match as well.

**SOLUTION 20.4** *(from page 210)*
The program prints "false". Static methods are invoked with reference to an object's declared type, not with reference to the particular object. The type of r is Firework, so r.flies() returns false.

**SOLUTION 20.5** *(from page 212)*

- *One argument for the presence of checked and unchecked exceptions*: The Java designers had it right: Listing `NullPointerException` and potentially dozens of other common exceptions on every method would needlessly clutter my code with dreck that I'd eventually learn to ignore.

- *On the other hand*: I think we can agree that we need an architectural approach to handling exceptions, and we need a solid test environment that minimizes the chances of runtime problems. Assuming that we had those facilities, what do we need the compiler to do for us, regarding exceptions? My answer is, "nothing." I'd prefer to have my IDE let me right-click on a method to see all the exceptions that can emerge, along with where they're caught in my architecture and what test cases cover these exceptions. Sound advanced? Maybe, but specifying exceptions as checked and unchecked merely papers over a complex topic that deserves much deeper consideration. While we await better IDE support, I'd vote for no having no "checked" exceptions and, as I say, an architecture that comprehends exception handling and a good test environment.

## TEMPLATE METHOD (Chapter 21)

**SOLUTION 21.1** *(from page 218)*

Your completed program should look something like:

```
package com.oozinoz.applications;
import java.util.*;
import com.oozinoz.units.*;
import com.oozinoz.fireworks.*;
public class ShowComparator implements UnitConstants
{
    public static void main(String[] args)
    {
        Rocket r1 = new Rocket(
            "Mach-it", 22.95, (Length) METER.times(1000));
        Rocket r2 = new Rocket(
            "Pocket", 2.95, (Length) METER.times(12));
```

```
Rocket r3 = new Rocket(
    "Sock-it", 9.95, (Length) METER.times(100));
Rocket r4 = new Rocket(
    "Sprocket", 3.95, (Length) METER.times(50));

List rockets =
    Arrays.asList(new Rocket[] { r1, r2, r3, r4 });

Comparator c = new Comparator()
    {
        public int compare(Object o1, Object o2)
        {
            Rocket r1 = (Rocket) o1;
            Rocket r2 = (Rocket) o2;
            double apogee1 =
                r1.getApogee().getMagnitude();
            double apogee2 =
                r2.getApogee().getMagnitude();
            return (int) (apogee1 - apogee2);
        }
    };

Collections.sort(rockets, c);
Iterator i = rockets.iterator();
while (i.hasNext())
{
    System.out.println(i.next());
}
}
}
```

## SOLUTION 21.2 *(from page 220)*

The code for `markMoldIncomplete()` passes the information about an incomplete mold to the material manager:

```
package com.oozinoz.aster.client;
import com.oozinoz.aster.*;
public class OzAsterStarPress extends AsterStarPress
{
    public MaterialManager getManager()
    {
        return MaterialManager.getManager();
    }
    public void markMoldIncomplete(int id)
```

```
        {
            getManager().setMoldIncomplete(id);
        }
    }
```

Note that the work involved in completing a TEMPLATE METHOD is similar to the work in supplying an ADAPTER. The difference between these patterns is that ADAPTER calls for you to translate an interface, whereas TEMPLATE METHOD calls for you to supply a step of an algorithm.

### SOLUTION 21.3 *(from page 222)*

What you want is a hook. You might phrase your request something like this: "I wonder whether you could be so kind as to add a call in your shutDown() method, after discharging the paste and before flushing? If you call it something like collectPaste(), I can use it to save the paste that we reuse here at Oozinoz."

The developers are likely to negotiate with you about the name of the method. The point is that by requesting a hook in a TEMPLATE METHOD, you can make your code much stronger than you can by working around an inadequacy in the existing code.

### SOLUTION 21.4 *(from page 224)*

The getPlanner() method in the Machine class should take advantage of the abstract createPlanner() method:

```
public MachinePlanner getPlanner()
{
    if (planner == null)
    {
        planner = createPlanner();
    }
    return planner;
}
```

After adding this method, you can delete the getPlanner() methods in the subclasses of Machine.

This refactoring creates an instance of TEMPLATE METHOD. The getPlanner() method lazy-initializes the planner variable, relying on the createPlanner() step that subclasses must supply.

## STATE (Chapter 22)

**SOLUTION 22.1** *(from page 226)*

As the state machine shows, when the door is open, a click will take the door to the StayOpen state, and a second click will start the door closing.

**SOLUTION 22.2** *(from page 229)*

Your code should look something like:

```
public void complete()
{
    if (state == OPENING)
    {
        setState(OPEN);
    }
    else if (state == CLOSING)
    {
        setState(CLOSED);
    }
}
public void timeout()
{
    setState(CLOSING);
}
```

**SOLUTION 22.3** *(from page 232)*

The code for status() relies on the state's class name and will report, for example, the status of an open door as "DoorOpen", instead of "Open". You can, of course, trim off the "Door" prefix, if you like.

**SOLUTION 22.4** *(from page 234)*

Your code should look something like:

```
package com.oozinoz.carousel;
public class DoorClosing extends DoorState
{
    public DoorClosing(Door_2 door)
    {
```

```
            super(door);
    }
    public void click()
    {
        door.setState(door.OPENING);
    }
    public void complete()
    {
        door.setState(door.CLOSED);
    }
}
```

**SOLUTION 22.5** *(from page 234)*

Figure B.25 shows a reasonable diagram. The code for this refactoring is in the com.oozinoz.carousel_sol package.

**FIGURE B.25:** This diagram shows the Door and DoorState classes sharing constants that DoorConstants defines.

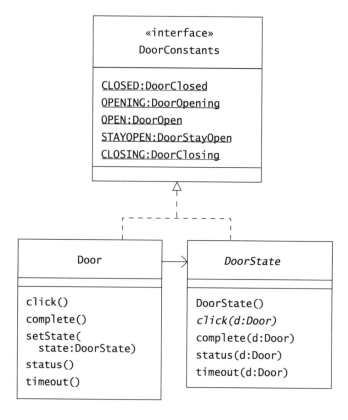

The code for DoorConstants is:

```
package com.oozinoz.carousel_sol;
public interface DoorConstants
{
    DoorState CLOSED   = new DoorClosed();
    DoorState OPENING  = new DoorOpening();
    DoorState OPEN     = new DoorOpen();
    DoorState CLOSING  = new DoorClosing();
    DoorState STAYOPEN = new DoorStayOpen();
}
```

The Door class now retains a single state object:

```
package com.oozinoz.carousel_sol;
import java.util.*;
public class Door extends Observable
implements DoorConstants
{
    private DoorState state = CLOSED;

    //....
}
```

The Door object passes itself as an argument when it forwards state transition calls to its state variable. This lets the receiving state update the Door object's state with setState(). For example, Door.click() is:

```
public void click()
{
    state.click(this);
}
```

And DoorClosing.click(door:Door) is:

```
public void click(Door door)
{
    door.setState(OPENING);
}
```

## STRATEGY (Chapter 23)

**SOLUTION 23.1** *(from page 242)*

The GroupAdvisor and ItemAdvisor classes are instances of ADAPTER, providing the interface a client expects, using the services of a class with a different interface.

**SOLUTION 23.2** *(from page 242)*

Figure B.26 shows one solution.

**FIGURE B.26:** The advertising policy at Oozinoz includes four strategies that appear as four implementations of the Advisor interface.

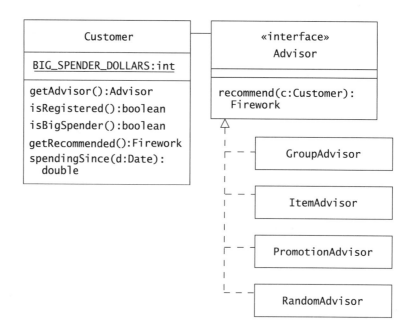

**SOLUTION 23.3** *(from page 244)*

The code for ItemAdvisor.java should look something like:

```java
package com.oozinoz.recommend;
import com.oozinoz.fireworks.*;
public class ItemAdvisor implements Advisor
{
    public static final ItemAdvisor singleton =
        new ItemAdvisor();
    private ItemAdvisor() {}
    public Firework recommend(Customer c)
```

```
        {
            return (Firework) LikeMyStuff.suggest(c);
        }
    }
```

This code creates a `singleton` object that uses the `LikeMyStuff` engine and that clients can use as an instance of the `Advisor` interface.

## SOLUTION 23.4  *(from page 245)*

Your code should look something like:

```
    public Firework getRecommended()
    {
        return getAdvisor().recommend(this);
    }
```

The `getAdvisor()` method still has a complex `if` statement, but once the advisor is known, polymorphism does all the work.

## SOLUTION 23.5  *(from page 246)*

The presence of multiple, similar singletons is reminiscent of the FLY-WEIGHT pattern, which organizes a group of similar, shareable, immutable objects. To this point, *Design Patterns* (Gamma et al. 1995) mentions that "STRATEGY objects often make good flyweights" (p. 323). On the other hand, the intent of FLYWEIGHT is to use sharing to support large numbers of fine-grained objects efficiently. It's a bit of a stretch to imagine that you'll ever have "large numbers" of alternative strategies.

## SOLUTION 23.6  *(from page 247)*

Is a reusable sort routine an example of TEMPLATE METHOD or an example of STRATEGY?

- *For* STRATEGY: According to *Design Patterns*, TEMPLATE METHOD lets "subclasses" redefine certain steps of an algorithm. But the `Collections.sort()` method doesn't work with subclasses; it requires a `Comparator` instance. Each instance of `Comparator` provides a new method and thus a new algorithm and a new strategy. The `sort()` method is a good example of STRATEGY.

- *For* TEMPLATE METHOD: There are many sorting algorithms, but `Collections.sort()` uses only one, a merge sort. Changing the algorithm would mean changing to, say, a heap sort or a bubble sort. The intent of STRATEGY is to let you plug in different algorithms. That doesn't happen here. The intent of TEMPLATE METHOD is to let you plug a step into an algorithm. That is precisely how the `sort()` method works.

## COMMAND (Chapter 24)

**SOLUTION 24.1** *(from page 250)*

Java Swing applications commonly apply the MEDIATOR pattern, registering a single object to receive all GUI events. This object mediates the interaction of the components and translates user input into commands for business domain objects.

**SOLUTION 24.2** *(from page 252)*

Your code should look something like:

```
protected JMenu fileMenu()
{
    if (fileMenu == null)
    {
        fileMenu = new JMenu("File");
        Font f = SwingFacade.getStandardFont();
        fileMenu.setFont(f);

        JMenuItem save = new JMenuItem("Save");
        save.setFont(f);
        fileMenu.add(save);
        save.addActionListener
        (
            new ActionListener()
            {
                public void actionPerformed(ActionEvent e)
                {
                    save();
                }
            }
        );
```

```
            JMenuItem load = new JMenuItem("Load");
            load.setFont(f);
            fileMenu.add(load);
            load.addActionListener
            (
                new ActionListener()
                {
                    public void actionPerformed(ActionEvent e) {
                        load();
                    }
                }
            );
        }
        return fileMenu;
    }
```

Although the actionPerformed() method requires an ActionEvent argument, you can safely ignore it. The fileMenu() code registers a single instance of an anonymous class with the Save menu item and a single instance of another anonymous class with the Load menu item. When these methods are called, there is no doubt about the source of the event.

**SOLUTION 24.3** *(from page 254)*

The testSleep() method passes the doze command to the time() utility method of the CommandUtil class:

```
    public void testSleep() {
        Command doze = new Command()
            {
                public void execute()
                {
                    try
                    {
                        Thread.sleep(2000);
                    }
                    catch (InterruptedException ignore)
                    {
                    }
                }
            };
        long t = CommandUtil.time(doze);
        assertEquals(2000, t, 50);
    }
```

**SOLUTION 24.4** *(from page 256)*

You can create the hook you need as an anonymous subclass:

```
package com.oozinoz.aster.client;
import com.oozinoz.aster.*;
public class ShowHook
{
    public static void main(String[] args)
    {
        AsterStarPress2 p = new AsterStarPress2();
        Hook h = new Hook()
        {
            public void execute(AsterStarPress2 p)
            {
                MaterialManager m =
                    MaterialManager.getManager();
                m.setMoldIncomplete(p.getCurrentMoldID());
            }
        };
        p.setMarkMoldIncompleteHook(h);
    }
}
```

**SOLUTION 24.5** *(from page 257)*

In FACTORY METHOD, a client knows *when* to create a new object but doesn't know what kind of object to create. FACTORY METHOD moves object creation to a method that isolates a client from knowing which class to instantiate. This principle also occurs in ABSTRACT FACTORY.

**SOLUTION 24.6** *(from page 257)*

The intent of the MEMENTO pattern is to provide storage and restoration of an object's state. Typically, you can add a new memento to a stack with each execution of a command, popping and reapplying these mementos when a user needs to undo commands.

## INTERPRETER (Chapter 25)

**SOLUTION 25.1** *(from page 266)*

The following program will shut down all the machines that MachineLine
controls, except for the unload buffer:

```
package com.oozinoz.robot.interpreter;
import com.oozinoz.machine.*;
public class ShowIf
{
    public static void main(String[] args)
    {
        Context c = MachineLine.createContext();
        Variable m = new Variable("m");
        Constant ub =
            new Constant(c.lookup("UnloadBuffer1501"));
        Term t = new Equals(m, ub);

        IfCommand ic =
            new IfCommand(
                t,
                new NullCommand(),
                new ShutdownCommand(m));
        ForMachines fc = new ForMachines(m, ic);
        fc.execute(c);
    }
}
```

The fc object is an interpreter; it interprets execute() to mean shut
down all machines except the unload buffer.

**SOLUTION 25.2** *(from page 267)*

One solution is:

```
package com.oozinoz.robot.interpreter;
import com.oozinoz.machine.*;
public class WhileCommand extends Command
{
    protected Term term;
    protected Command body;

    public WhileCommand(Term term, Command body)
    {
```

```
            this.term = term;
            this.body = body;
        }

        public void execute(Context c)
        {
            while (term.eval(c) != null)
            {
                body.execute(c);
            }
        }
    }
```

**SOLUTION 25.3** *(from page 268)*

The intent of INTERPETER is to let you define composite classes that interpret, or bring meaning to, an operation, based on the type of composition they represent. This lets you create a "language," or infinite pattern of executable operations. The intent of COMMAND is merely to encapsulate a request in an object. Can an interpreter work as a command? Sure. The question of which pattern applies depends on your intent. Are you defining an infinite pattern of executable operations, or are you encapsulating requests in objects?

**SOLUTION 25.4** *(from page 270)*

One solution is: If the possible compositions of an interpreter hierarchy are a "language," the job of a parser is to translate elements of a textual language into corresponding elements of the interpreter language.

## Introducing Extensions (Chapter 26)

**SOLUTION 26.1** *(from page 277)*

The complete code should look something like:

```
package com.oozinoz.machine;
import java.util.*;
public class BinStack
{
    public static final int STACK_LIMIT = 3;
    private Stack stack = new Stack();
```

```
synchronized public Bin pop()
{
    while (stack.size() == 0)
    {
        try
        {
            wait();
            Thread.sleep(500);
        }
        catch (InterruptedException ignore)
        {
        }
    }
    if (stack.size() == STACK_LIMIT)
    {
        notify();
    }
    return (Bin) stack.pop();
}

synchronized public void push(Bin b)
{
    while (stack.size() == STACK_LIMIT)
    {
        try
        {
            wait();
            Thread.sleep(500);
        }
        catch (InterruptedException ignore)
        {
        }
    }
    if (stack.size() == 0)
    {
        notify();
    }
    stack.push(b);
}

public int size()
{
    return stack.size();
}
}
```

**SOLUTION 26.2** *(from page 277)*

The call to notify() in the pop() method will wake up a thread that was waiting for the stack to make some room. The awakened thread must then wait to obtain the monitor. Because the pop() method is synchronized, it holds the monitor until the method completes.

**SOLUTION 26.3** *(from page 279)*

The problems in the model are as follows.

- The Rocket class can't extend two classes.
- The Rocket.clone() method can't have the same signature as and a different return type from the method it overrides.
- The Rocket.clone() method can't reduce visibility from protected to private.
- The Rocket.clone() method can't throw an extra exception. You could cure this problem if you made RocketCloneException an extension of CloneNotSupportedException.

**SOLUTION 26.4** *(from page 280)*

Questionable aspects of the model follow.

- The FireworkCollection class is useful as a collection that contains only a certain type of object. However, such a collection is either a list or a set, and it should be named accordingly.
- The FireworkCollection class stores Firework objects in a set instead of a list. This makes it difficult to imagine what a call to, say, get(0) will return.
- The FireworkCollection class has an iterator() function, which is good, but it returns Iterator, which is questionable. The returned iterator will have a next() method that returns an Object that the caller will have to cast to Firework. This defeats the idea of having a separate collection class for fireworks.
- The fireworks hierarchy comprehends the fact that a firework's type does not always indicate whether the firework will explode.

For example, rockets may or may not explode, although firecrackers always explode and sparklers never do. The `setExplodes()` method allows flexibility in modeling firework types but also allows setting a `Sparkler` object to be an exploding type of firework. You should avoid this type of modeling error. In this case, it might work to create an `ExplodingFirework` subclass of `Firework`.

• The `setExplodes()` method of `Firecracker` throws an `IllegalArgumentException` if the argument is false, as all firecrackers explode. It is inconsistent to have this method throw an exception without extending this thought to `Sparkler`, whose instances should never explode.

• The hierarchy partitions fireworks into types of fireworks but also includes the `FireworkSimulator` subclass. A class's subclasses should usually not overlap. In this example, it's easy to imagine a class that is both a simulator and, say, a rocket.

## SOLUTION 26.5 *(from page 283)*

Whether LSP applies in this case is a matter of judgment. LSP specifically maintains that an object should function as an instance of its superclass. If you think of interfaces as pure abstract classes, LSP implies that an instance of a class that implements an interface should function as an "instance" of the interface. Given this interpretation of LSP, the `Arrays.asList()` method, at least through JDK 1.4, breaks LSP.

It seems inconsistent to me to declare that a class implements an interface but then throw an exception when some methods of the interface are called. An interface is a contract for the behavior of the class. Exceptions to LSP should be rare, as should the use of `UnsupportedOperationException`.

## SOLUTION 26.6 *(from page 284)*

To add observability to a class, you can provide it with an attribute of type `Observable` from the `java.util` package or type `PropertyChangeSupport` from the `java.beans` package. Add the operations you need to your class, and implement them by forwarding each call to the attribute. For example, if you call your class's attribute `changeSupport` and initialize it to a PropertyChangeSupport object, you can implement the method:

```
protected void firePropertyChange(
    String propertyName,
    Object oldValue,
    Object newValue)
{
    changeSupport.firePropertyChange(
        propertyName,
        oldValue,
        newValue);
}
```

Note that you have no obligation to reimplement every operation from the class to which you delegate.

**SOLUTION 26.7** *(from page 285)*

A. *True.* To provide operations that manipulate strings, the simplest approach is to create a utility class with operations that accept a string and return a transformed version of it.

B. *True.* Multiple references to `OoString` objects would be affected by one another's changes to the object.

C. *False.* You can generally create simple subclasses of classes that expect strings. For example,

```
import java.io.*;
public class OoStringReader extends StringReader
{
    public OoStringReader(OoString ooString)
    {
        super(ooString.getString());
    }
}
```

Note that operations that expect a `StringReader` object will accept an instance of `OoStringReader`.

D. *False.* There is no obligation to support all the operations of the class you delegate to. The `getString()` method of `OoString` lets clients extract the underlying `String` object if they need an operation that `OoString` does not supply.

E. *True*. In particular, Java compilers will interpret a sequence of characters between double quotes as an instance of String:

```
String answer = "Yep, strings are special";
```

# DECORATOR (Chapter 27)

**SOLUTION 27.1** *(from page 296)*

One answer is:

```
Writer out = new PrintWriter(System.out);
out = new WrapFilter(new BufferedWriter(out), 15);
((WrapFilter) out).setCenter(true);
out = new RandomCaseFilter(out);
```

Alternatively:

```
WrapFilter out =
    new WrapFilter(
        new BufferedWriter(
            new RandomCaseFilter(
                new PrintWriter(System.out))),
        15);
out.setCenter(true);
```

The com.oozinoz.applications package includes classes ShowFilters2 and ShowFilters3, which apply these two methods, respectively:

```
package com.oozinoz.applications;
import java.io.*;
import com.oozinoz.io.*;
public class ShowFilters3
{
    public static void main(String args[])
    throws IOException
    {
        BufferedReader in =
            new BufferedReader(new FileReader(args[0]));
        WrapFilter out =
            new WrapFilter(
                new BufferedWriter(
                    new RandomCaseFilter(
                        new PrintWriter(System.out))),
```

```
                    15);
            out.setCenter(true);

            while (true)
            {
                String s = in.readLine();
                if (s == null)
                {
                    break;
                }
                out.write(s + "\n");
            }
            out.close();
            in.close();
        }
    }
```

Running this program looks something like:

```
> java -classpath \oozinoz\classes com.oozinoz.applica-
tions.ShowFilters3 demo.txt


ThE "SPacesHot"
SheLl hOVers aT
100 MeterS For
2 to 3 MINUTeS,
 ERuptinG StAr
BURStS EVErY 10
 sEconds THat
   gENeRatE
   abUnDant
 REAdIng-LEvEL
  liGhT for a
    TypIcaL
   sTaDium.
```

**SOLUTION 27.2**  *(from page 297)*

One solution is:

```
package com.oozinoz.io;
import java.io.*;
public class RandomCaseFilter extends OozinozFilter
{
    protected RandomCaseFilter(Writer out)
```

```
    {
        super(out);
    }
    public void write(int c) throws IOException
    {
        out.write(
            Math.random() > .5
                ? Character.toLowerCase((char) c)
                : Character.toUpperCase((char) c));
    }
}
```

## SOLUTION 27.3 *(from page 306)*

Your solution should be pretty close to:

```
package com.oozinoz.function;
public class Exp extends Function
{
    public Exp(Function f)
    {
        super(f);
    }
    public double f(double t)
    {
        return Math.exp(source[0].f(t));
    }
}
```

## SOLUTION 27.4 *(from page 307)*

You might build up the equation by using several Function variables or by defining all in one shot:

```
package com.oozinoz.applications;
import com.oozinoz.function.*;
public class ShowBrightness
{
    public static void main(String args[])
    {
        FunPanel p = new FunPanel();
        p.setPreferredSize(
            new java.awt.Dimension(200, 200));
```

```
                                  Function brightness =
                                      new Arithmetic(
                                          '*',
                                          new Exp(
                                              new Arithmetic(
                                                  '*', new Constant(-5), new T())),
                                          new Sin(
                                              new Arithmetic(
                                                  '*',
                                                  new Constant(Math.PI),
                                                  new T()))));


                                  p.setXY(new T(), brightness);
                                  com.oozinoz.ui.SwingFacade.launch(
                                      p,
                                      " Brightness");
                          }
                      }
```

**SOLUTION 27.5**  *(from page 311)*

Listeners provide flexibility in how an application behaves, but they do not include the idea of composition. The intent of DECORATOR is to let you *compose* an object's behavior, not merely alter it.


## ITERATOR  (Chapter 28)

**SOLUTION 28.1**  *(from page 317)*

A working program is:

```
        package com.oozinoz.applications;
        import com.oozinoz.fireworks.*;
        public class ShowFireworkList
        {
            public static void main(String[] args)
            {
                FireworkList flist =
                    Promo.getPromotionalFireworks();
                FireworkList.Itr i = flist.iterator();

                while (i.hasNext())
                {
                    Firework f = i.next();
```

```
                    System.out.println(
                        f.getName()
                            + ", $" + f.getPrice()
                            + ", "  + f.getType());
                }
            }
    }
```

## SOLUTION 28.2 *(from page 323)*

As Chapter 16, FACTORY METHOD, describes, iterators provide a classic example of the FACTORY METHOD pattern. A client that wants an iterator for an instance of a ProcessComponent knows when to create the iterator, but the receiving class knows which class to instantiate.

## SOLUTION 28.3 *(from page 329)*

You need to change the next() code to not return the node of a composite that you're iterating over. You also need to pass along the value of the showInterior Boolean to subiterators you create:

```
public Object next()
{
    if (peek != null)
    {
        Object o = peek;
        peek = null;
        return o;
    }
    if (!visited.contains(node))
    {
        visited.add(node);
        if (showInterior)
        {
            return node;
        }
    }
    return nextDescendant();
}

protected Object nextDescendant()
{
```

```
        while (true)
        {
            if (subiterator != null)
            {
                if (subiterator.hasNext())
                {
                    return subiterator.next();
                }
            }

            if (!children.hasNext())
            {
                return null;
            }

            Iterable i = (Iterable) children.next();
            if (!visited.contains(i))
            {
                subiterator = i.iterator(visited);
                subiterator.setShowInterior(showInterior);
            }
        }
    }
}
```

**SOLUTION 28.4** *(from page 331)*

The go() routine launches a new thread that can wake up at any time. If you run the code repeatedly, you may get varying results, depending on your compiler, your virtual machine, and the environment in which you are running. The output indicates that in the given run, the go() method retains control through three iterations, printing the list from index 0 to 2:

```
Mixer1201
ShellAssembler1301
StarPress1401
```

At this point, the second thread wakes up and places "Fuser1101" at the beginning of the list, bumping all the other machine names down one slot. In particular, "StarPress1401" moves from index 2 to index 3.

When the primary thread regains control, the go() method prints the remainder of the list, from index 3 to the end:

```
StarPress1401
UnloadBuffer1501
```

**SOLUTION 28.5** *(from page 335)*

To make a clone of a collection before iterating over it, you have to ensure that the source collection is cloneable. Create a synchronized version of the collection for general access, and synchronize on this collection when cloning the underlying source collection:

```java
package com.oozinoz.applications;
import java.util.*;
public class ShowConcurrentMutex2 implements Runnable
{
    private ArrayList sourceList;  // note the type change
    private List synchList;


    protected static ArrayList upMachineNames() // here too!
    {
        return new ArrayList
            (
                Arrays.asList
                (
                    new String[]
                    {
                        "Mixer1201",
                        "ShellAssembler1301",
                        "StarPress1401",
                        "UnloadBuffer1501"
                    }
                )
            );
    }

    protected void go()
    {
        sourceList = upMachineNames();
        synchList =
            Collections.synchronizedList(sourceList);
        List copy;
        synchronized (synchList)
        {
            copy = (List) sourceList.clone();
        }


        Iterator i = copy.iterator();
        int j = 0;
```

```
            while (i.hasNext())
            {
                j++;
                if (j == 1)
                {
                    new Thread(this).start();
                }
                System.out.println(i.next());
            }
        }

        public void run()
        {
            synchList.add(0, "Fuser1101");
        }

        public static void main(String[] args)
        {
            new ShowConcurrentMutex2().go();
        }

    }
```

It is important to synchronize on the right mutex object when cloning the underlying collection. The synchronizedList() method creates an object that wraps the source collection. This object synchronizes on itself when accessing to the source list. To clone the source safely, you need to synchronize on this same object: the synchList object in the program.

As before, this program prints out a valid list of "up" equipment. The difference is that now, the second thread is not blocked while the primary thread iterates over its clone—a critical distinction in practice!


## VISITOR (Chapter 29)

**SOLUTION 29.1** *(from page 339)*

The difference is in the type of the this object. The accept() method calls the visit() method of a MachineVisitor object. The accept() method in the Machine class will look up a visit() method with the signature visit(Machine), whereas the accept() method in the MachineComposite class will look up a method with the signature visit(MachineComposite).

**SOLUTION 29.2** *(from page 342)*

One solution is:

```
package com.oozinoz.applications;
import com.oozinoz.machine.*;
import com.oozinoz.dublin.*;
public class ShowFind
{
    public static void main(String[] args)
    {
        MachineComponent f = OozinozFactory.dublin();
        System.out.println(new FindVisitor().find(f, 3404));
    }
}
```

This program successfully prints out:

```
StarPress3404
```

**SOLUTION 29.3** *(from page 344)*

A solution is:

```
package com.oozinoz.dublin;
import com.oozinoz.machine.*;
import java.util.*;
public class RakeVisitor extends MachineVisitor
{
    private Set leaves;
    public Set getLeaves(MachineComponent mc)
    {
        leaves = new HashSet();
        mc.accept(this);
        return leaves;
    }
    public void visit(Machine m)
    {
        leaves.add(m);
    }
    public void visit(MachineComposite mc)
    {
        Iterator i = mc.getComponents().iterator();
        while (i.hasNext())
        {
```

```
                    ((MachineComponent) i.next()).accept(this);
                }
            }
        }
```

**SOLUTION 29.4** *(from page 349)*

One solution is to add a Set argument to all the accept() and visit() methods, so that the set of visited nodes gets passed around. The Process-Component class should then have a concrete accept() method that calls its abstract accept() method, passing it a new Set object:

```
public void accept(ProcessVisitor v)
{
    accept(v, new HashSet());
}
```

This design is similar to the approach that Chapter 28, ITERATOR, used to create an iterator for the ProcessComponent hierarchy.

The ProcessAlternation, ProcessSequence, and ProcessStep sub-classes in the ProcessComponent hierarchy pass the set to a visitor's visit() method:

```
public void accept(ProcessVisitor v, Set visited)
{
    v.visit(this, visited);
}
```

Now visitor developers must create classes with visit() methods that accept the visited set. This is a significant hint that using the set is a good idea, although the visitor developer retains the responsibility for populating the set.

**SOLUTION 29.5** *(from page 351)*

Alternatives to applying VISITOR follow.

- Add the behavior you need to the original hierarchy. You can achieve this if you are in good communication with the hierarchy developers or if you are in a shop that does not recognize code ownership.

- You can let a class that must operate on a machine or a process structure just traverse the structure. Note that you don't need visitor to extend, say, a *list* of items. The reason VISITOR pops up with hierarchies is that the hierarchy contains various types. But you can detect an object's specific type with `instanceof` or by building in Booleans, such as `isLeaf()` and `isComposite()`.

- If the behavior you want to add is of a significantly different thrust than the existing behavior, you can create a parallel hierarchy. For example, the `MachinePlanner` class in Chapter 16, FACTORY METHOD, places a machine's planning behavior in a separate hierarchy.

# APPENDIX C: **UML AT A GLANCE**

THIS APPENDIX briefly explains the features of the Unified Modeling Language (UML) that this book uses. UML provides conventional notation that this book applies to illustrate the design of object-oriented systems. Although UML is not overly complex, you can easily underestimate the richness of the features it provides. For a rapid introduction to most of the features of the UML, read *UML Distilled* (Fowler with Scott 2000). For a more thorough review, read *The Unified Modeling Language User Guide* (Booch, Rumbaugh, and Jacobson 1999). By learning to use standard nomenclatures and notations, we learn to communicate at a design level, making us all more productive.

## Classes

Figure C.1 applies some of the UML features for illustrating classes. Following are notes on class diagrams.

- Indicate a package by placing the name of the package in a rectangle left-aligned with a larger box that may show classes and interfaces. Figure C.1 shows a portion of the com.oozinoz.fireworks package.

**FIGURE C.1:** The fireworks package includes the Firework and Classification classes.

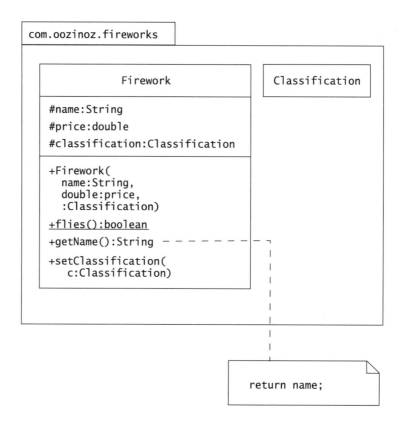

- UML does not require that a diagram show everything about a portrayed element, such as the complete contents of a package or all the methods of a class.

- Draw a class by placing the name of a class centered in a rectangle. Figure C.1 shows two classes: `Classification` and `Firework`.

- You can show a class's instance variables in a rectangle beneath the class name. The `Firework` class has instance variables `name`, `price`, and `classification`. Follow the variable's name by a colon and the variable's type.

- You can show a class's methods in a second rectangle beneath the class name. The `Firework` class has a constructor, a method with the same name as the class. The class also has at least three other methods: `flies()`, `getName()`, and `setClassification()`.

- When a method accepts parameters, you should usually show them, as the `setClassification()` method does.

- Variables in method signatures usually appear as the name of the variable, a colon, and the type of the variable. You may omit or abbreviate the variable name if its type implies the variable's role.

- You may indicate that an instance variable or a method is protected by preceding it with a pound sign (#). A plus sign (+) indicates that a variable or a method is public, and a minus sign (-) indicates that a variable or a method is private.

- Indicate that an instance variable is static—and thus has class scope—by underlining it, as the `flies()` method shows.

- Make notes by drawing a dog-eared rectangle. The text in notes may contain comments, constraints, or code. Use a dashed line to attach notes to other diagram elements. Notes can appear in any UML diagram, although this book uses notes only in class diagrams.

## Class Relationships

Figure C.2 shows a few of UML's features for modeling class relationships. Following are notes on class relationship notation.

- Show a class name or a method name in italics to indicate that the class or method is abstract.
- Use a closed, hollow arrowhead to point to a class's superclass.
- Use a line between classes to indicate that instances of the classes are connected. Most commonly, a line on a class diagram means that one class has an instance variable that refers to the other class. The classes `MachineComposite` class, for example, uses a `List` variable that contains references to other machine components.
- Use a diamond to show that instances of a class contain a collection of instances of another class.

**FIGURE C.2:** A `MachineComposite` object contains either `Machine` objects or other composites. The `Customer` class depends on the `LikeMyStuff` class without instantiating it.

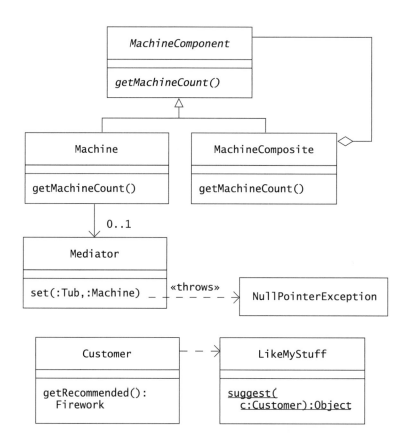

- An open arrowhead indicates navigability. Use it to emphasize that one class has a reference to another and that the pointed-to class does not have a back reference.
- A multiplicity indicator, such as 0..1, indicates how many connections may appear between objects. Use an asterisk (*) to indicate that zero or more instances of an object of a class may be connected to objects of an associated class.
- To show that a method may throw an exception, use a dashed arrow pointing from the method to the exception class. Label the arrow with a «throws» stereotype.
- Use a dashed arrow between classes to show a dependency that does not use an object reference. For example, the Customer class uses a static method from the LikeMyStuff recommendation engine.

## Interfaces

Figure C.3 shows the basic features for illustrating interfaces. Following are notes on interfaces.

- You can draw an interface by placing the text «interface» and the name of the interface in a rectangle, as Figure C.3 shows. You can use a dashed line and a closed, hollow arrowhead to show that a class implements the interface.

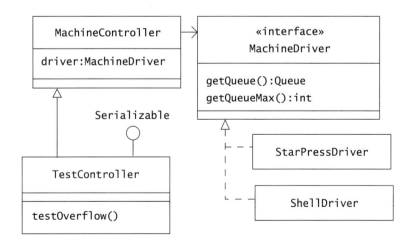

**FIGURE C.3:** You can indicate an interface with either an «interface» stereotype or a lollipop.

- You can also show that a class implements an interface by showing a line and circle, or "lollipop," and the name of the interface.
- Interfaces and their methods are always abstract in Java. Oddly enough, interfaces and their methods do *not* appear in italics, unlike abstract classes and abstract methods in classes.

## Objects

An object diagram illustrates specific instances of classes, as Figure C.4 shows. Following are notes on object diagrams.

- You can show an object by giving its name and type, separated by a colon. You may optionally show just the name, or just a colon and the type. In any case, underline the name and/or type of the object.
- Use a line between objects to indicate that one object has a reference to another. You can use an open arrowhead to emphasize the direction of the reference.

**FIGURE C.4:** Depictions of objects indicate the objects' names and/or types. A sequence diagram shows a succession of method calls.

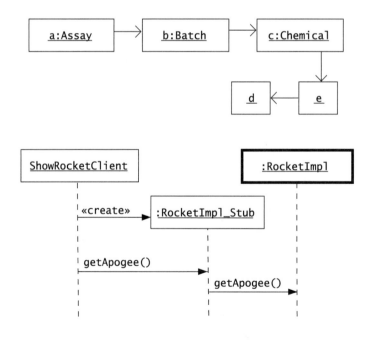

- You can show a sequence of objects calling methods of other objects, as the lower part of Figure C.4 shows. The order of method calls is top to bottom, and the dashed lines indicate the existence of the object over time.
- Use the «create» stereotype to show that one object creates another.
- Draw a bold outline box around an object to indicate that it is active in another thread, process, or computer.

## States

Figure C.5 shows a UML statechart diagram. Following are notes on illustrating states.

- Show a state in a rectangle with rounded corners.
- Show state transitions with open arrows.
- A statechart need not map directly to a class diagram or an object diagram, although you may arrange for a direct translation, as Figure 22.3 in Chapter 22, STATE, shows on page 230.

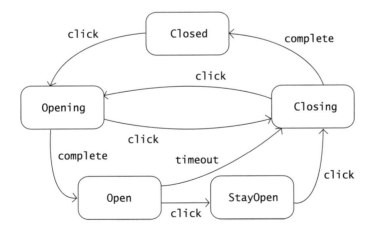

**FIGURE C.5:** A statechart diagram shows transitions from state to state.

# GLOSSARY

| | |
|---|---|
| ABSTRACT CLASS | A class that cannot be instantiated because it either contains abstract methods or is declared to be abstract. |
| ABSTRACT METHOD | A declaration of an operation that concrete subclasses must implement. |
| ABSTRACT SYNTAX TREE | A structure, created by a parser, that organizes input text according to a language's grammar. |
| ABSTRACTION | A class that depends on abstract methods that are implemented in subclasses or in implementations of an interface. |
| AERIAL SHELL | A firework that is fired from a mortar and that explodes midflight, ejecting and igniting stars. |
| ALGORITHM | A procedure, or sequence of instructions, that accepts inputs and produces outputs. |
| API | See APPLICATION PROGRAMMING INTERFACE. |
| APOGEE | The greatest height that a fired or flying firework achieves. |
| APPLICATION PROGRAMMING INTERFACE | The interface, or set of calls, that a system makes publicly available. |

**449**

| | |
|---|---|
| ASSAY | An analysis, usually of a chemical mixture. |
| BUSINESS OBJECT | An object that models an entity or a process in a business. |
| CAROUSEL | A large, smart rack that accepts material through a doorway and stores it. |
| CLASS DIAGRAM | A drawing that shows definitions of and relationships among classes and interfaces. |
| COMPOSITE | A group of objects in which some objects may contain others, so that some objects represent groups and others represent individual items, or leaves. |
| CONCRETE CLASS | A class that can be instantiated; unlike an abstract class. |
| CONSOLIDATION LANGUAGE | A computer language, such as Java, that absorbs the strengths and discards the weaknesses of its predecessors. |
| CONSTANT | A field that is static and thus widely accessible and final, with a fixed value. |
| CONTEXT | An object that contains information about the setting in which a group of other objects are operating. In particular, a context may record which object of a group is current or active. |
| CONTEXT-FREE LANGUAGE | A language that can be described with a grammar. |
| CORBA | Common object request broker architecture; a standard design, or common architecture, for facilitating, or brokering, object requests that pass between systems. In many applications, the use of CORBA has been displaced by RMI. |
| CYCLE | A path in which a node, or object, appears twice. |

| | |
|---|---|
| DEEP COPY | A complete copy of an object in which the new object's attributes are complete copies of the original object's attributes. |
| DEMO | An example that shows how to use a class or a subsystem. |
| DESIGN PATTERN | A pattern—a way to pursue an intent—that operates at about a class level. |
| DIMENSION | An aggregation of a physical measure's exponents of length, mass, and time. |
| DIRECTED GRAPH | A graph in which edges have a direction; they point. |
| DOUBLE DISPATCH | A design in which a class B object dispatches a request to a class A object, and the class A object immediately dispatches a request back to the class B object, with additional information about the class A object's type. |
| DRIVER | An object that operates a computer system, such as a database, or an external device, such as a line plotter, according to a well-specified interface. |
| DUD | A firework that does not work correctly, particularly a firework that is designed to explode but doesn't. |
| ENTERPRISE JAVABEANS | A specification of an $n$-tier, component-based architecture. |
| EXTENSIBLE MARKUP LANGUAGE | A textual language that relies on tags, or markup, to contain information about the text and that specifically separates classes or types of documents from their instances. |
| FAIL-FAST | An algorithm that fails as soon as possible when it cannot adjust to a problem in its inputs; specifically, when the inputs change during the algorithm's execution. |

| | |
|---|---|
| FIREWORK | Any combustible composition that may burn, fly, or explode, providing entertaining visual and aural effects. |
| FOUNTAIN | A ground-based firework that emits a spray of sparks. |
| GRAMMAR | A set of composition rules. |
| GRAPH | A collection of nodes and edges. |
| GRAPH THEORY | A mathematical conception of nodes and edges. When applied to an object model, a graph's nodes are usually objects, and a graph's edges are usually object references. |
| GRAPHICAL USER INTERFACE | In an application, a layer of software that lets a human interact with (graphical depictions of) buttons, menus, sliders, text areas, and other components. |
| GUI | See GRAPHICAL USER INTERFACE. |
| HOOK | A provision that a developer places in his or her code to give other developers a chance to insert code at a specific spot in a procedure. |
| HOPPER | A container that dispenses chemicals, usually into a machine. |
| HYPE | Overexcitement about a technology's potential value. |
| IMMUTABLE | Unchangeable; specifically, an object with values that cannot change. |
| IMPLEMENTATION | The Java statements that make up the bodies of a class's methods. |
| INTERFACE | The collection of methods and fields that a class permits objects of other classes to access. Also, a Java interface that defines the methods that an implementing class must provide. |

| | |
|---|---|
| INTERPRETER | An object composed from a composition hierarchy in which each class represents a composition rule that determines how the class implements, or interprets, an operation that occurs throughout the hierarchy. |
| JAVA DEVELOPMENT KIT | A collection of software that includes the Java class libraries, a compiler, and other supporting tools; usually refers specifically to kits available at `java.sun.com`. |
| JDBC | An application programming interface for executing SQL statements. JDBC is a trademarked name, not an acronym. |
| JDK | See JAVA DEVELOPMENT KIT. |
| JUNIT | A testing framework, written by Erich Gamma and Kent Beck, that lets you implement automated regression tests in Java. Available at `www.junit.org`. |
| KIT | A class with `create-` methods that return instances of a family of objects. |
| LANGUAGE | Usually, a set of strings but generally a set of objects that follow a pattern established by a collection of rules. These rules typically include composition rules, or grammar, and may include other rules, such as the rule that identifiers must be declared before they are used. A language that can be fully described with a grammar is a context-free language. |
| LAYER | A group of classes with similar responsibilities, usually collected in a single Java package, and usually with well-defined dependencies on other layers. |
| LAZY-INITIALIZE | To instantiate an object when it is first needed. |
| LEAF | An individual item within a composite. |

| | |
|---|---|
| LOOSE COUPLING | A comparatively small and well-defined amount of responsibility that interacting objects bear to one another. |
| MEAN TIME BETWEEN FAILURE | The amount of time that is expected to elapse from the time a machine comes up to the time it fails to operate correctly. |
| MEASURE | A combination of a magnitude (a number) and a dimension. |
| MESSAGE | Usually, a method call but generally a portrayal of communication between objects, as in a sequence diagram. |
| METHOD | An implementation of an operation. |
| METHOD LOOKUP | The algorithm for deciding which definition of a method to use when a client calls an object's method. |
| MODEL/VIEW/ CONTROLLER | A design that separates an interesting object—the model—from user interface elements that portray it—the view and the controller. |
| MOLALITY | A count of the number of molecules in a batch of a chemical substance. |
| MOLE | A number—Avogadro's number—defined as the number of atoms in 12 grams of carbon 12. The beauty of this number is that it lets you apply chemical equations while working with measurable quantities of chemical batches. If you know that the molecular weight of a chemical is mw, mw grams of the chemical will contain one mole of the chemical. |
| MONITOR | A lockable object aspect that represents possession of the object by a thread. |
| MORTAR | A tube from which an aerial shell is fired. |
| MTBF | See MEAN TIME BETWEEN FAILURE. |

| | |
|---|---|
| MUTEX | An object shared by threads that contend for control of the object's monitor. The word mutex is a contraction of the words *mutual exclusion*. |
| MUZZLE VELOCITY | The speed at which an aerial shell leaves the mortar from which it fires. |
| N-TIER | A type of system that assigns layers of responsibility to objects running on different computers. |
| OOZINOZ | A fictional fireworks company named for the sound of an audience at an exhibition. |
| OPERATION | A specification of a service that can be requested from an instance of a class. |
| PARALLEL HIERARCHY | A pair of class hierarchies in which each class in one hierarchy has a corresponding class in the other hierarchy. |
| PARAMETRIC EQUATIONS | Equations that define a group of variables, such as x and y, in terms of a standard parameter, such as t. |
| PARSER | An object that can recognize elements of a language and decompose their structure, according to a set of rules, into a form suitable for further processing. |
| PATH | In an object model, a series of objects such that each object in the series has a reference to the next object in the series. |
| PATTERN | A way of doing something; a way of pursuing an intent. |
| PERSISTENT STORAGE | Storage of information on a device, such as a disk, that retains the information even when powered down. |
| POLYMORPHISM | The principle that method invocation depends on both the operation invoked and the class of the invocation receiver. |

| | |
|---|---|
| RANDOM CASE | A STRiNG like thIS wHOSE ChARActErs MAY bE uPPeR OR LOwERcaSe, AT RANdom. |
| REFACTOR | To change code to improve its internal structure without changing its external behavior. |
| RELATION | The way in which objects stand with regard to one another. In an object model, the subset of all possible references from objects of one type to objects of a second type. |
| REMOTE METHOD INVOCATION | A Java facility that lets objects on different computers communicate. |
| RICH COMPOSITE | A composite that includes multiple ways for grouping subcomposites. |
| RMI | See REMOTE METHOD INVOCATION. |
| ROLLOVER | A GUI component effect that changes the look of the component when the cursor is over it. |
| ROMAN CANDLE | A stationary tube that contains a mixture of explosive charges, sparks, and stars. |
| ROOT | In a tree, a distinguished node or object that has no parent. |
| SEQUENCE DIAGRAM | A drawing that shows a flow of messages between objects. |
| SESSION | The event of a user running a program, conducting transactions within the program, and exiting. |
| SHALLOW COPY | As opposed to deep copy, a shallow copy limits the depth to which it copies an object's attributes, letting the new object share subordinate objects with the original. |
| SHELL | See AERIAL SHELL. |

| | |
|---|---|
| SIGNATURE | A combination of a method's name and the number and types of its formal parameters. |
| SPARKLER | A wire coated with a combustible paste saturated with iron filings that, do, in fact, sparkle. |
| SQL | See STRUCTURED QUERY LANGUAGE. |
| STAR | A compressed pellet of an explosive mixture, usually part of an aerial shell or a Roman candle. |
| STATE | A combination of the current values of an object's attributes. |
| STATIC METHOD | A method that is bound to a class and that can be invoked against the class or against an object whose declared type is the class. |
| STRATEGY | A plan, or approach, for achieving an aim given certain input conditions. |
| STREAM | A serial collection of bytes or characters, such as those that appear in a document. |
| STRUCTURED QUERY LANGUAGE | A computer language for querying relational databases. |
| STUB | A method that does nothing; a class that implements an interface with methods that do nothing. |
| TIER | A layer that executes on a computer. |
| TITLE CASE | A String Like This Whose Characters Are Uppercase If They Follow Whitespace. |
| TREE | An object model that contains no cycles. |
| UML | See UNIFIED MODELING LANGUAGE. |
| UNIFIED MODELING LANGUAGE | A notation for illustrating design ideas. |

| | |
|---|---|
| UNIFORM RESOURCE LOCATOR | A pointer to a resource on the World Wide Web. (See `java.net.URL` for more information.) |
| UNIT | A standard measure; a standard magnitude or amount of a particular physical dimension. |
| URL | See UNIFORM RESOURCE LOCATOR. |
| UTILITY | A class that has all static methods. |
| WORKBOOK | A student's book of problems and exercises. |
| WIP | See WORK IN PROCESS. |
| WORK IN PROCESS | Partially manufactured goods in a factory. |
| XML | See EXTENSIBLE MARKUP LANGUAGE. |

# BIBLIOGRAPHY

Alexander, Christopher. 1979. *The Timeless Way of Building*. Oxford, England: Oxford University Press.

Alexander, Christopher, Sara Ishikawa, and Murray Silverstein. 1977. *A Pattern Language: Towns, Buildings, Construction*. Oxford, England: Oxford University Press.

Alpert, Sherman R., Kyle Brown, and Bobby Woolf. 1998. *The Design Patterns Smalltalk Companion*. Reading, MA: Addison-Wesley.

Alur, Deepak, John Crupi, and Dan Malks. 2001. *Core J2EE Patterns: Best Practices and Design Strategies*. Upper Saddle River, NJ: Prentice-Hall.

Ambler, Scott W. 1999. *More Process Patterns: Delivering Large-Scale Systems Using Object Technology*. Cambridge, England: Cambridge University Press.

Ambler, Scott W. 1999. *Process Patterns: Building Large-Scale Systems Using Object Technology*. Cambridge, England: Cambridge University Press.

Arnold, Ken, and James Gosling. 1998. *The Java™ Programming Language, Second Edition*. Reading, MA: Addison-Wesley.

Beck, Kent. 1996. *Smalltalk Best Practice Patterns*. Upper Saddle River, NJ: Prentice-Hall.

Booch, Grady, James Rumbaugh, and Ivar Jacobson. 1999. *The Unified Modeling Language User Guide*. Reading, MA: Addison-Wesley.

Brown, William J., Raphael C. Malveau, William H. Brown, Hays W. McCormick III, and Thomas J. Mowbray. 1998. *AntiPatterns: Refactoring Software, Architectures, and Projects in Crisis*. New York: John Wiley & Sons.

**459**

Buschmann, Frank, Regine Meunier, Hans Rohnert, Peter Sommerlad, and Michael Stal. 1996. *Pattern-Oriented Software Architecture, Volume 1: A System of Patterns*. New York: John Wiley & Sons.

Carey, James, Brent Carlson, and Tim Graser. 2000. *SanFranciso™ Design Patterns: Blueprints for Business Software*. Boston, MA: Addison-Wesley.

Chan, Patrick , Rosanna Lee, and Doug Kramer. 1998. *The Java™ Class Libraries, Second Edition,Volume 1*. Reading, MA: Addison-Wesley.

Coad, Peter, Mark Mayfield, and David North. 1996. *Object Models: Strategies, Patterns, and Applications*. Upper Saddle River, NJ: Prentice-Hall.

Cooper, James W. 2000. *Java™ Design Patterns*. Boston, MA: Addison-Wesley.

Coplien, James O. 1992. *Advanced C++ Programming Styles and Idioms*. Reading, MA: Addison-Wesley.

Coplien, James O., and Douglas C. Schmidt, eds. *Pattern Languages of Program Design*. 1995. Reading, MA: Addison-Wesley.

Cormen, Thomas H., Charles E. Leiserson, and Ronald L. Rivest. 1990. *Introduction to Algorithms*. Cambridge, MA: The MIT Press.

Flanagan, David. 1997. *Java™ Examples in a Nutshell*. Sebastapol, CA: O'Reilly.

Flanagan, David. 1999a. *Java™ Foundation Classes in a Nutshell*. Sebastapol, CA: O'Reilly.

Flanagan, David. 1999b. *Java™ in a Nutshell*, 3rd ed. Sebastapol, CA: O'Reilly.

Flanagan, David, Jim Farley, William Crawford, and Kris Magnusson. 1999. *Java™ Enterprise in a Nutshell*. Sebastapol, CA: O'Reilly.

Fowler, Martin. 1996. *Analysis Patterns: Reusable Object Models*. Reading, MA: Addison-Wesley.

Fowler, Martin, with Kendall Scott. 2000. *UML Distilled, Second Edition*. Boston, MA: Addison-Wesley.

Fowler, Martin, Kent Beck, John Brant, William Opdyke, and Don Roberts. 1999. *Refactoring*. Reading, MA: Addison-Wesley.

Gamma, Erich, Richard Helm, Ralph Johnson, and John Vlissides. *Design Patterns*. 1995. Reading, MA: Addison-Wesley.

Gosling, James, Bill Joy, Guy Steele, and Gilad Bracha. 2000. *The Java™ Language Specification, Second Edition*. Boston, MA: Addison-Wesley.

Grand, Mark. 1998. *Patterns in Java™*. New York: John Wiley.

Hamilton, Graham, Rick Cattell, and Maydene Fisher. 1997. *JDBC™ Database Access with Java™*. Reading, MA: Addison-Wesley.

Harrison, Neil, Brian Foote, and Hans Rohnert. 1999. *Pattern Languages of Program Design 4*. Reading, MA: Addison-Wesley.

Honderich, Ted, ed. 1995. *The Oxford Companion to Philosophy*. New York: Oxford University Press.

Larman, Craig. 2002. *Applying UML and Patterns, Second Edition*. Upper Saddle River, NJ: Prentice-Hall.

Lea, Doug. 2000. *Concurrent Programming in Java™, Second Edition*. Boston, MA: Addison-Wesley.

Liskov, Barbara. May, 1987. *Data Abstraction and Hierarchy*. SIGPLAN Notices, volume 23, number 5.

Martin, James, and James J. Odell. 1995. *Object Oriented Methods—A Foundation*. Englewood Cliffs, NJ: Prentice-Hall.

Martin, Robert C., Dirk Riehle, and Frank Buschmann, eds. 1997. *Pattern Languages of Program Design 3*. Reading, MA: Addison-Wesley.

Metsker, Steven J. 2001. *Building Parsers with Java™*. Boston, MA: Addison-Wesley.

Mowbray, Thomas J, and Raphael C. Malveau. 1997. *CORBA Design Patterns*. New York: John Wiley & Sons.

Plato. 1991. *The Republic of Plato, Second Edition*. Allan Bloom, ed. New York: Basic Books.

Pree, Wolfgang. 1994. *Design Patterns for Object-Oriented Software Development*. Reading, MA: Addison-Wesley.

Rising, Linda. 2000. *The Pattern Almanac 2000*. Boston, MA: Addison-Wesley.

Russell, Michael S. 2000. *The Chemistry of Fireworks*. Cambridge, England: Royal Society of Chemistry.

Schmidt, Douglas, Michael Stal, Hans Rohnert, and Frank Buschmann. 2000. *Pattern-Oriented Software Architecture, Volume 2, Patterns for Concurrent and Networked Objects*. New York: John Wiley & Sons.

Vlissides, John. 1998. *Pattern Hatching*. Reading, MA: Addison-Wesley.

Vlissides, John M., James O. Coplien, and Norman Kerth, eds. *Pattern Languages of Program Design 2*. 1996. Reading, MA: Addison-Wesley.

Weast, Robert C., ed. 1983. *CRC Handbook of Chemistry and Physics*, 63rd ed. Boca Raton, FL: CRC Press.

Wolczko, Mario, and Randall B. Smith. 1996. *Prototype-Based Application Construction Using SELF 4.0*. http://www.cs.ucsb.edu/oocsb/self/.

# INDEX

## Symbols

#, +, -, meaning in UML, 443

Underscores in class names, 17

## A

Abstract classes
Component class as, 51
contrasted with interfaces, 14–15, 359
defined, 449
in *Design Patterns*, 13
refactoring into bridge classes, 70–73
role in abstractions, 65
subclassing, 26

ABSTRACT FACTORY, 175–182
families of objects and, 175–179
function of, 156
look-and-feel and, 180–182
object type unknown in, 422
overview of, 175
packages and, 179–180
summary of, 182

Abstract methods
concrete methods dependence on, 70–71

defined, 449
Abstract syntax trees, 350, 449
Abstractions
defined, 449
drivers as example of, 65
implementing, 65
JDBC driver example, 67–68
AbstractTableModel class, 27–28, 364
accept( ) method, 338–339, 343, 436
ActionListener interface, 252, 420
actionPerformed( ) method
BinStack object and, 278
overriding, 252, 420–421
polymorphism and, 249–250
active object
in an example, 129
UML, 446
ADAPTER, 21–35
class and object adapters, 26–31
driver instances of, 65
foreseen adaptation, 21–25
recognizing, 33–34, 366
summary of, 34–35

unforeseen adaptation, 31–33
Advisor interface, 242
Aerial shells
construction of, 171
cyclic composites and, 319
defined, 449
manufacturing model for, 59–63
overview of, 1–2
RocketSim example, 22
Alexander, Christopher, 1
Algorithms
compared with strategies, 237
defined, 206–207, 449
implementing in a method, 215
sorting and, 215–216
TEMPLATE METHOD and, 218–221
Analyses. *See* Assays
Anchoring a chain of responsibility, 135–136
API (application programming interface)
defined, 449
INTERPRETER and, 260
JDBC as, 66

Function decorators (cont'd)
setXY( ) method,
299–300
T subclass, 304–305
FunPanel class, 299, 301
Fuser class, 173, 402

## G

Gang of Four, 5
getAdvisor( ) method, 419
getClass( ) method, 274
getMachineCount( )
method, 52–53, 56,
368
getRecommended( )
method, 240
getResponsible( ) method,
134–135, 387–388
getStepCount( ) method,
62–63
GoF, 5
Grammars
defined, 269, 452
development of, 350
Graph theory
applying to object
modeling, 54–56
defined, 452
Graphical user interface.
*See* GUI
GroupAdvisor class,
240–242, 418
Groups, 51. *See also*
COMPOSITE
GUI (Graphical user
interface)
defined, 452
GUI factories, 182
GUI mediators, 103–108
GUI objects, copying,
186–187
GUI objects, separating
from business
objects, 94, 98, 381
in JTable, 26
.gz file extension, 292
GZIPOutputStream class,
290–291

## H

HashSet.clone( ) method,
334
Headers, method declara-
tion and, 209
Hook methods, 221–222,
254–255
Hooks, defined, 452
Hoppers, 452

## I

Image proxies, 115–122
ImageIcon objects, 116–120
getIconHeight( ) method,
119, 385
getIconWidth( ) method,
119, 385
ImageIconLoader class,
120–122, 386
ImageIconProxy objects,
117–120
ImageProxy class, 119, 385
Immutability of objects
defined, 452
extracting immutable
part, 141–143
FLYWEIGHT and, 140–141
Implementation, defined,
13, 452
Inner classes, instantiation
control with, 145
Input/output streams.
*See* Streams,
DECORATOR
Interface patterns. *See*
ADAPTER, BRIDGE,
COMPOSITE, FACADE
Interfaces, ordinary, 13–20
beyond ordinary
interfaces, 20
contrasted with abstract
classes, 14–15
defined, 13, 452
facade classes and, 37
Leaf and Composite
classes and, 52
methods, 14–15, 360–361

obligations implied in,
15–16
placing constants in,
16–19
summary of, 19–20
UML, 445–446
INTERPRETER, 259–270
compared with
COMMAND, 268, 424
example, 260–268
languages and parsers
and, 268–270
overview of, 259
summary of, 270
Interpreters
defined, 453
function of, 213
*Introduction to Algorithms*
(Cormen, Leiserson,
and Rivest), 206
IOException, 211
isTree( ) method, 207
ItemAdvisor class, 240–242,
418–419
iterator( ) method
composite iterator and,
323, 328
FACTORY METHOD and,
167–168, 433
Object class returned by,
399
ITERATOR, 313–335
accessing collections of
class instances, 287
iterating over composites,
318–328
overview of, 313
summary of, 335
thread-safety, 329–334
type-safety, 313–318
Itr class, 315–316

## J

Java
class libraries, 49,
367–368
database connectivity in,
66

STATE (cont'd)
modeling, 225–229
overview of, 225
refactoring to, 229–234
summary of, 235
Statement object, queries
with, 371
Static methods
defined, 457

## U

UIKit class, 184–185,
406–407
*UML Distilled* (Fowler and
Scott), 6, 441
UML sequence diagrams
JDBC application, 67
showing class relation-
ships with, 69, 371
use of notes in, 443
UML (Unified Modeling
Language), 441–448
class relationships,
444–445
classes, 442–443
defined, 457
distinguishing between
operations and
methods, 205–206
interfaces, 445–446
objects, 446–447
states, 447
why this book uses, 6
Unchecked exceptions, 212,
412
Underscores in class names,
17
Underline, meaning in UML
objects, 446
static methods, 443
Undo operations, 194,
196–197
UnforgivingBuilder class,
161–162, 396–398
Unified Modeling Language.
*See* UML
*The Unified Modeling
Language User Guide*
(Booch, Rumbaugh,
and Jacobson), 6, 47,
358, 441
Uniform resource locator
(URL), 458
UnitConstants interface,
24–25
Units of measure
defined, 458
Oozinoz, 24

URL (uniform resource
locator), 458
User environments,
standardizing,
180–182
Utility class
contrasted with facade
classes, 47–49, 367
defined, 47, 458

## V

Variables, UML, 443
Visibility modifiers
controlling instantiation
with, 145, 392
inappropriate access to
code and, 80–81,
376
method modifier types,
209
Reservation constructor
and, 159, 395
visit( ) method, 341–343,
350, 436
VISITOR, 337–351
adding operations
without changing
class, 287
controversy regarding,
349–351
extending, 339–345
overview of, 337
summary of, 351
VISITOR cycles, 345–349
VISITOR support, 337–339
Visualization class, 195
Visualization2 class, 197,
250

## W

wait( ) method, 274–276,
278
WindowAdapter class, 16
WIP (work in process), 86,
458
Workbook
defined, 458

value of workbook
approach, 6–7
WrapFilter class, 294–295,
345
www.oozinoz.com, 355

## X

x values, in parametric
equations, 40–42
XML (Extensible Markup
Language), 157, 451

## Y

y values, in parametric
equations, 40–42

## Z

Zip utility, 292
ZipOutputStream class, 291

# Also Available from Addison-Wesley

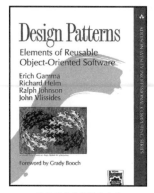

0201633612

0201184621

0201432935

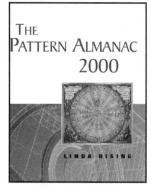

0201615673

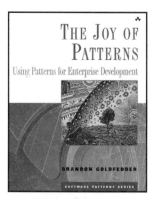

0201657597

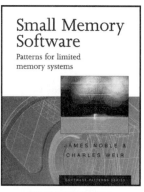

0201596075

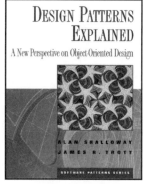

0201715945

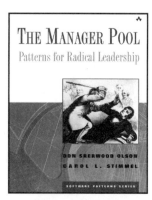

0201725835

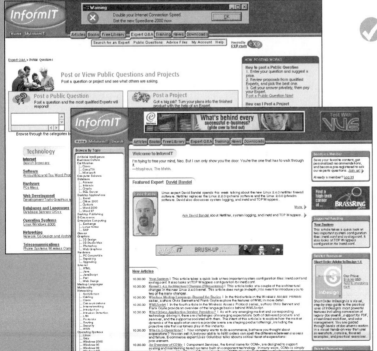